THE
INTELLIGENT
TRADER

THE STEP-BY-STEP GUIDE TO WALL STREET'S
MOST PROFITABLE TRADING STRATEGIES

DAVID A. HOFFMAN

Book Cover Design by ebooklaunch.com

ISBN: 978-0-578-84445-9

Published by Andrew Publishing LLC

ANDREW

Learn more from the author at

DavidAHoffman.com

This book is dedicated to my wife, Mariam, who challenged me for ten years to make this book the most readable and beneficial version for my readers. I will always be grateful for her passion and dedication to being the best.

And to my three children, Jessica, Harry, and Jacob, whose love and support have forever brought me comfort and pride!

Table of Contents

THE
INTELLIGENT
TRADER

Introduction

Trading is a wonderful, glorious way to have fun, challenge your mind, and ultimately make money. This book is dedicated to providing you with the same skills world-class traders use every day to succeed in the markets.

As a trader, you become the entrepreneur of any business you choose. Even if you do not have enough capital to start your own business, you still become an integral part of any startup you invest in by purchasing the shares of a company. The investments you make drive the businesses of the world, from drug discovery, clean energy, and electric cars to game development, restaurants, and sports betting.

Yet, choosing the securities to trade and understanding how to analyze your investments can be a daunting task. Many investors look for easy answers and shortcuts. For many readers, the shortcuts and systems in easy-money books have failed them because the markets are too smart to allow an easy system to beat it.

The Intelligent Trader is designed to help you navigate the path that real traders take to succeed in one succinct but thorough guide! If you are either trying to learn how to be a trader for the first time or you are a seasoned professional looking to correct some faults in your trading style, then this book will help you. In a sense, this book is the prequel to all other trading books because I will help you explore all aspects of fundamental trading in a step-by-step manner. We will start by studying the psychology of the high-performing trader and the inner preparation needed to succeed. Then, I will help you find trade ideas and show you how to put those trade ideas into action! You will learn how the market works before and after you execute a trade, which will prepare you to maximize your return and minimize the amount of money others take away from you.

In these pages, I will present the core elements of trading in a way that most readers have never seen or heard before. Most authors do not understand how to describe what makes the market function or what is happening to you when you interact with the market. In reality, trading begins in the mind. Your heart may give you the desire, but it is up to your brain to do the work that is required to outperform other professionals.

As a form of business in which you are trying to make a living, trading is unique. You have no salesforce; neither are you marketing a product or service. You are not drilling for oil, with your oil well against the earth's geology. When you trade, there is a human on the other side who has decided at that moment to take an equal and opposite bet against you. It is his mind against yours. You need to be profitable to survive. You will need a fundamental framework about all aspects of trading to not only survive but also thrive.

I can assure you that no "one secret" will make you money. Super trading systems are more of a myth than a reality. Once a system is in the public domain, it never works very well as a trading advantage. If all there is to trading are hard-and-fast rules like capital preservation and using stop-loss orders, then we would all be rich right now!

Rather, in these pages, you will gain fruitful insights into all aspects of trading. This book can jump you to the head of the class because most traders never stop to learn the fundamentals of what makes the market tick properly.

There Are No Universal Truths in Trading—Only Best Practices

Let's begin with this thought: there is no perfect answer to anything in trading—there are only best practices. The market is always evolving, often making hard-and-fast rules obsolete as soon as the ink dries.

The markets were here long before any of us were ever born. They will still be here, unconquered and *partially unsolved*, when we are long gone. I claim "partially unsolved" here because there are skills that, when applied consistently, will give you an advantage—skills that will help you navigate the trading issues you face.

Trading is a never-ending mix of variables, and the trader applies best practices to win over time. As a trader, there are skills, disciplines, and strategies you will put in your toolbox to use as the markets evolve and change every day.

The Many Views of Trading

Most students of trading do not accept this premise. Instead, they believe their job is to devour a mass of information, searching for universal truths that apply in all cases. Other students focus on a specialty. For example, mathematically inclined students seek out the best formulas, as they believe the market is one giant regression equation. Moreover, other students read the trading classics, figuring that replicating what great traders do is the key to success. Finally, other students study technical analysis in the belief that market information can be understood through charts.

But for every "trading skill" that is learnable, there is also an art to trading. As I'll describe, the art of trading comes from mastering your mind, your heart, and your interactions. Combining that mastery with a set of best practices will allow you to compete as a trader at the highest level.

My Track Record

I have traded the capital for many of the largest financial institutions in the world, including Deutsche Bank (Germany's largest bank), Merrill Lynch (which was bought by Bank of America), and Nomura Securities (the largest Japanese brokerage shop). I have been a junior trader, a head trader, a global head trader, and a portfolio manager. I finished my trading career as the Head of Proprietary trading for Nomura in my hometown of New York City. Along the way, I traded the futures exchanges in Chicago and London and even did a stint in Japan!

In my career, I have made and lost millions of dollars on trades. I have had a few losing years, when I lost more than ten million dollars. Fortunately, I have had many more winning years, including a run from 2006 to 2012, when I made over 250 million dollars for my institutions. I have also trained and supervised dozens of traders, whose trading performance under my supervision or, ultimately, on their career paths totaled billions of dollars.

Like many of you, I have traded my own capital as well. I owned a seat on the American Stock Exchange from 1990 to 1992 and traded equity options for my account. I recently incubated a new fund, the Lucullus Fund, which has performed well during the 2020 COVID-19 crisis. These experiences have brought me a wealth of insight, expertise, and knowledge that have formed the basis for this book.

Why I Wrote This Book

I wrote this book because I love the markets. I am passionate about what I do, and I never stop learning. With this book, I hope to spur on many more great traders I might otherwise never have the chance to mentor. My goal is to transmit what I have learned into a collection of anecdotes and best practices for you to use. The ideas you learn here will always be a part of what makes you a great trader.

Now, a few more disclosures are in order. As an author of a trading book designed for interested novices and experienced traders alike, I have had to choose the level of basic knowledge that I assume the reader possesses. For this book to be most useful to novice and professionals alike, I have assumed that all readers understand basic terminology such as what a "buy order" and a "sell order" are. I have also had to draw the line on how basic I should get in special categories, such as options or technical analysis. If you have never encountered basic terminology about markets or get lost in one of the sections of this book, I refer you to footnotes throughout the book. Throughout those notes, I reference many excellent books on the subjects explored in that particular chapter.

Finally, I will do my utmost to balance the use of "he" versus "she" in my writing. I apologize in advance for being trained to write in the masculine form, and I understand the overuse of the word "he" can be offensive. I'd like to note that I have strived to help bring women into the trading world. While my track record on that front is better than most, the industry is still biased towards men even though women traders are easily just as talented as men.

Overview

To begin, I will explore how great fundamental traders need to connect the best practices in trading with the mental and emotional aspects set off each time we act. Next, this book will explain the basic tenets of fundamental research. I will go on to describe other popular trading styles so you can understand how multiple trading styles can harmoniously interact with each other in the marketplace.

Later chapters will cover critical aspects of designing a trade. I will address how to size a trade, manage your risk, and, finally, how and when to take your profit. This book will also provide a section of sample trades from idea generation to taking profit, with all the steps outlined in between. Then, the book will delve into more challenging topics such as options, crisis management, and using leverage. The concluding chapters deal with a trading business's costs, fighting slippage in your trading, and understanding risk reporting.

I will use every technique in my power to help you learn. In the end, you will see that having an insatiable appetite to learn more about the markets—as I do—is part and parcel of what lifts a trader from good to great. In addition, while you search for knowledge, you will simultaneously engage the markets because trading and understanding the results you achieve are part of the learning process.

Perfection in trading is a goal that is never attainable but forever approachable. In yoga, your goal is to reach the perfect form of each position while knowing all along that one can never achieve the ideal position. Yet, as you practice and stretch, your body moves in ways you never thought possible. Your mind relaxes, and you achieve beautiful forms that allow you to move toward your goals of health in body, mind, and spirit.

So, too, in trading, we can never learn all the lessons there are to know and apply them correctly in every situation. We challenge ourselves to learn what there is to learn and apply the lessons better each time we find ourselves in similar situations. By doing so, we begin to relax and draw upon our experiences, even in the most emotional of times.

In the end, most traders become ex-traders because of losses. The corollary to this, though, is that most traders do not understand how to design trades or think about the market to give them winning trades in the first place.

If my book is successful, I will have given you an entirely new perspective on how to trade, and you will still be asking me to learn more! Your quest for knowledge will expand as opposed to being satiated. If I leave you with that feeling, I will have succeeded in training another great trader.

SECTION I

PREPARING THE INNER BEING FOR A LIFETIME OF TRADING

CHAPTER 1

It Starts with Preparation

As a trader, my goal is to find the discipline within myself to react with the highest probability of success in all markets. I hope to trade without letting my heart, my mind, or the influence of others lead me astray from the craft I have worked so hard to hone.

The Intelligent Investor[1] is considered the classic book on the fundamental analysis of corporations. Nonetheless, Ben Graham (the author) and his legendary disciple, Warren Buffett, are not telling you the whole story when they imply that trading is about finding hidden value and nothing else. Trust me that a chill still goes up their spines when a trade they put on went wrong, when news followed that was unexpectedly bad, and when the moment arrived that they had to decide to stay in or get out!

Let me give you a simple example. Most trading books tell you it is incredibly essential to use stop-loss orders as a way to protect yourself against significant trading losses when the market is going against a trade you put on. However, few of those books explain to you that your brain is not calm when a stop-loss trade is in order. At that moment, the brain is going through a massive number of calculations: "Is this the right level to stop out, or should I adjust it somehow? How could I have been so wrong about this trade that I now have to get out at a loss? Why didn't I trade this differently at the beginning?"

In addition, your heart is kicking out some emotions at you. You may feel physically nervous. You may feel depressed or angry. In reality, you may be blinded enough by these physical and mental factors that you have trouble answering your brain when it's asking you all these questions about your stop.

I accept all this and more is coming at you. Through my anecdotes, I will try to show you what trading is, so that when those moments of pain or uncertainty come

---

[1] *The Intelligent Investor*, Benjamin Graham, HarperCollins, 1973

your way, you will embrace them as part of the process and not as something to fill you with dread.

I love analogies, and you will read lots of them in this book. They are a great way to learn and retain information. Learning how to trade by starting with heavy math is pretty tough. Try using an analogy about a second-order differential equation!

I teach through stories, and here is my first one: Trading is most analogous to surfing. As you read below about a surfer's life, play along with this analogy and think about how surfing relates to trading. Then, I will follow up this analogy with all the comparisons I feel are essential to trading.

To be a great surfer, you need to have a specific set of core skills, which we can think of as the building blocks of surfing. For example, you need to be physically strong enough to stand up on a surfboard in a moving ocean. Thus, before you ever enter the water, you have to be physically fit. Also, you must have the proper equipment, including the right outfits and surfboards.

Your next set of building blocks is learning how to surf. Surfing lessons begin on land, where you learn how to lie on a board, pop up in the water, balance yourself, and even how to fall off the board properly so you avoid injury as much as possible.

The surfer's next order of business is to learn where the waves are. All good surfers know that every beach has different sets of waves every day. Even famous surfing beaches have varying conditions that may or may not allow for surfing on a particular day. Therefore, researching the wave conditions before you go to the beach will enable you to avoid disappointment upon arrival and maximize your surfing experience.

Armed with this preparation, the surfer heads to the right beach and prepares to enter the water. Good surfers know that the ocean has no emotional attachment to them. Its waves are not there to help or hurt them. If our surfer enters the water and rides the waves successfully, the ocean does not care or judge. If he fails to ride the waves, gets hurt, or even drowns, the ocean goes on unemotionally.

If he is an expert, the surfer knows he can enjoy a safe ride if he applies his skills, no matter how big the wave. Indeed, the best surfers are dropped onto giant waves by helicopters or towed out to them on jet skis. However, size is not the only factor that determines whether he can ride a wave. The surfer's skills, training, physical fitness, and discipline determine which surfers can ride which waves.

In short, not every surfer can ride all waves. The same surfer can ride high waves one day and may struggle to ride similar waves the next day. The best surfers know the ocean may get the better of them on certain days. The best surfers do not question the skillsets they have honed throughout years of training just because they did not ride the waves successfully on a particular day. Instead, they ask their friends what went wrong, what information they missed, or whether conditions were not as optimal as they initially appeared to be. Overall, they try to learn from information gathering.

When the surfer is not successful or cannot stay on a wave any longer, he focuses on his safety. He knows that he could be seriously injured or even killed if he does not manage his risk while out on the ocean. He knows it is better to abandon poor conditions and live to surf again than to risk it all on one wave. When he is surprised and knocked off his board, he knows that he must manage his escape from the wave's backwash in a calm manner, using his skills and physical fitness to get back on the board and escape to more tranquil waters.

Catching the Waves

Some days, the surfer catches the waves, riding each one. As he approaches the beach, he abandons the ride, letting the wave finish its last few meters of life before breaking onto shore. The surfer wades in the shallow water next to his board, triumphantly enjoying the moment of his successful ride. And seemingly without effort, but helped by small riptides, he gets back on his board, belly down, facing the ocean, and quietly paddles back out to sea to wait for his next wave.

The more the surfer is in rhythm with the ocean on a good day, the more he can maintain this pattern with ease and fulfillment. But at times, the waves are not as predictable and can be inconsistent. Out of frustration or boredom, the surfer rides a wave beneath his standards and tries to make do with the circumstances. The ride is bumpy and less controllable, the wave collapses sooner than he expects and in a way he has not seen before. He is fooled to the point that his washout into the ocean is uncomfortable and even a little scary. He hits the water in an unfamiliar direction, with excessive water getting into his mouth and nose. He swims extra hard to regain control because he is caught in the wake of the wave, which still has some power left in it. Our surfer has to make quick decisions that involve risk. He must choose to either swim to shore and try to find a new rhythm or turn back toward the ocean without the help of a friendly riptide to give him a boost. Our surfer knows it is not the ocean's fault. He knows it has no feelings for him. It is the innate risks of the sport, and so he knows he must use his best practices to get him out of this lousy cycle of wave patterns or else the day is lost.

In the end, the surfer evaluates his successes and failures for the day in a measured way. No matter how the day went, he knows he cannot change the past. Yet, he can assess how to improve his preparations to make his future surfing experience more successful. He can also gather his thoughts about his great rides of the day, remember all the things he did right to catch those waves, and determine what he can do to keep repeating that success.

Big Spills Are Integral to Successful Rides

The expert surfer knows that big spills are an integral part of significant successes. The two cannot be separated for long. Surfing higher waves means bigger falls from time to time. The ocean is too unpredictable for it to be otherwise.

Big spills are scary, even if they happen to the surfer less and less often. The surfer does not question his overall level of skills, but understands that not all dangers are visible when he takes on the wave. The surfer does not judge any particular spill as a measure of his ability, but he does make changes on days when he falls more than rides. He assesses whether his research of the conditions was what it should have been.

In conclusion, our surfer friend takes the ups and downs of surfing as a package: a life chosen when dealing with forces greater than himself matched against his skills, preparation, and best practices. After all, isn't that what makes surfing a lifetime passion?

The Similarities Between Surfing and Trading

How did you do with this analogy? Did you see some similarities between surfing and trading? Let me detail all the ways the surfer's skills, capabilities, and decision-making are analogous to the disciplines needed to be a great trader.

Like the surfer, a trader must have the necessary skills before she even begins to attempt to trade. Basic math, an understanding of the specific exchange rules she is trading on, and knowledge of the products she uses are three simple examples of these skills.

Traders also have to learn the basics of how to trade, the techniques of putting in orders, sizing trades, and taking profits. There are many other basic building blocks of trading. For example, for traders who use models or analytical tools, understanding the derivation, mathematics, and the history that comes before them can be assets for the trader to use.

Then, once the trader has developed the basic building blocks that are precursors to making a trade, she must do research before entering the market. That is, she must study information about the products she wants to trade and understand the current pricing, market conditions, and recent news.

Most traders enter their trade and immediately assign either a benevolent or cruel personality to the market. If the trade goes well right off the bat, the market is deemed cooperative or kind to the trader. If the trade goes wrong, the average trader assumes that the market is against her and is hunting her down for daring to take a risk.

But for the most part, the market is analogous to the ocean and our surfer. The surfer knows that the ocean is neither friend nor foe; it has no feelings and cares nothing about whether the surfer experiences a great ride or takes a spill. So too must a trader think about the market. The market is there for all to enter. It has no prejudice against you, and winners and losers play out through the process of trading. Again, the market has no hidden agenda against you or anyone else.

By maintaining this mindset, the trader can become more successful by focusing on the task at hand and using her knowledge and trading acumen to enter at the best price. She will manage her winning and losing trades with a steely attitude, devoid of emotions whenever possible.

At times, many trades do well; the pattern of entering and exiting feels as smooth as the surfer who rides the waves and then uses the gentle undertow to take him out to the next breaker. When trading is seamless, traders exit trades toward the end of a move in the market. They do not worry about missing the very top price when they exit a trade. A great trader is not distracted by the emotion of other traders, who, in a panic, buy at the top and desperately try to get into the trade. Where others are jumping in at the end, the successful trader uses that time to assess what next great opportunities are available and prepare to enter the market ahead of the crowd.

At other times, one weak trade follows another, followed by an even worse trade. The market seems to toss the trader around like a surfer who has fallen off his board. At such times, it is best to remember that the market has no bias and would have rewarded you had you traded on the other side. Nonetheless, by closing out losing trades according to your plan, you can sooner or later exit from a nasty undertow, reorganize yourself, and enter the market again at the time and place of your choosing.

Alternatively, the trader will have big wins when everything goes right. Profitable traders know significant gains are often followed by big losses as the market moves up and down. Winning and losing trades are tied together and are not a full reflection of the trader's ability to time the market.

A Collection of Positive and Negative Outcomes

In the end, a trader should think of her trades as a collection of expected positive and negative outcomes. She should judge her results as a blended benchmark of a set of trades, with each transaction maximized to its potential (maximized can also mean stopping out losers as close to the original loss tolerance level as possible).

Like a surfer who thinks a typical good day still includes getting his board flipped by the ocean four or five times, a great trader thinks about her trades in the same way. She tries to win them all, but she accepts losses as nothing more than part of her larger objective: to win over time. She does not question her trading acumen with each fall. Rather, she tries to learn from apparent mistakes, knowing all the while that anyone who tries to trade markets must be prepared for falls when conditions take an unpredictable turn.

As you dream about being a trader, remember on one beautiful Sunday to go and mingle at Dukes in Malibu Beach, or hang out at Bonsai Beach in Oahu, or at Belmar on the Jersey Shore. Watch some surfers, and as you do, think about their lives and their steadfast commitment to doing something they love. Watch them fall and see them get up time and again, and think about how the apparent failure of falling off the board is a natural act for them. Take heart that even the best of the best are scared when they fall and get emotional when they ride the waves. They are greedy when they want to do it again right away and competitive when they catch a wave that others don't. They even grow jealous when they miss a wave that others found.

As in surfing, the highs and the lows of trading cannot be separated, and they do not have to be. Knowing in advance you will face all these thoughts and emotions is an essential part of preparing yourself to trade and is as important as learning math or mastering your computer. Understanding the building blocks will make you successful because you prepped in advance instead of winging it on the spot.

CHAPTER 2

Facing Your Fears: Who Are These People I Am Trading Against?

Another critical step in preparing your mind to trade is to reduce the anxiety you feel about the people who are trading against you.

The novice trader is often wholly intimidated by the marketplace and the powerful beings she may be dealing with. People on the other side of the trade—the ones you meet on the phone, through Bloomberg, through electronic trading platforms on the web, or an exchange—seem to know it all. But in reality, this is only because you see one thing: the execution of their trade.

When faced with being on the opposite side of a well-known market participant, even experienced traders will quickly assign attributes to that individual that are rarely justified. "He must know something," the trader thinks to herself. "He's probably calling lots of other people to make the same trade. I have to get out or I will be crushed."

Believe You Are an Equal

While self-criticism is vital to help manage your trading risk, it is often best to take a much more sanguine approach to your fears. It's okay to be fearful, but it's also okay to stand by your beliefs and know you are an equal participant in the fight.

Let's think back to a childhood hero for some of us: the fictional boxer Rocky Balboa, portrayed so elegantly by Sylvester Stallone in the "Rocky" film series. As you may recall, Rocky had already beaten Apollo Creed in a great testament to his willpower and training. But now, Rocky was facing an opponent who tried to unleash fear on him and defeat him mentally before they ever threw a punch at each other.

Rocky knew that Clubber Lang—his next opponent—was strong and tough. Still, Rocky also knew that the discipline he had put into training should make him equal to the task of beating Lang. It was okay for Rocky to be fearful but confident; there was nothing wrong with getting into the ring as long as he had done his training and research. In short, he was prepared for the fight. He did not know if he would win, but he had a plan for each contingency that could occur during the battle.

Clubber, on the other hand, just wanted to rely on his reputation; he stopped doing his homework a long time before the fight. He was confident solely because his track record made him feel smart and unbeatable, even though every match is different.

Once in the ring, Rocky took Clubber's first set of punches. He knew he could take the pain after months of training for Clubber, and he began to shout during the fight, "You ain't so bad!" Not only was it imperative for Rocky to be in shape to take the punches, but he also knew he had to avoid being intimidated by Clubber. Granting Clubber the power to intimidate him would give Clubber an edge and prevent Rocky from fighting to his strengths.

By the same token, big traders know they can make the markets fearful, and for a short time, their comments can move the price by merely publicly talking about their trades. For instance, Bill Gross of Pimco Investment Management was one of the most famous bond traders of our time. He is well-known for publicly talking about his trades to scare others into following him for fear of being run over.

As a trader, you must not empower your counterparts with extra strength. Suppose everyone you trade against is deemed to be smart and informed. In that case, your mind will not accept the possibility that you have superior knowledge.

Read Your Opponent's Personality

One of the best poker books ever written is called *Texas Hold'em.*[2] The author is the legendary Phil Hellmuth, one of the most successful poker players of our generation. What makes Phil so likable is his confidence that his skills, discipline, and ability to read other players give him an advantage over time. He does not characterize anyone he plays against as better than him. Instead, he assigns characteristics to each of his opponents in the form of animal personalities.

For example, the scared player is the Mouse, who is always more frightened than confident and only plays with super-strong hands. The crazy player is the Jackal, who likes to be involved in so many hands that it's frustrating because no one can have a good hand all the time. The Elephant plays randomly for big money and does not seem to know the odds very well, but his bets are so big that it's expensive to bet

---

[2] *Phil Hellmuth's Texas Hold'em*, Phil Hellmuth, HarperCollins, 2009

against him if you turn out to be wrong (even though you know his play is not well thought out). The Lion is tough because he plays good hands and bluffs well, making for a fierce competitor.

Finally, the Eagle is the player who knows there are only a few times when all players are vulnerable. If he has a high hand or can perform a skillful bluff, he can significantly leverage his winnings. He is the most formidable player of all to beat because he uses *all* his skills *all* the time, knowing that discipline wins out in the end.

By assigning opponents these animal personalities, Phil Hellmuth can play the game without fear. He understands it's not perfect knowledge of the cards that makes these players do what they do, but their unique style of play.

On the other hand, Phil is unabashedly self-critical. He understands he will lose more times than he will win because poker is a game of long-term averages. He complains when an amateur beats him simply because there were not enough hands played yet for Phil to leverage his experience and training to beat his opponent. Yet, his confidence remains unshaken, as Phil knows beginner's luck plays a part in poker (as it does in trading). Early hands can make someone a winner, but eventually, that person will be a loser against a pro like Phil.

The Person on the Other Side Is a Trader Just Like You

Trading works the same way. Do not personify the person to whom you sold your S&P futures contract as anyone more than a trader just like you. On your own, know the odds of the possibilities that can happen when you put a trade on. Independently quantify those odds, and do not rely on others such as stockbrokers, analysts, or web chats to tell you how the market will go. Do not empower others to manage your risk, and do not fear that they know something special you don't.

To help calm your fears, think of your trading counterparts in the way Phil Hellmuth thinks about his poker opponents. For example, I have always thought of certain hedge funds as Jackals because of their need to be in every trade. Aggressive hedge funds know that by being very visible about their execution, they get other traders to think, "Wow, there must be a good reason for this trade." That reason may not be well thought out at all, but the hedge fund hopes to draw other traders into the same trade simply by trying to trade in an intimidating fashion!

To counter other traders, face your fears like our pals Rocky and Phil. Know that your counterparts are a mix of characters who interact with the market in different ways, but this interaction does not equate to knowledge. Often, other participants in the marketplace have anxieties similar to yours. Some may be loud and boisterous, always trying to look smart and confident. But none of the traits create superiority unless you empower them as such. At the end of the day, remember that other traders' posturing has no bearing on the homework you do for your trading ideas. They also have no bearing on the construct of your trade and its ability to be successful.

The next time you see that fast-talking, boisterous know-it-all in the marketplace, think to yourself, "You ain't so bad!"[3]

---

[3] *Rocky III,* directed by Sylvester Stallone, 1982

CHAPTER 3

Overcoming Games That the Mind (and the Heart) Can Play on You

H ave you ever thought about owning a food franchise? Maybe something fun, like a Dunkin' Donuts or a Dairy Queen? Or how about a nice Boston Market chicken store? Well, if you've ever had those thoughts, then you have something in common with almost every trader in the universe.

In its heyday, Boston Market was one of the most popular franchises ever conceived. It was one of the first fast-food chains to offer fresh food instead of fried. It was the first to have side dishes that seemed healthy compared to onion rings and French fries. Within a few years, just the fee to have the right to build a store (forget the cost of building the store) was nearly $500,000.[4] No franchise in history had ever seen the mania that went into competing to own one of these stores.

I can't even count how many traders told me they wanted to buy one. But if you think the reason they all wanted to buy a Boston Market is that their years of financial training made it evident to them that it was an excellent investment, you are mistaken. Everyone knew that Boston Market was quickly replicated and overpriced as an investment—they just wanted one because it seemed like a great way to get away from trading! To most traders, it seemed like a more relaxing way to make a living than enduring the mind games trading played on them. No matter that the job entailed mopping sticky floors at eleven at night or smelling like a roasted chicken when you got home—that was nothing to them compared to the pain and sorrow of a trade gone wrong.

---

[4] "Coming Home to Roost?" *Washington Post*, Margaret Webb Pressler, October 19, 1997

Prepare for Your Own Mind Games

Your mind can be very cruel to you. It will tell you that the market has you beat or that you won't have a winning trade at any time in the future. These thoughts come with the territory.

When people ask me how to deal with the stress when things go wrong, I advise them to do the following: imagine that the market was waiting for you—just you and no one else—to come along. You make winning trades every time you enter a buy or sell order. Think of all those people, all those computers, all those who have come and gone before you, and no one else figured out how to win on every trade until you came along.

Does the thought of winning every transaction you ever put on seem preposterous? Of course. Yet, we struggle with handling losses in our mind when it's so logically a normal part of trading.

Your mind grants you great powers when you win on a trade and gives you a high that allows you to feel confident for hours, days, and even weeks. When you are earning on a trade, you may also receive a shot of adrenaline, courtesy of your brain that wants you to keep seeking this incredible feeling of success.

But when you are wrong on a trade, your mind saps your energy. It blinds you. It will not allow you to enjoy other aspects of your life while losses are building. It fills you with dread. Even though one part of your mind can completely understand the impossibility of winning on every trade, another part can't seem to comprehend this and tortures you all the same.

It's not just your brain you have to watch out for. Your mind might get depressed, but your body will not leave it at that. It seems that every part of your body wants in on the action. Your heart might serve up some sadness, your back might tighten up, your shoulders might hurt, or your sciatic nerve might even kick in. Your eyes may get a little blurry or watery. Your mouth might get dry, and of course, your stomach will hurt or churn. You could even begin to yawn—a sure sign of nervousness that is also one of my personal demons. Your knees might shake, or move up and down un-controllably. I used to work in between two traders who both bounced their knees up and down when they were nervous about a trade. I used to forget that they were doing this and would wonder if I was feeling the tremor of an impending earthquake!

Train Yourself to Manage Your Risk

The best traders balance the pain and pleasure the mind serves up while a trade is taking place. Many of the feelings, emotions, and anxieties the brain serves up have a purpose: they tell you that things are not going as planned. But you need to calm your internal alarms down by showing yourself that you are in control.

Prepare a checklist when you trade and train yourself to use it each time things go wrong. Your checklist will train your mind to feel you are a disciplined trader—one who is capable of managing risk. You need to train your mind and body to understand that you have exit strategies when things go wrong. You've learned the skills to assess what is happening in real-time and make necessary adjustments, and have the capability to close out a losing trade if the analysis determines that is the best course of action.

It is critical to understand that if you master the skills of managing risk, your mind and body will release you more and more from servitude to them. They will trust you can manage the stresses of the market. You will thus be able to live a life in parallel with your trading world. Trading and living life can offer a positive, balanced lifestyle instead of an all-consuming feeling that leaves you unable to focus on anything but your losing trades.

Straight Talk About the Mind and the Heart

The mind, the heart, and the business of trading cannot be separated from one another. That's okay; your mind is there to give you instant feedback, good or bad, whether you ask for it or not. Your heart is there to let you know you care about all of this, which is a good thing given that the best traders love what they do and would not want to do anything else.

Your brain and your heart are never going to be great partners. They are more like annoying little siblings who you wish would stop hanging around with you and your friends. But even a little brother can remind their older brother to buckle his seatbelt!

Like your little brother, know that you cannot ditch your partners (your mind and heart) in this beautiful vocation. Embrace the fact that they will always be there. Remember that most traders never deal with how they react in the heat of the moment and have no idea how to handle their reactions until it's too late. The untrained novice trader's mind will play tricks on him, but yours will give you alerts and be part of your trading team. The heart of an inexperienced trader will discourage him when times are tough, but yours will renew your spirit after losses and give you strength to meet the next trading challenges.

A False Sense of Confidence

Let us delve even deeper into the emotional and mental highs that come with trading.

Understanding your reaction to the high you get from winning trades is critical. It can make the difference between leveraging your winning trades in a disciplined way or being lulled into a false sense of security. If you let your mind trick you into thinking you are a super trader, you will put less work into future trades. When you lose perspective of the market's normal flows, winning trades can give you a false sense of confidence that your knowledge base is so superior that you can now set aside market discipline and risk management.

One allure of trading is that when one is successful, it creates income irrespective of time. This may seem like a simple statement, but in reality, it is one of the most important things to understand about how your mind is affected by trading. Most people growing up had at least one job where they were paid on an hourly basis. Your performance doing that job had no short-term effect on how you made money. Unless time went by and the clock crossed into a new hour, you weren't earning a penny more.

But now, you are a trader, and time appears to not affect your compensation. When trades are winning, they create income seemingly immediately. If you feel confident, winning trades will allow you to raise the amount of capital you apply to the market, increasing your profitability by any factor you are willing to risk!

This circumstance sets off a robust collection of emotions and thoughts in the trader's heart and brain. Feelings of happiness, self-worth, and even greed stem from the heart. Meanwhile, the brain is racing much farther ahead. It is contemplating financial freedom, power, and control over those with whom the trader interacts in the marketplace.

There's Danger in Overconfidence

Many of these robust thoughts and feelings are riddled with danger. When you feel you have control over something as powerful as the stock market, it can lead to sloppy execution, wasteful decisions, costly errors made from overconfidence, and eventually losses. Significant losses come from a failure to understand it wasn't your power and self-worth that helped you trade successfully in the past. Instead, the ability to apply a set of financial and mental skills led you to success in a marketplace where wins and losses occur in balance.

As quickly as the mind understands that money can be made irrespective of time, it also begins to realize that if a trader blows up, she faces the terrible and daunting future of having to go back to a "real job." Now, when trades start to go wrong, her thoughts of losing the ability to control her financial destiny are an equally powerful engine of fear and depression. These thoughts are why it is critical to tackle the mind and the heart early on, lest they take control of your actions regardless of the amount of training you've had.

Winning Trading Should Be a Source of Pride

A winning trader should feel proud of his accomplishments. Winning trading is an acquired skill. A winning trade in isolation can be the result of luck, but a series of winning trades cannot be repeated consistently over time without a knowledge base. Unlike sports or singing, where genetics plays a more prominent role than your mental capacity, trading skills can be learned and enhanced throughout one's life. When harnessed, the desire to learn more—fed by both winning and losing trades—results in a powerful feedback loop. It helps create a purpose and value from losing trades, and channels negativity into positive energy.

Winning trades can be analyzed as well. Was it fear that prevented the trade from being sized correctly? Was the exit level of a trade chosen because it was researched and planned, or was it done because there was a profit to take? Did your emotional side want to grab it and feel good about booking a winning trade?

Overall, treat yourself as someone worth studying and worth investing in. Think of the irony here—you are reading a book on how to trade, and what you have been reading so far is essentially a self-help guide on dealing with your mind and heart! Until you are willing to battle with what's inside you, books about how to trade will not help you much. If they did—and if trading were not intermingled with one's mind and heart—one of the hundreds of trading books already written would have proven to be the bible on the subject.

Each reader is his or her own ecosystem that will react differently when applied to real markets with real money. In a very real sense, I have to train each of you individually because you will each understand, internalize, and use the same market information differently.

Studying Yourself

I have worked with hundreds of traders for over thirty years. I know that no two individuals learn in the same way. They cannot, because each individual's interaction with the market is personal. One person's mind sees the exact price movements differently from the traders to her left and right.

What should you investigate about yourself? You can start by stereotyping yourself. Here, I will talk about two well-known trading stereotypes: aggressive and passive personalities.

Aggressive-Personality Trader: If you are an aggressive trader, you like to win by having a take-no-prisoners attitude. When you trade, you want to add to a position quickly when it seems to be going your way. You often find yourself buying or selling at your limits.

To many observers, being aggressive is equivalent to being an obnoxious or cocky trader—and someone to be despised. But there is nothing wrong with being an aggressive trader, and that style has its pluses and its demons (which must be dealt with).

Aggressive traders often win and lose bigger than the average trader, which makes the highs higher and the lows lower. If you are an aggressive trader, you have to know that fact going in and be prepared to deal with it.

An aggressive trader typically acts faster and is willing to exploit short-term data, rarely trading in a slow, static market. Aggressive traders like to assess where the market is trending and are less concerned with long-term fundamentals. Their focus is often on short-term technical factors, such as which side is being squeezed by unexpected movements.

When you trade in this aggressive way, you have to focus on stop-loss skills, since significant positions obtained quickly will usually have higher volatility than the average trade. Therefore, you can suffer higher losses than expected. Often, aggressive traders do not calculate a stop-loss limit because they know they will be out of the trade quickly if something goes against them. The ability to fearlessly and quickly dump a losing position comes from acquired knowledge and the confidence that very soon you will be back into the next trade. Why even fret over an issue as minor as the loss of a stopped-out trade?

Aggressive traders travail in someone else's pain. They look for opportunities to push a market that may have recently reversed from a clear trend. Aggressive traders do not need additional validation; rather, they trade with the knowledge that whatever information is available and disclosed is enough to move the market a long way in a short time. An ideal move is big enough for the trader to get in and out without worrying that new information will come along and invalidate the most recent facts. Aggressive personalities are often characteristic of athletes, along with those who value street smarts over book smarts, and those who see trading as more of a game of wits among the participants.

Passive-Personality Trader: On the other hand, the stereotypical passive trader sees the idea of trading as a fundamental mind game in which he: (1) researches a thesis; (2) tries to convert the argument of what will fundamentally happen into a model of how the market will move; and (3) uses the model to design and test trading strategies until one strategy is ultimately ready for launch in the real marketplace.

Maybe you are a passive trader. When you played sports, you liked to sit back and wait for a mistake, like a good tennis player who stays on the baseline waiting for his opponent to take too big of a chance. A passive trader does an intense amount of research, so he tends to see what is right and wrong very clearly. He is unconcerned about short-term movements, except for the fact that they can cause short-term aberrations that create exceptional entry levels for longer-term trades.

Aggressive traders see passive traders as suckers since passive traders often sit on the sidelines. Aggressive traders will jump ahead of passive traders on important news flashes. In contrast, passive traders will take their time and get the data right, checking all the facts. By comparing new data to old data, passive traders see if their trading view is worth initiating.

To the passive trader, the market is the sum of good and bad entry points. The emotions of the other participants are irrelevant. All that matters to passive traders is that they eventually want to buy or sell at a price that represents a miscalculation by the market compared to the research they have done.

These are but two of the many stereotypes you can assign to yourself. You could be a Disciplined Market Maker, an Options Guru, or an Algo Specialist, to name just a few more stereotypes. Once you have created a stereotype about yourself, your next step should be to build a checklist in your mind as to how your type of personality feels empowered to deploy a trade.

For instance, will you have done hours of research on a particular topic and feel vindicated by the data you uncovered about a stock or bond? Will you react quickly to an economic news release, knowing that you have studied the market expectations of what the data should look like? Are you entering as a disciplined market maker who has spent a considerable amount of time perfecting your computer model to make the best bid-offer spread possible?

If your heart and mind know you are a prepared person, you will remain calm during the various scenarios unfolding in the marketplace playout for or against your trade. Your checklist will include tools you will use to re-evaluate your decision as new information comes along. For example, if you are a market maker, you will do sanity checks on your model to ensure it is up-to-date and spitting out correct prices. If you watch headlines, you will be searching for news in an unbiased manner, willing to look objectively as news flashes affect your trades.

Your checklist will also include your exit strategies: both stop-loss orders and take-profit orders since you are willing to accept the path on whichever way the market takes you. In addition, your checklist will play through some disaster scenarios that will prepare you in case of an emergency, like a fire drill at school. For instance, how will you handle it if your live data feeds stop working or there is news of a terror threat in your area?

Your mind and heart are watching all the time. They will see what kind of checklists you have and how disciplined you are. They will be impressed if you are consistent and do what you plan to do. Your heart will still beat faster in moments of stress, but your mind will calm your heart because it will see you are taking the evasive action you had planned. Your mind will be analyzing what went wrong when you lose on a trade, but your heart will not crush you with sadness because it is confident that this is part of the usual ebb and flow of the business.

In summary, your teammates—your heart and your mind—can be sources of power instead of conflict. Your heart can give you hope instead of dread. Your mind can be working on the next trade instead of kicking you for being wrong about your last trading decision. As a result, you can have a distinct advantage over your trading peers because they are untrained and bogged down by the torments of their hearts and minds. If you are in control, you are already ahead of 90% of the traders out there, who on the surface may seem to have it together, but on the inside, are ripping themselves apart.

You have prepared your heart and mind by specializing in a discipline and trading style that suits you. In return, they are empowering and encouraging you.[5]

---

[5] *Trading in the Zone*, Mark Douglas, Penguin, 2000

SECTION II

THE BUILDING BLOCKS OF TRADE IDEAS AND TRADE DESIGN

CHAPTER 4

The Origin of a Trading Idea

Most trading books begin their instruction at the point where your trading idea is known. Many authors assume that trading ideas are a dime a dozen, plucked magically from some sort of "fountain of wisdom."

Taking the trading idea as a given, authors will then proceed to explain the skills of money management, the discipline of stop-loss orders, the power of adding to a winning trade, and the hundreds of other skills needed to execute your trading idea.

Copying Others' Ideas

Coming up with a trading idea is far from a given. In fact, it is an "unnatural act" because trading idea generation involves "seeing" correctly what others do not see—or what they ultimately fail to value. No matter how sophisticated your methodologies for deriving an asset's value, it is only a trading idea if you decide that the market has it wrong and that you have it right.

But alas, we are social creatures, and we like to copy what others do. It feels natural to borrow trading ideas from others because we take comfort that our fellow human beings agree with us and do what we do. Therefore, traders copy ideas from everywhere: published research, media stories about what other traders are doing, or charts with fancy technical analysis.

Why You Should Own Your Own Trade Ideas

But to be a great trader, you have to generate original ideas. Even if others ultimately come to the same conclusion you do and put on similar trades, it is essential to own your thoughts about what to trade. There are several reasons why this is true.

First, it is human nature to resist questioning authority. When an idea comes from a well-respected source, we tend to take it as truth instead of challenging the thesis. But by generating our own independent trading ideas, we validate the origins of the information for ourselves.

Second, when we take an idea from others, we do not control that idea's distribution. Therefore, we must consider the likelihood that if the concept is in the public domain and has been reviewed by other market participants, there is probably little value left in that idea.

Third, ideas generated by brokers, analysts, or banks are often driven by the desire of these sources to earn commissions from you. Because of this underlying motivation, these sources are likely to bring you many ideas of inferior quality, yet they hope you can execute an increasing number of trades through their organization. That is not to say, however, that all their ideas will be inferior.

Finally, in trading, you are trying to take money out of the market. But the market is not a well full of dollars. It consists of people, many of whom are trading against you. But how can you take money from them if you are buying on their own ideas?

The bottom line is this: it is more plausible that, over time, you will be more successful trading on ideas you generate for yourself than those gleaned from external sources. If market participants do not know your concept ahead of time, then other traders cannot prepare for the idea. They, therefore, cannot modify their trading strategy to take advantage of your trade.

How to Form Your Trading Ideas

How do you, the reader, begin to form your trading ideas? I will devote several chapters to this critical process. First, I will explore what resources you bring to the table, which will profoundly affect the types of trading ideas to look for. Then, I will delve into the special processing skills needed when dealing with the reams of information in the marketplace. Next, we will devote time to reviewing the trade-related research available through the financial industry and how to extract real value from it. Finally, we will look at ways that you can develop your independent trade ideas. When you are done with this section of the book, you will not only be able to create unique trading ideas, but you will do so with a mindset that fits your personality and skillset.

Honing Your Best Skills

Remember—no trader can trade all the many styles that exist in the marketplace. While it is possible to develop expertise in many trading styles, it is unnecessary to be an expert in more than one style. The goal of trading is to take money out of the market and put it into your pocket—not to be an expert in many trading styles.

Imagine you are Mariano Rivera, one of the greatest relief pitchers of all time. You are thirty years old but still looking to improve. You have a choice between improving your batting swing for the few times a year you might hit in a game, or using that same time to develop another pitch. Learning to hit a little better will not get you paid a penny more, but adding a devastating curveball to your repertoire might extend your career and get you paid more money even farther into the future.

It is the same principle with trading. Honing your own area of expertise and ability to generate trade ideas is critical. Again, you need not be a master of many trading styles. The market is sufficiently large, so having your area of expertise will easily allow you to accomplish your goal of making more money over time.

Your Unique View of the World

You are a child of your environment. You were born in a particular country and you were taught a specific language. You were educated uniquely from the millions of other people who enter the market each day.

"What do you mean?" you might ask. "I know hundreds of people who went to the same high school or college I attended. They had the same teachers and learned the same material that I did. I am not unique."

As I hinted at earlier, it matters little how many people sat to your left or your right during Algebra I. It only matters how you absorbed that information and that you can apply it to the world in your own unique way.

When you enter the marketplace, you will not be taking a standardized test. You will not be asked to determine the proper weight load for a steel beam in a building, and there is only one correct answer. You will not be landing a plane where only one trajectory will get you down without crashing. Instead, you will be an actor in a dynamic place where your entrance into the marketplace changes that dynamic. Understanding your personal building blocks will lead you to trade ideas that are uniquely yours.

How You Process Information

Let us look at a simple example. Suppose you were a kindergarten teacher trying to teach a class of ten children. In that case, you might notice that some kids can repeat a word after a single try, while others need several attempts. But the ones who need several shots might be better at painting a picture. Other students who do not paint well or learn words quickly may nonetheless be the fastest at picking up a basic math concept. Moreover, others who are weaker at these first three tasks may be more socially adept than the other children and learn more easily from their classmates' interactions.

Now, let us look at this situation from a student's perspective. Do you remember your days in school? Do you recall your greatest triumphs and failures? I was the worst artist in my class. I have always been a terrible artist, as I do not absorb things visually very well or think in a visual way. But I was good at figuring people out. I quickly figured out who the bullies were and how they thought. Since I was not a big kid, I quickly learned to befriend them, even if I was just pretending, so I could make my life easier. I also developed the skill of "reading" people, which has especially served me well throughout my trading life.

Maybe your skill was numbers and so you were proud that you found math easy. From that ability, you developed an enjoyment of the many things having to do with math throughout your school days because that part of your brain seemed to work best. You enjoyed knowing that math homework and tests would be easy for you. Later in your schooling, you thought of leveraging that knowledge into your career so you had the confidence of knowing you would get paid to do something that comes more naturally to you than to most people.

Understanding How Others Process and React to Information

Today, I still look at information in terms of not only how I process information, but also asking myself how others will process that information and how they will react to it once they have done so.

I think about who these other people are. They may be other traders who are on the opposite sides of my trades—I may even know some of them personally. I think about how they react to bad news and in what time frame they might act. I also ask myself how far would they go to get out of a trade if they thought something was wrong? Furthermore, I think about how they would begin to change their minds entirely about an asset's price and where they might drive that price once they are set in their new perspective.

To learn more about my trading style as outlined above, consider reading George Soros's book *The Alchemy of Finance,*[6] in which he discusses a theory he calls

---

[6] *The Alchemy of Finance,* George Soros, John Wiley & Sons, 1987

"reflexivity." Essentially, reflexivity is the theory that price movement is partially derived from a feedback loop of how people react to an asset's initial information. By using reflexivity as a trading style, one can focus on people's reactions to the price movement from fresh news and design trades by taking advantage of assessing these reactions. Often, this style of trading does as well as the more famous method of anticipating the initial causes of the price movement.

Since this trading style involves <u>my</u> skillset of reading other people, using this style allows me to place trades in front of other traders based mainly on how I think they will react to information instead of creating some valuation model based on the genuine worth of a security.

Others who are more mathematically oriented than I am might take the very same news that I learned and use it solely for its value as an input into their analytical equation. That is, they might make a bet using a model irrespective of how others, including me, might act. An economist might look at the market as a gigantic econometric model that can be solved if the correct inputs are used. A philosopher or psychologist might see the same market as the sum of human emotions and want to trade when emotions become irrational. And good for all of them. They do what they are good at, and I do what I am good at, and that is what makes markets go!

Your Traits and Trading Style

Now, it is time to reach into your soul and understand who you are. What are your personality traits? What did you excel at on a consistent level dating back to your childhood? What comes naturally to you? In what situations do you find yourself being the smartest person in the room? What subjects are you strongest in? How do you solve problems in your mind? Do you judge things analytically or emotionally? Do you seek out knowledgeable resources when faced with a dilemma, or do you trust your instincts? How do you interact with people?

Answering these questions will give you insights into your trading style and strategies. As you begin to answer these questions, try to match your strengths with individual trading styles. If you have already been a trader, do you find that the type of trading you do matches well with your innate skills? Or is there a contradiction between your trading style and your natural inclinations and abilities? Have you ever struggled to emulate a trading style because you thought it was the correct way to make money but found it was contradictory to your fundamental nature?

If you have never traded before, you are in luck because you can start your trading with a style that best suits your strengths. Go out and reverse-engineer the type of trader you want to be. Instead of reading about what some "cool" trader does and trying to emulate that person, find out what trading style seems cool to you, no matter what others say about it. Find a method that plays to as many of your strengths as possible.

Do Not Let Others Decide What Kind of Trader You Should Be

For over two decades, I was part of teams at Deutsche Bank and Merrill Lynch, recruiting new traders out of college and graduate school. We went to the best schools in the country to meet the best and the brightest. Ninety-five percent of those we met had not traded before but had read about trading and were interested in getting a job in the field. They particularly wanted to work for a big bank or investment bank because we had training programs that lasted over a year, which would give them an additional leg up on the competition. The people we interviewed represented the top 10% of the resumes we reviewed. Even then, we only took one out of every ten people we interviewed to be in our training program.

After a year of training, only one out of every two people we trained were assigned to be a trader. In other words, after going through this extensive selection process to find the best minds in the world, we were right only 50% of the time! Worse yet, only one out of the two people we picked to be a trader ultimately made the bank any money!

Why was there such a high failure rate in the recruiting and selection process? It is not just because trading is hard and takes a unique skill set. And certainly, it was not because those selected were weak in analytical skills. Quite the contrary—successful trading goes well beyond building a great spreadsheet or understanding high-level math.

It is because so many people, including the best and the brightest, do not assess how they process information and why they might not be suitable candidates for one style (in this case, market making) versus another style more natural to them.

As you have already learned from this chapter, as a trader, you will process the same information everyone else receives in a way that is unique to you. You may process it quickly or slowly. You may make snap judgments based on this information, or you may prefer to combine several pieces of information and make long-term judgments. You may know some things innately because they are subjects in which you are an expert, or you were culturally exposed to how that information should be processed through years of experience.

Thus, it should come as no surprise that you feel more comfortable making specific trades that are structured to take advantage of your expertise. A scientific mind might be attracted to deriving trades generated from an algorithm. A mind that likes to look at a series of factors and reserve judgment until much more is known might be more attracted to stock trading, because the pricing of stocks involves collecting and assessing multiple points of reference. A mind that focuses on human behavior might be attracted to day trading or market making because other people's reaction function greatly influences prices in the short run.

If you focus on your unique talents, the trading style that suits you will drop into your lap. If you process information as naturally as possible to your expertise, ideas will come to you more readily and trade designs will make sense because you will be trading in a style that is, well, uniquely you!

CHAPTER 5

The Beginnings of Fundamental Research

In this book, research is defined as thoughts and ideas about markets or individual securities intended to help you determine the fair value of a security. When you conclude from your research that a security you analyzed has a different valuation than what is currently priced into the market, your trade idea is born.

In the early decades of stock trading (around 1970), fundamental analysis dominated the mindset of how a trading idea germinated. With the advent of the computer age, fundamental information grew exponentially. For many, there is too much fundamental information available for it to be applied with any rigor to a trade. This led to the rise of other categories and trading styles, which we will address in Chapter 14.

For now, I wish to focus the reader's attention on one salient point: if I told you the stock market would close next Friday and not re-open for five years, what questions would you ask about a stock before you traded it? Would you care about how the chart looked five years earlier, or would you rather know how it generated its profits and cash flow over that time? What good is a chart if the company you were high on five years earlier is no longer in business?

Another way to think about the idea that fundamental value is the core of every analysis is to imagine trying to derive the cost of an Initial Public Stock Offering (IPO) or a new bond issue without doing fundamental research. With no prior price history or relevant factors to compare it to, a new stock or bond must be valued based on its business's core components. Often, a team of trained analysts from the world's top investment firms takes months to provide a valuation. This valuation is then tested among potential investors who verify or reject the price based on their independent analysis. When the judgments of the investment firms and the investors merge into a tightly formed price range, the market is then prepared for the launch of a new asset.

Dislocations in the stock market price often result in a quandary, which only fundamental thinking can resolve. We witnessed after the burst of the tech bubble in

2000 and with the COVID-19 crisis of 2020 that recovery of the fundamentally strong stocks occurred first. Within the first few weeks of each crisis, investors quickly separated what would be valuable in the future world, given the reality of much weaker financial conditions.

I am biased towards fundamental ideas as the basis of any trade idea. In later chapters, we will explore other means of generating trade ideas that rely on charts or machines to remove as much of the human element as possible from idea generation. Yes, humans are flawed, and the depth of available information to form a total view of an asset is cavernous indeed. But no security can have a price worth trading if it does not have an intrinsic value, and intrinsic value comes from fundamental research. (The corollary to this principle is if something loses its intrinsic value, such as a Bernie Madoff investment fund or Enron, it is fundamental research that will expose it—not a line on a graph!)

Let's divide research into three categories: (1) research that is presented to you by the financial industry; (2) news headlines and stories directly related to a financial security; and (3) ideas about trading a security that you, the reader and trader, generate independently. Though these are all very broad-based categories, they apply in almost all cases and help you compartmentalize your thinking as "research" comes streaming in.

In the first category, research presented to you by the financial industry (street research) almost always comes with a trade idea attached to it. That makes this type of analysis very tempting to use because the work is already done for you.

In the second category, one needs to take the headline's information and devise a trade idea around it. This is a slightly more challenging task than using street research, but it is still appealing.

Finally, we have the third category where we go looking for information that is valuable in affecting the price of a security and then creating a trade idea around it. This is the most challenging research of all, and one that most traders tend to avoid because it takes initiative (and a lot of extra work).

Street Research

For the rest of this chapter, we will focus on the first category: research produced by the financial industry, or, as it is more affectionately called, "street research" ("street" as in Wall Street).

Street research comes with an inherent bias. The trade ideas produced professionally by financial firms are used as tools to sell their clients' financial services or products. Those services result in commissions for trades executed by the firm, fees for the use of proprietary software, exchange fees, and a host of other ways that financial firms can think of to extract money from you.

Because these services are so profitable, Wall Street firms' quality and packaging of trade ideas are usually quite good. Top research on almost any financial subject is available in beautifully printed booklets, generally with the firm's name and author printed right on the front. Thus, if you like the research from a particular firm or some of its analysts, it is easy to subscribe to future reports, which are often available on the web. Typical street research will involve a hypothesis about future price movement in a security due to an observable trend in data or expectations of a change in future data.

The research report's analyst/author attempts to support her hypothesis using a combination of historical data, relationships to similar securities, or predictions of certain future conditions. In the case of research of a single security, the author will typically try to identify the circumstances that led up to the current price. She will then present comparative information about similar securities to demonstrate how the security's current valuation compares to other securities given the same economic conditions. When she shows the specific security compared with other securities over time, it's typically because there is some deviation from the mean that is the motivation for writing the research in the first place.

Finally, the author will make certain suppositions to explain a potential price movement in the near future. She may predict how the security will perform due to possible economic conditions to come or how it may revert to its normal proportional relationship to other securities. (I use the word "predict" because that is all it is—a prediction. However, expect to see the word "projection" instead of "prediction" in future instances, as "projection" sounds so much more plausible.) Since predicting the future price of securities is challenging and rewarding, when an analyst makes a correct call, she will develop a reputation for accuracy relative to her peers. Such analysts become well-known over time, and some of them have even become household names.

Critiquing Street Research

How do we critique institutional-quality research? If every research piece written made correct predictions of future market movements, there would be no need for trading books, algorithmic computer models, or Mike Bloomberg's vast data network. Instead, we would just gather the street's research on our favorite stocks, take a few minutes to read the reports, and make profitable bets. If their track record were even slightly better than 50/50, it would be a well-publicized accomplishment worthy of yearly awards in *The Wall Street Journal*.

The fact that neither you nor I have ever identified authors on Wall Street who continually publish winning trade ideas is no surprise to experienced traders. Still, it may be a surprise to the novice.

What are the factors that make predicting price movements difficult? How do we learn to be critical when we have grown up to believe the written word, particularly Wall Street research, which often sounds a lot like the economics textbooks we read in school?

When we read a well-constructed financial argument, our brains revert to a basic premise we adopted to survive as we were growing up. In short, we are trained to take in the word of our instructor. We are encouraged to accept whatever textbook he or she gives us to read. We define learning as acceptance of authoritatively written documents to be memorized and regurgitated.

This learning system does not encourage debate, much less questioning what is taught. There is simply no time. It would slow things down, and we would never cover the entire required curriculum before year's end.

Imagine that you are presented with a well-written, well-constructed, and well-researched thesis on a particular security. Remember, your instincts are first and foremost *not* to question authority. Therefore, it is only natural that we think these professional trade presentations are good ideas.

We also have a deep need to be right. As traders, we feel embarrassed when we get a trade wrong. We feel doubly ashamed when we are wrong about a trade that, seemingly, most others got right. What can be more humiliating than getting a trade wrong when the very idea of the trade was presented to you as a beautiful research piece? A document that you know was circulated to other professionals, all of whom executed on the idea you passed on!

When we read the research, we have to fight the primal instincts drilled into our heads over a lifetime of education. We need to question the preamble, the premises, the assumptions, and even how the conclusions are drawn. Once we learn that it is all right to challenge the thinkers and researchers in our industry, we can begin to use research as a tool to enhance our trading ideas.

Analysts' Biases

Let's start with the understanding that authors have a bias. That is, they often have a predetermined belief about an asset and set out to find evidence to prove their case. This process is opposite to what you might assume it to be, as most readers think the researcher lets the facts determine the conclusion.

For example, imagine an analyst at Citibank presupposes that oil prices are going higher and that analyst has a Ph.D. in thermodynamics. In that case, it will be reasonably easy for him to write a research piece suggesting that oil prices are going up. As the reader of this research, we are likely to assume that the analyst was neutral before he drew his conclusions.

Since we cannot know who has a bias and who does not, we have to assume that all authors have a preference. Their bias can be innocent in that they honestly believe that their conclusions come from assessing the facts and not from some hidden conviction lodged in their subconscious. Their bias can also be insidious, and can even manifest as an attempt to further their career by choosing a controversial stance in the hope that if they are proven right, they will receive acclaim for predicting something will happen that no one else saw coming! As it turns out, career advancement and fame are big-time motivators for analysts to make risky predictions, even if their real goal should be to help their clients succeed in the market.

One way to deal with bias is to pit leading analysts against each other and compare what they say about the same asset. It is much more likely that you will feel better informed if you compare the Citibank analyst's view with those of the Goldman Sachs and Bank of America analysts.

Focus on the Depth of Research and Factual Persuasiveness

When we critique research, we need to focus on the depth of research and the persuasiveness of the facts. Depth of research refers to how much detail an institutional author may use to convince their reader that a security is mispriced. The author can use many well-laid-out arguments supported by an array of facts, figures, and logic.

This can be a valuable recommendation when you see that the thought process is detailed and the analysis is thoroughly researched. On the other hand, a trade recommendation made by using just a few facts suggests that these ideas may only partially explain which way the market will go next.

The foreign exchange market provides an excellent example of the depth of analysis one can conduct about a market. It is generally understood that many factors cause a foreign exchange rate to go up or down. Most times, the market is balanced, with many factors offsetting each other. Thus, it is quite natural for an FX analyst to be persuasive about the direction of a currency by making only a few basic arguments on why the market can tip one way or another with the advent of just a few new facts. But in reality, a few points may not be very persuasive to large market participants and have little effect on the actual price.

You must challenge the arguments to see if they are new, relevant, well-supported, and, most importantly, would sway others in control of enough capital to move the market. Therefore, when analyzing the information, consider the sources the writer is using. Do they come from unique research, or are they general thoughts already present in the public domain?

For example, banks often have proprietary information on trade volumes and flows that may be unavailable to the trading public. This type of information tends to be more valuable than regurgitating newspaper stories about how traders react to the market. Individual analysts often have access to key decision-makers such as central bankers or politicians, presenting a unique perspective that cannot be found in other publications.

Good sources also include hard data that may not be readily available in the public domain. A good analyst will do the digging for you where others will not. Data on commodities, sales trends for stocks, and central bank data on bond purchases are all examples of information in the public domain, but only relevant in the hands of a professional analyst who knows what the data means.

On the other hand, it is quite natural for an analyst to regurgitate what they have read in the newspaper. Maybe it is comments from a central banker that were widely publicized in the financial press but are being restated as a trading idea. Or perhaps the source is another trader who is hyped as being knowledgeable but does not see the markets any more clearly than you do. Or it may be information gathered from chats on social media, which is impossible to fact-check and should be treated more as gossip than research.

When one reviews street research, we need to overcome our biases and those of the analysts who authored the analysis. We need to question authority. If we come to the same conclusion that the analyst does after we (1) test the hypothesis, (2) challenge the assumptions, and (3) check the data, we can then be more confident in whether we should bet our capital on the trade proposal or not.

Again, we want to dig for the sources, determine if they are credible, and draw our conclusions to determine if the information is unique and timely or repetitive and in the public domain. If we follow these market practices on filtering what we read, we will quickly build a stable of analysts and sources that we trust. That will be our first step in sound idea generation.

CHAPTER 6

Integrating News Items into Your Trading

N ews headlines about stocks, bonds, foreign exchange, and other investment vehicles constantly flow from global media, affecting prices and valuations continuously. Technically, all news, by definition, is unexpected. However, planned announcements often come with an expectation of what the result will be. For example, with stocks, there are often earnings estimates available before the actual announcement.

We will categorize headlines in two ways: (1) those that have an estimate before the headline (which, for our purposes, are news releases), and (2) those that are mostly unexpected, which we call news announcements.

Examples of news releases are quarterly earnings, monthly sales reports, and central bank policy meeting summaries. Examples of news announcements can be political events, takeover announcements, or weather incidents. In most cases, both types of headlines can affect preconceived notions that you have about a particular trade. If you have already put a trade on, you may have to respond to a surprise headline by modifying your position, often under duress. If you are still gathering research on a security, you must incorporate the news in an unbiased manner. Altogether, you must accept the facts even if the new data is contradictory to your original thinking.

Managing News Items

Many financial securities have known dates in the future where new facts will be published that will confirm or alter our view as to the valuation.

For example, all publicly traded stocks have quarterly earnings announcements, with dates set up to a year in advance. Each company releases the previous quarter's results for sales, earnings, and cash flow, as well as future estimates. There are monthly estimates of oil reserves, crop reports, and metals data in the commodities industry. The financial sector likewise has dates for central bank announcements and economic data that are released by local and national governments.

In almost all cases, analysts in the financial industry publish their predictions for the data to be announced using their historical databases, regression analyses, and anecdotal information. As their predictions are distributed and read by the traders, the predictions are incorporated into the security's price. Ultimately, the analysts' forecasts become the "expected" result of the soon-to-be-released information. The degree to which the actual announcement hits or misses the expected outcome will affect the degree and timeliness in which traders recalculate the security value. The larger the shock or surprise value, the more likely it is that the security will be re-priced instantaneously.

How do we manage news items as part of our research toolbox? Are we to just take the news as the risk of what we do and hope for more good news than bad over time? Or is there some way to manage news releases and headlines in a more structured approach to give our trading an edge over others?

As usual, with trading, there is no set formula on how to deal with news—just best practices. We all want news headlines to go our way when we are already invested in a security. When considering a trade, we want news headlines to provide us with a great entry point or confirmation of our thinking. But since wishing is not what professionals do, we have to devise best practices to manage headline risk.

Research the Market Consensus

The first best practice for headline management is to research the market consensus for a predicted news release concerning the securities you have decided to trade. Not only do you want to know the consensus estimate, but also whether that estimate has a tight distribution.

Suppose the distribution of the forecasts is close to the average estimate. In that case, markets approach the pending news with everyone thinking the same way. On the other hand, if there is a broad distribution of estimates compared to the average, you know there is uncertainty. The more uncertainty that exists, the higher the volatility of the price of the security.

Thanks to the web and data service providers such as Bloomberg or Barron's, researching the consensus is easier than it used to be. Many services publish estimates for earnings, economic releases, commodity reports, and central bank policy forecasts. Often, if you dig, you can find the range of estimates as well.

Compare Latest Data with Past Average Estimates

The second-best practice is comparing the average estimates in the past with the actual data that comes out. Some securities, like utilities or industrial companies, tend to provide accurate forecasts of future earnings. Thus, it is no surprise that the estimates by analysts covering these companies come exceedingly close to the actual data.

On the other hand, specific securities, such as growth stocks, are dependent on data that is quite hard to accurately predict. Your research should reflect how often estimates for news releases are missed by a significant margin and what the subsequent reaction was in the price. (By "subsequent," I mean the next few seconds or the next few days as the data gets absorbed by the marketplace.)

As a researcher, the questions for you are the following:

A) Am I involved in a security that is often affected by surprises in planned news releases?

B) Am I confident in my research about what that news release will be, or am I reliant on others for that data?

C) If I am reliant on others, how often is the data missed, and what is the market's typical reaction?

Answering these questions will help frame your thinking about when you should enter the market. If you have high confidence in a forecast, you'll want to enter the market before the planned announcement. If you're going to play it safe, then you'll want to avoid planned announcements and look to enter the market days or even weeks later, after you have quantified the announcements' effect on the price.

The Difficulties Surrounding Management of News Items

Realistically, it is hard to have market practices for news events. By definition, news events are unexpected, which makes it difficult to evaluate their significance in advance. However, over the past ten to fifteen years, we have witnessed extreme events, including war, terror, disease threats, natural disasters, oil shocks, fraud of all types, and political events. Looking back now, we can study the data on how most securities reacted to these shocks.

As traders, when we choose our trade design, we must take into account the possibilities of a significant move after a surprising piece of news. Would the risk of a 10% or 15% drop in the price of our security in one or two days (no matter how unlikely) lead us to consider buying an option rather than directly purchasing the security? How volatile is our security during news events? Have the markets in the past ignored your security when global news hits? (For example, utility stocks tend to be ignored if the news item is not weather-related.) Is it a stock people are fearful of when bad news hits? (For example, the travel industry typically gets hurt following terrorist events.)

Traders must prepare for the possibilities of news events for the securities they research and plan to trade. First, run scenarios using historical data (use percentage changes from the past so you can compare like for like data over time) to see how often your security has a significant jump up or down in price.

Next, determine the potential holding time of your trade. The longer the holding period, the more likely your trade timeline will cover a news event or two. However, an option's cost will most likely be too prohibitive to buy solely based on the small chance of a single news event. A more extended holding period may make the same option more attractive, given the higher likelihood of a series of news events.

In summary, with research headlines, we care about the estimates and the distribution of those estimates. The larger the range and the more extensive the forecast's dispersion, the less confidence the market has in the future price path of the security in question.

We also look for accuracy. The less accurate the historical track record is of estimates, the more we have to rely on our own knowledge base of that security when we plan to trade it.

Finally, we want to use historical data to understand how the asset we are interested in handles news events. This helps shape our thinking about the potential volatility of our security, even if extreme events seem unlikely. The higher the volatility risk, the more you should consider implementing alternative trading strategies, such as buying an option instead of the security or waiting for a planned news release before entering your trade.

CHAPTER 7

Processing Incoming Information

Trade ideas begin with research. However, the market does not remain stagnant while your plan germinates. Instead, new information comes in that you will have to process.

What does it mean to process information like a trader? Speed is a critical component of being successful in trading. While speed alone is not the only determining factor, there is no denying its success in today's marketplace. Somewhere between 60% and 80% of the volume on an average day of New York Stock Exchange trading is done by traders using super-fast computers loaded with algorithmic equations.[7] If speed were not an issue, we would see a greater mix of trading styles, as we did before the age of fast computing.

Most Futures Commission brokers (that is, FCMs for "Futures Commission Merchants") report that their clients who use some form of computerized trading are more profitable and have greater career longevity than those who do not. As an example, some computers are programmed to read news headlines and react when they see words like "surprise," "miss," or "greater than expected." Other computers are programmed to: (1) do math comparing an earnings release or an economic release to the number that was expected, and (2) follow a specific rule set when the difference between the numbers is more than one standard deviation from the mean expectation.

Information Advantage May Be Interwoven into Speed

Interwoven with the need for speed is the understanding that others may have an edge, which gives them an advantage over you and others in the same security.

---

[7] "Machines Are Driving Wall Street's Wild Ride, Not Humans," Chris Isidore, CNN Business website

In the excellent trading classic, *Reminiscences of a Stock Operator,*[8] a book about how the stock market operated from 1900 into the 1920s, the author, Edwin Lefevre, explains how the market seems at times to move to an unusual new valuation. When this happens, he says, traders should go with the latest trend because, very often, news comes along afterward to justify the move. That is, by the time one hears the story, it's too late to make money. The move has already happened.

Lefevre further explains his theory that "news comes to justify the move," citing a famous example when railroad stocks began a once-in-a-lifetime rally, with no news ahead of time to explain such a significant move. Only after the big move was on its way would the story become apparent: the Great San Francisco Earthquake of 1906 had occurred, and rails would be needed to move material to help rebuild an entire city.

What is implied by Lefevre's writings is that the market is smarter than any trader; somehow, markets figure out what good news or bad news is coming. In reality, someone always has the correct information. Even back in Lefevre's day, someone knew of the Great Earthquake and figured out how to make a profitable trade before others did. The person with the information knew he was right. He could thereby trade with greater conviction and continue to buy until others who had sold to him were forced out of the trade and began to buy too, even if they did not know why they were doing it!

When someone has information before others, it is called an Information Advantage. When others believe they are trading with someone with an Information Advantage, they will avoid that marketplace lest they lose a lot of money. For decades, regulators have been concerned with the public perception that an Information Advantage rigs the markets against the average investor. Congress responded beginning in 1933 with the Securities Act of 1933 and followed with another set of laws in 1940.[9]

Since 1940, the rules and regulations have been updated to meet the challenges presented by each new form of information dissemination. These processes were put into place to level the playing field through legislation and by granting power to the Securities and Exchange Commission (SEC) and the Commodity Futures Trading Commission (CFTC), among other agencies, to enforce the law. Banning insider trading, regulating how and when corporations release material information, and

---

[8] *Reminiscences of a Stock Operator*, Edwin Lefevre, George Doran and Company, 1923
[9] Law.cornell.edu/wex/securities_act_of_1933

standardizing the timing of press releases on economic data are some of the more public policies that the federal government has established concerning information dissemination.

Speed Is an Advantage That Cannot Be Regulated Away

As a trader in 2020 and beyond, one must recognize that speed is an advantage that cannot be regulated away. Information travels faster and faster, and computers interpret that information faster and faster as well.

At its September 18th, 2013 meeting, the Federal Reserve decided to maintain its policy that was in effect at the time. The Fed continued purchasing $85 billion in US bonds each month, at least for the time being. The market had been expecting a "tapering" or reduction in the number of bonds the Fed would purchase each month. Computers at the CFTC detected that traders began to buy bonds within 3/100 of a second after the announcement was released—faster than any human could process the data. The reaction was so fast that it was doubtful that a computer could receive the data quick enough and decide whether to buy or sell in 3/100 of a second.[10]

Whether there was either an illegal early leak of the data or that computers have reached a new plateau of processing speed is of little consequence. What is important is that you, as a trader, need to accept that the speed of information processing, with or without an Information Advantage, is a critical part of trading. It is a golden goose, as it were, for the multitudes of traders who attempt to succeed in trading by merely using faster and faster processors.

If you are so analytically inclined, you, too, can pursue trading as a "speed war" and focus your skillset on winning that battle. Suppose you are not sufficiently well-capitalized or not as interested in a trading style dedicated to high-speed computer algorithms. In that case, you need to identify speed as an influence on the marketplace and adjust your processing of information to include how high-speed traders are reacting. In other words, to combat the speed advantage of others, you need to have a two-step process: (1) you must analyze the information on its merits, and (2) you must study how traders faster than you have assessed and reacted to the news.

For example, in the case of the September 18th, 2013 Fed meeting, within seconds of the Fed announcement, the ten-year US government bond interest rate had already

---

[10] *The Financial Review*, Edition 49, M.A. Goldstein et al, pages 177-202

rallied 13 basis points. As a trader, one then had to assess for herself: (1) if the announcement was indeed a bullish event, and then (2) evaluate to what degree the fast algo traders have it right: was a 13-basis-point rally too much, too little, or just right?

Just to give you some perspective on how vital speed is becoming, think about this little anecdote. I recently attended a presentation featuring Jack Schwager, author of *The Market Wizards*,[11] a collection of stories and trading theories from many of the recognized "great" bank traders of our generation. Two of the individuals Schwager wrote about in the book were invited to speak to the audience. One of these traders commented that he might never have been written about in Jack's book had he grown up in the current trading environment. When he started in the business, his trading edge was getting up at 5:00 a.m. and getting to the place in Manhattan where the first issues of that day's *The Wall Street Journal* were delivered. By reading the paper before anyone else did, he found stories a few times a week that could move markets. In other words, he profited by acting before the majority of traders had digested the same article.

Listening to that story, I had to admit I had made many a dollar reading an article and trading on it before the overall market picked up on the information. Today, critical articles by the most widely followed writers in the *Journal* are reacted to within seconds of the story's release by traders reading the online version of the paper. As we say in the industry, "By the time the ink is dry, the story is too old to trade on!"

The Ability to Filter

Third, in addition to understanding speed and Information Advantages, you must have the ability to filter.

In the digital age, information is expanding at a frightening speed. One calculation has it that 80% of all the world's digital information currently in storage was written in the last five years. To put it another way, all the data from the beginning of time until 2015—over 5,000 years of history—represents only 20% of the total information stored today.[12]

Thus, as a trader, you have the unenviable job of filtering through a rapidly growing array of data and prioritizing it to assess value in the marketplace. Some data can be

---

[11] *Market Wizards,* Jack Schwager, John Wiley & Sons, 1989
[12] Sciencedaily.com, May 22nd, 2013

worthless for evaluating the price of a security, whereas other data can be so crucial that they are universally accepted as market moving. Still other data may have a substantial influence initially on a minority of traders, but over time, sway the majority. This data is often the most influential on the market and the area in which great traders like to operate. This is because as influential data begins to sink in, more and more capital will be applied to move the price of a security.

A great example of data that matters, but which is typically ignored by market participants, is 10K and 10Q filings by corporations. The SEC requires public companies to file these reports in a timely manner and release them to the public. These filings contain all the relevant financial information of a corporation's earnings in such meticulous detail that many traders ignore them and choose to read the abbreviated corporate press release instead.

Yet, these filings often reveal essential nuances such as cash management, sales trends, and new risks that the company has identified in the competitive landscape, along with investments in research and development. These small nuances can ultimately affect the company's valuation, particularly as larger investors dig into the reports.

Data Ranking Is Critical to Trading Success

Finally, the corollary of filtering data is ranking data. Often, there will be conflicting pieces of information that will cause debate as to whether a security is likely to go up or down, so being able to rank data is critical to trading success. In ranking data, the goal is to rank it by its ability to influence a security's price and the degree to which the price will be affected.

Ranking data includes identifying which data has expired in terms of its influence on the market. A particular data point can be worth a 10% movement in a commodity price, but that same data point can wither in value as time elapses. For instance, the weekly report on crude oil supplies can often move the market dramatically at the time of the report's release. However, within days, trading on that report alone would have little to no effect on the market, which typically moves on to other, more up-to-date factors.

Furthermore, data ranking is not merely about the age of a report but also about the significance of one data point versus another. The monthly US jobs report is probably the most famous continuous example of this idea. On the first Friday of each month, the US Department of Labor publishes the most recent jobs report. The report includes various figures, such as the unemployment rate, the total of non-farm jobs created, the average number of hours worked per week, and the average income earned per week. All this data hints at the real-time health of the US economy. When it comes to traders, they typically rank the data in this report by what is more critical to Federal Reserve members, who may act on this data in the future.

Thus, the modern-day trader needs to filter the available information and this filter must process data quickly. As there is an ever-growing array of information, the filter must also delineate market-moving data from unrelated data to security pricing. Finally, data that is deemed essential must be ranked as to its ultimate value because different data will have different effects on an asset's price in the market.

CHAPTER 8

Independent Research—
How to Generate Your Own Ideas

ndependent research is defined as research produced by the reader that is obtained by sources other than street research from the financial industry designed for general distribution.

This definition can be quite broad and encompass a great deal of information. Articles on the web or in a newspaper may be uninteresting to some but may represent excellent research material for you. For instance, a day at the mall might mean a fun shopping trip for your spouse. Still, for you, it might be an excellent opportunity to research sales trends at the very source where the consumer votes with their wallet! These days, even listening to a game or app that a 10-year-old finds popular might lead you to an idea about a company worth checking out. Think Roblox or Fortnite!

Independent research might also mean traditional forms of research. Searching through your local libraries to read excerpts on historical market conditions is an excellent way to discern similarities between markets today and those of the past. For example, the policy initiatives taken by the Federal Reserve beginning in 2010 to boost the economy were taken right out of the playbook of the US Treasury and the Federal Reserve, from their actions dating 1932 through 1937 during the Great Depression.[13]

Independent research can also mean reading publications of thought leaders or academics, which might expose new policy ideas that will be picked up by politicians or central bankers—thereby having a direct effect on the market. A great example of this is Modern Monetary Theory.[14] This theory, which recently (2019) came back in prominence, is based on the idea that large governments with dominant currencies

---

[13] *A History of the Federal Reserve: Volume 1*, Allan Meltzer, University of Chicago Press, 2003
[14] "Modern Monetary Theory, Explained," Dylan Matthews, Vox.com, April 16th, 2019

can print money to solve short-term economic problems. They can do this without fear of inflation because they can always pay back the debt created with the currency they own. This theory, which for years existed as a small corner of the academic world, has suddenly taken hold as actionable with the COVID-19 outbreak of 2020.

There is no right or wrong answer about where to go for information. But it is critical that you develop a knack for independent thinking and challenge yourself to open your mind to the notion that there are trading ideas everywhere in the real world. Remember that independent research is a two-way process—you can have an idea and look for data to back up your hypothesis, or you can get a trading idea from what you read or observe.

Estimating Future Value

The most critical part of independent thinking for one's research is to develop a methodology for future conditions. While predicting the future is an imperfect process, it is necessary to assess a security's prospects to trade successfully. Remember, you are expressing a futuristic opinion by the mere act of trading, whether it was formally developed or not.

In reality, we predict the future with every financial transaction we conduct. We buy a car not just based on our current needs but also considering our future demand for driving that car. When we loan money to someone, we predict the future likelihood of being paid back. We borrow money to pay college tuition based somewhat on our predicted earning power of a college degree. Fear not the concept of estimating potential future value; we do it all the time.

Making Future Assumptions About a Bond

What predictions should we make or consider about an asset? Let's consider two popular investments: bonds and stocks.

For a bond, the objective of our prediction is clear: we just want the issuer to pay us our interest and principal. No matter how successful a corporation might be in the future, if we invest in bonds, they will only pay us interest and principal. The rest goes to the stockholders. Thus, we want to make projections about the company's future creditworthiness. We do this by assessing how much money they have currently borrowed relative to their cash flow. (We can do this with state or local government debt as well.) By doing so, we can assess if the bond is collateralized by an asset such as a machine or property, which may give us some assurance that the company would rather pay back the bond than risk losing that asset.

We can also look at the management team's culture and assess whether they are risk-takers with a propensity to borrow lots of money. Furthermore, we can ask ourselves these questions: will management leave investors wondering whether they will get paid back (think casino operators, as an example)? Or does the management consist of conservative stalwarts whose very value is based on their strong creditworthiness (think Berkshire Hathaway, as an example)?

We then sum up these simple predictions along with as many other external factors as the investor can consider. Examples are: industry risk, central bank interest rate policy, and inflation—all affect the value proposition. Often, our analysis of different bonds will lead us to rank our predictions in order of confidence. These rankings should guide us in terms of how we commit our capital.

Lastly, many bond services rank and rate bonds of all types. As a prudent trader, you would do well to compare your predictions with one of these services to see where you agree and disagree. Be a good devil's advocate with yourself by challenging why an independent source does not support the bonds you think are reliable. If you remain committed to your prediction, what information could come in the future that would make you reconsider?

Making Future Assumptions About a Stock

Predictions about stocks involve a great deal of information processing. The goal is to determine what is happening with the business to date and how past trends might play out in the future.

Two of the most common predictions are on growth and value. Growing companies are companies whose sales rise year over year, often from a new product or innovative service. As the company builds out its marketing team, it can reach many customers, leading to higher year-over-year revenues. Often, profits follow revenues. Therefore, making predictions about growth trends is the leading driver of trading ideas for stocks.

To most investors, it is most comfortable to simply project historical growth trends into the future, determining which profits could be generated if those sales predictions come to fruition. Professional traders, however, look for deeper insights than just trends. They look at market share and the ability of a particular company to gain more—i.e., is the company's product or service so innovative and market-leading that it will drive growth and sales? Or is the company competing on price alone, and if so, will competitors lower their prices and hurt profits for everyone? Is the product global or regionally centric? Growth trends can expand for longer if the product or service can extend beyond its home country borders. Ask yourself: what does it cost for the company to acquire a customer (marketing, advertising, word of mouth, etc.)? The cheaper, the better. If marketing can go viral, even better. Finally, is the product digital? One of the main reasons that the growth of technology companies has been like no other in history is software and Internet companies' ability to create and recreate their products digitally. Digital copying involves virtually no cost to make or distribute—something no company could have dreamed about before 2000.

In contrast, value investing tends to look more at the protectability of a company's product or service. Patents, quasi-monopolies, and brands all create value that is hard to duplicate. Value companies have loyal customers who cannot shift to alternatives quickly. Whether an electric company, which is given a quasi-government monopoly to operate, or a brand so storied in history, such as Louis Vuitton, a value company has a market share that can be counted on for years to come.

Typically, value companies have limited growth year to year. But on the other hand, they avoid dramatic changes in their competitive landscape and can invest over the long haul. Pharmaceutical companies are ideal value models where patents protect their current sales portfolios. At the same time, new investments in drug discoveries fill the pipeline for future years.

Consider New Structural Trends

Growth and value are two of the most common ways of predicting (or projecting) a future price in the fundamental analysis world. Still, there are many styles of fundamental analysis to choose from. Sometimes investors can generate ideas from companies just being born, focusing purely on these companies' potential.

For example, investors today are looking at artificial intelligence, virtual reality, and quantum computing strictly for their potential, even if successful applications are not yet visible. Often, investors will bet on smart management teams and prototypes at the birth of innovation—doing so is high risk but high reward! On the other hand, fallen angels (stocks that were once popular but have since lost their cache) can rise again with creative management and a new structural idea.

Does anyone recognize the chart below of this fallen high-flyer dating back to 2000 who has made a bit of a comeback since?

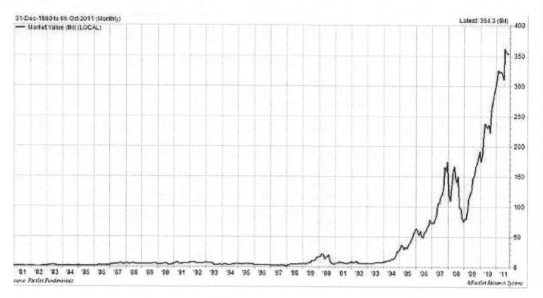

Of course, it is Apple (APPL). Many thought Apple dead in the water when it lost momentum building Mac computers in the late '80s and mid '90s. It took a rejuvenated Steve Jobs about five years upon his return to Apple to design brand-new technology and reinvigorate a stodgy company. Today, that fallen angel has become the greatest comeback kid of all time.

Though shoppers were amazed when they first saw the iPod in 2001, many investors had a bias against Apple, given its previous 20 years of fits and starts. Overcoming those past biases took three years from iPod's introduction. Then, Apple stock began its long 16-year ascent that seems obvious in hindsight.

Best Practices for Vetting Your Trading Idea

Whether you find an idea independently or are presented with an idea you want to research, you need to conduct a best-practice methodology to validate your premise. Critique your concept in the same manner you would expect a professional analyst to review his facts before presenting it to the public as a trade recommendation.

In some instances, critiquing your trade idea is easy because many securities you would consider trading already have professional trade recommendations on them, enabling you to simply compare your independent logic with the professional's view.

Take Apple, for example, where you go online to compare your trading thesis with several analysts from major financial institutions. Challenge yourself to be as professional as you can with due diligence on your view. Google the good and bad about a stock you are interested in and see if any critiques you find get you to change your mind.

If your ideas are researched well and you have challenged them intellectually, you will feel more confident when you create a trade around them. Your research should help you not only determine the direction of the trade, but also what your profit objective should have. It should also include the time frame needed for the trade to be successful. Finally, consider what adverse price action might cause you to think that there is contradictory information out there that is superior to your reasoning for making the trade.

What follows is my list of the top ten sources of independent information for trade ideas. Use this list as a starting point while learning to open your mind to the notion that trading ideas can come from anywhere. Ultimately, you will develop your own top ten list, which will probably be better than mine. After all, it will be personalized for you and will most likely contain unique sources that you care most about.

My Top Ten Sources for Independent Trade Ideas

1.) *Thought Leaders*

Read and listen to entire speeches or discussions with central bankers or ex-central bankers. Hear out current and former CEO or corporate board members. Seek out what the founders of the company think and what makes their approach novel. Often the Chief Technology Officer or Chief Science Officer knows the company's vision better than the company's CEO and can see the future for the product or service they are developing.

In the Twitter age of 140 characters, too many rely on headlines and nothing else for their information. Yet, an entire speech or quarterly press release will often have a much deeper understanding than some reporter's headline. By reading the whole text, you can do what no algorithmic machine can do—i.e., understand the intonation, context, and emphasis on what is and what is not crucial to the speechmaker. What is emphasized often resonates with the listener. At the same time, headlines can often put the wrong accent on what was important.

2.) *Experts from Academia Who Look at Data as Impartially as Possible*

Academics publish papers that are read and reviewed by other scholars in a process called peer review. Therefore, they operate under a much higher standard to support their theories with facts. These papers are valuable tools for trade ideas because academics' goal is to improve current thinking and challenge the norm in new ways. In doing so, they must support their arguments with further research since their arguments will not be published if their data is not an advancement of what has been written before.

3.) *Data and Projections by Large Independent Organizations*

These organizations include the World Bank, the International Monetary Fund (IMF), or the Organization for Economic Cooperation and Development (OECD).

Funded by member countries, these global organizations publish global, regional, and country-specific data and economic projections. This data is valuable when considering long-term trends, demographics, or determining if there is enough economic growth to help companies bolster sales or investment.

4.) *The Red Herring*

"Red herring" is an old term that refers to the red ink used on background documents prepared by companies for investors just before they issue a bond or stock to the public. In today's world, this term means anything published by corporations or bond issuers that explains their current financial and business conditions. These publications include quarterly reports (including footnotes), documents prepared for bond issuance, financial projections, or press releases.

Often, lazy traders will let a news service condense these documents into a few short headlines. These traders will make decisions based on the angle of the news reporter instead of reading the report themselves and developing their own view of the company or bond issuer.

5.) *Flow of Funds*

Where are money and business moving? We can find the answer in the money-flow information.

For example, when central banks publish the number of reserves they have, they tell us which currencies are being accumulated. Sales data tell us what is being bought or sold both in a broad economic sense and at a micro level. Which companies are growing sales and which are declining? Data on crops or oil demand help show the flow in these commodities.

Most flow data is now available for free on the web. Still, if you need more real-time data, you can look to data publishers who charge a fee for their services, such as Standard & Poor's, Bloomberg, or FactSet.

There have also been developments in artificial intelligence services that offer to do the digging for you in real time (many of these firms use the ".ai" domain extension to denote they do this type of research). Many of these services will provide you with a list of criteria you can use to screen thousands of stocks at once for things like credit card sales, miles traveled, or stores that are popular based on geolocation services!

This flow data is exciting and daunting at the same time. Remember that making an effort to support your hypothesis with facts will help you build a lasting trade idea that can take the marketplace's ups and downs.

6.) Conversations with Other Traders

Other traders are putting their capital at risk just like you, and they collectively drive the market. Traders are an amazingly diverse bunch of people, so seeking them out and learning what motivates them can open new ways of thinking about your markets.

Though some traders consider what they know to be proprietary and will not discuss it, many see value in exchanging knowledge because both sides get to learn something. Many business news channels interview leading traders; those interviews are available on these channels' websites. Top traders also speak at conventions or retreats, and their speeches are usually published the same or next day.

7.) Exchange Data

Ultimately, most securities that are traded are cleared by a financial exchange. Thus, exchanges have a deep set of information worth studying.

Exchanges publish a "tape," which is a stream of trades in order of which security has most recently traded and at what price. "The Tape" has been watched by traders for a century, dating back to the early 1900s. Even the best-kept trade secret shows up on the tape because to profit from a good idea, one must eventually go to the exchange and execute a trade, which the exchange then publishes to the world!

Personally, I check the tape a few times a day, even for just 15 minutes, to look for symbols that repeat and appear to be exploding up or down. The brain and its visual contextualization are an excellent computer. Do not underestimate its ability to pick up unusual movements in stock prices. Following up on the why will often lead to news or information that you will formulate into a new trading idea. With the advent of speedy computers, one can achieve the same results using alerts set on electronic tape-reading platforms. For example, services like Benzinga Pro provide up to the minute lists of stocks that are on the move over the last hour or day. Try different settings with these alerts, such as new year-to-date high, double average volume, double average intra-day move, etc.

8.) Implied Volatility and Put/Call Skew

Most securities have a settlement price, which attempts to be a neutral point where the security will trade next. Some securities, however, are poised to move much more than others. By studying the option prices of the securities we are interested in trading, we can discern if the market is expecting large future movements based on their implied volatility.

We derive implied volatility using an option price formula (see Chapter 17 on options). The higher the volatility assumptions, the more the market expects the security will jump in the future. Also, by studying the Put-Call Skew (which answers the question, "Are Puts more or less expensive than Calls, given the same percentage difference from the current stock price?"), we can determine if the market has a bias for our security to go up or down in the future.

9.) Historical Data and Charts of Price Changes

Humans are visual creatures. Often, when presented with a chart of historical prices, humans cannot help but see a pattern that makes them believe where a security might trade next. No matter the sum of past prices resulting from traders moving the security based on the news and the valuation at the time, many traders still make predictions of where prices will go in the future solely on the pattern of a chart.

Thus, it is essential to understand these traders' perspectives since a tremendous amount of capital is willing to be invested based exclusively on a chart pattern.

10.) News That Affects Related Securities

Always think of the coin as two-sided: if the news is good for my stock, maybe it is bad for another stock. Perhaps selling the stock of the bad company is as good a trade as buying the stock of a good company!

For instance, when the news is good for electric cars' growth, it means that the story is terrible for gasoline producers. Alternatively, trying to pick who the winner will be among Netflix, Amazon, or Hulu may be more challenging than the more straightforward trade idea that Blockbuster Video will be wiped out.

Go and Build Your Top Ten List of Sources

Suppose you found my top ten list unfulfilling. That means you are already thinking about your sources of inspiration that make you a unique trader.

Again, my top ten list is a starting point. Add or subtract from my list by focusing on which sources you find lead the market. There is a mass of information out there; use your filters and focus on the sources that deliver the goods.

Above all, remember that the useful information you gather has to change your valuation proposition and also motivate others to change their view, so other capital will be used to move the security you care about in the direction you predicted.

CHAPTER 9

The Valuation Proposition

I n theory, if you could absorb all the institutional research, news headlines, and independent research available to you and place the information presented in some sort of supermatrix, trade ideas might fall out logically. Many of the world's largest investment firms aggregate massive amounts of data with the help of an army of analysts and a load of supercomputers. They promote their trade recommendations under the premise that they have indeed sorted through all of the relevant information for us.

But in reality, no one holds a monopoly on ideas. Some ideas are birthed simply from taking the counterview of what the majority thinks! Therefore, our job is to develop our unique process for generating ideas based on the best market practices of using the information we get from our research sources.

The first best practice of developing a valuation assessment is to understand the difference between finding the valuation and finding a trade idea. Our goal is to find valuations in the securities we analyze that are significantly different from the current estimates in the market to warrant the risk, the cost, and the effort to make a trade. When we study valuations, we must not have any inherent prejudice against the current market price. In fact, by ignoring current pricing, we can reach our own conclusion about the valuation. If it turns out that our assessment is similar to current pricing, we have achieved a reasonable outcome. When we come to a different valuation than the current market price, we have the beginnings of a trade idea; we need to assess this difference.

The second-best practice is to develop a level of confidence in our valuation assessment. No trade is sure to work. Instead, we have varying degrees of confidence in our valuation assessment. We gain confidence when we check our research sources and look for other supporting sources for our valuation. Our confidence can also grow when new incoming data validates the model we are using to predict future prices. (Examples of this new data could include updated projections of sales or social media exposure.) Confidence can likewise come from a speech or comment by an influential market participant who shares your valuation view. In the end, you will develop a sense of the level of confidence you assign to each valuation judgment you make.

Valuation Premises for the Four Major Financial Instruments

We now understand that our valuation assessment and the methods we use to confirm that assessment are critical to having trading ideas that can succeed. Let us now delve deeper into the value we are trying to determine with each of the four primary financial instruments we might trade—equities, bonds, commodities, and foreign exchange.

There are other asset classes outside of the four instrument types I am about to describe. Still, the core elements of how we think about valuation are the same and worthy of simplification. What follows are the basic valuation premises for each of these instruments; in each footnote, I provide you with an excellent starter book on valuing each of these types of assets in more detail.

1. Equity Valuation Premise:

We compare current market capitalization to future expected market capitalization.[15]

2. Bond Valuation Premise:

We estimate the bond issuer's ability to make the cash payments due for a bond, from today going forward, and the potential change in interest rates (interest, principal, and price appreciation).[16]

3. Commodity Valuation Premise:

We derive whether the terminal scarcity value of a commodity will be significantly different from what is perceived today.[17]

4. Foreign Exchange Premise:

We estimate if the value of one currency will appreciate in relation to another currency.[18]

---

[15] *One Up on Wall Street*, Peter Lynch, Simon and Schuster, 1989
[16] *Inside the Yield Book*, Martin Leibowitz, Prentice Hall, 1972
[17] *Hot Commodities*, Jim Rogers, Random House, 2004
[18] *The Art of Currency Trading*, Brent Donnelly, John Wiley & Sons, 2019

How These Premises Differ

Notice how the value proposition is quite different for each instrument type. We need to train our brains to think differently about each model.

For example, suppose we compare the bonds issued by Procter and Gamble with the shares of stock issued by the same company. In that case, we will need to think very differently about the valuation. The bond will not pay a penny more than the interest rate implied at the time of purchase. The bond will also generally remain around the same yield if market interest rates stay the same, even if the company's prospects get better over time.

On the other hand, the company can grow earnings, pay dividends with excess cash, or even acquire other healthy companies, thereby producing a larger equity valuation. P&G was founded in 1837 and still seems able to grow in the foreseeable future. Ironically, if the company expands quickly and aggressively—investing in new markets—its credit rating could go down, thereby causing its bond price to go down. Yet, the stock price might even go up! Or, at the same time, the sales prospects of P&G could go down. Still, company management could remain so conservative that the bond might also rise in price while the stock price goes lower.

In contrast, commodities never change—a bushel of wheat or a side of pork belly is physically the same today, tomorrow, and the next day. Wheat and meat pay no dividends or coupon interest. Their only value is whether the scarcity of the item goes up or down before consumption. If the market believes there will be future shortages of a commodity relative to future demand, the price will go up. If, on the other hand, the market believes suppliers will continue to make the item irrespective of demand, the price will decline.[19] To develop a sound trading idea, your valuation assessment must be centered entirely on information that helps you determine the scarcity of a commodity.

Our last instrument type is currency. Currency is a medium of exchange, typically issued by one country (though a group of European countries issues the Euro) that is the sole legal medium of exchange citizens can use to purchase goods and services in a

---

[19] For many decades, commodity prices were also driven by inflation fears. In some countries today where inflation is rampant, prices do rise in expectation that the currency used to purchase the commodity will devalue. Yet, in the last few decades in most of the developed world, inflation has been an inconsequential factor.

particular country. Since the government is the single controller of the supply, it can limit the creation of the currency or open up the printing presses and create a massive supply of that currency. If the supply is too large, prices of goods and services in a country or group of countries will rise because users of a currency will lose faith that it can hold its value relative to other currencies. For instance, the Turkish Lira from 2018-2020 was an excellent example of a currency whose supply was massively increased by the government. Relative to our currencies, the Turkish Lira depreciated by almost 100 percent over this period relative to the US dollar, thereby causing massive inflation in Turkey.

Of course, there are a limitless number of factors that affect the valuation of each of these types of trading instruments. I have simply given you a guide to help frame the general issue: the kind of financial instrument you trade changes the valuation methodology you use. The same good news that boosts a stock price could cause a commodity price to decline. Also, knowing the core components of what affects valuation will help you filter data faster. For example, knowing how a machine husks corn before it is put into a can will not help you value corn's price—but knowing that the US government has recently stopped demanding that ethanol, which is made from corn, be used as an additive to gasoline, will affect corn's price because this information affects scarcity value and is thus essential.

The next section of this chapter will cover valuation methods for equity securities that I have found particularly valuable and unique. To be clear, the following section will cover my "tricks of the trade"—methodologies that can be applied to other asset classes as well. You, as an individual trader, will ultimately develop your own repertoire.

Valuation Methods for Equities

Generally, the market valuation for publicly trading companies derives from the number of shares a company has issued times the current price of each share. This valuation is irrespective of whatever obligations a company may have, be it future tax payments, debt, pension obligations, etc. Rather, the market takes this valuation into account via the free-market mechanism that determines the price per share. As a result, knowing the total market value of a company tells us little about the company's prospects because we do not know the earnings a company has achieved to justify the market value.

For example, let's compare two companies: Salesforce and Oracle, which both sell computer software. As of the closing of May 22nd, 2020, both stocks had a market capitalization of approximately 160 billion dollars. However, Oracle earns nearly 10 billion dollars a year while Salesforce earns around 3 billion dollars a year! Why is Oracle, which makes 3.3 times more money than Salesforce, worth the same amount?

The answer is simple: in the eyes of the market, the two companies' prospects appear to be the same. That is, there are attributes of Salesforce that appear to be more intrinsically valuable in the future. Therefore, the market will pay more for Salesforce today (as measured by its current earnings) than it will for Oracle. Perhaps the market feels Oracle is already big and cannot grow quickly anymore, or that the products it sells will be less valuable in the future. On the other hand, the market may feel Salesforce is just getting started and may ultimately surpass Oracle's profitability and growth potential.

While there are hundreds of factors that contribute to a valuation assessment of a stock price, I will review five important factors that will give you a basis for thinking about the hidden value beyond the current sales and earning metrics.

First, the most common factor for valuation is the ability to deliver growth. If a business is growing, it always has new and more significant revenue to help solve problems. In short, success begets success. Sales growth convinces others to try the product and momentum builds. Success can come from a powerful marketing team selling a standardized product (EMC)[20] to a brilliant pair of social misfits who happen to have one of the world's best products (Google).

Growth metrics vary, and one has to open their mind to how growth can be monetized over time. Who would have thought 20 years ago that growing "tweets" or "TikTok videos" could be translated into real dollars?

Traditional growth metrics include standard variables as sales, earnings, customers, and distribution channels. One can add to that a plethora of digital metrics such as page visits, subscribers, user time, and yes—even likes! If you are uncertain about measuring growth for a particular company, review corporate press releases or the company's public filings. There, you will find discussions of the growth metrics that management itself deems crucial. You can also track if management has hit its goals as time moves on.

---

[20] "Addicted to Analytics-EMC's Marketing Science Lab," Mona Patel, Blog.dellemc.com, April 11th, 2013

A second factor we want to look at in evaluating successful companies—also related to growth—is evidence that the company is deferring its earnings to invest in growth. In other words, if management believes the return on capital kept in the business is higher than giving it back to shareholders in the form of dividends, then the company can grow through reinvesting its earnings. (Most corporate tax laws allow corporations to reinvest their earnings tax-free.) Reinvesting profits will often make earnings per share look lower than they are. Still, investors will take this reinvestment into account when they value the company.

Often, fast-growing companies will have extremely high price-earnings ratios. Companies such as Amazon grew so fast that it needed all their earnings to be plowed back into the company for its first sixteen years in business.[21] Pharmaceutical companies are likewise classic for plowing profits into research to further enhance their portfolio of medicines as far into the future as possible.

A third factor to consider is the "intrinsic" value of the product or service. If the product or service offered is regarded as a necessary good, the company will likely maintain a core valuation that one can count on in both good and bad times. For example, a patented product such as a drug or an iPhone can become such a core part of our lives that the company producing it can count on consistent sales.

Many companies produce critical goods that we may not realize are part of our daily lives: fertilizer, chemicals, coding for computer chips, and specialized fiber to move light waves along the Internet are all examples of intrinsic products that are not often thought about yet produce significant value for the companies that sell them. Intrinsic value can also encompass quasi-monopolies such as wireless carriers, movie studios, cable networks, banks, and consumer product companies.

All these companies exemplify instances in which market size or regulation has allowed them to form a quasi-monopoly subject to little competition year in and year out. While many of these companies are mature and slow growers, they also benefit from large reliable sources of revenue each year, which allow them to acquire fast-growing innovative startups! Walmart may be the best example of an intrinsic-value company using its vast resources to buy new companies to support growth.[22]

---

[21] "Amazon Records First Profitable Year in Its History," Juan Carlos Perez, IDG News Service, January 28th, 2004

[22] "20 Companies You Didn't Know Walmart Owned," Liz Flynn, 2019, Moneyinc.com

A fourth factor to consider is the change in the company's number of employees. The principle here is pretty simple: successful companies, no matter how digital they are, need more people to grow. When companies feel confident in growing their employee base, it often follows that their sales are rising.

Take a look at the Netflix employee chart below. Neither you nor I have ever probably met a Netflix employee, as the company is fully digital. Yet, from the table below, we notice Netflix has added nearly 7,000 employees over the last decade!

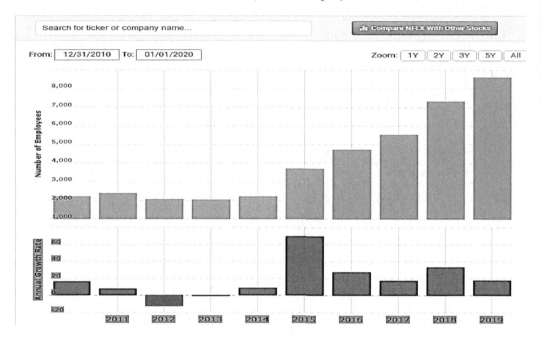

When Amazon began to accelerate its growth, there was concern that it was killing jobs at America's retail stores. While there is no denying that jobs have been lost in large droves, particularly in small stores, Amazon had to take in many of those displaced workers to fuel its growth—close to 700,000, to be exact, in the last decade alone—making it the second-largest employer in America as of 2020!

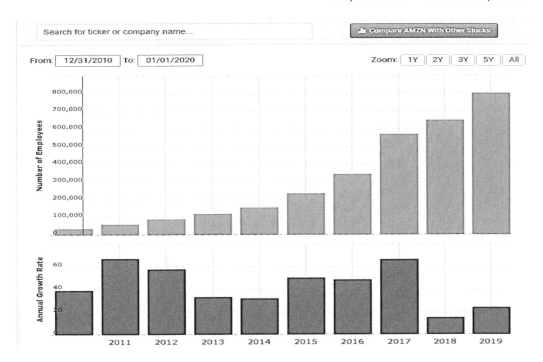

A fifth factor to consider is the number of common shares outstanding that a company has issued. Traders may not realize how frequently this number changes: the number of shares outstanding can change daily for most companies. The amount issued can rise for reasons such as stock options being exercised for key employees, stock being granted for compensation to officers and employees, or stock being sold by the company to raise additional capital.

On the other hand, stock outstanding can decline as well, most commonly when the company repurchases its stock in the marketplace. Companies buy back stock to reduce the number of shares outstanding, which increases their earnings per share. This can be a much more tax-efficient way to manage the company's cash than merely paying out a dividend. Companies that efficiently manage their outstanding shares, notably by limiting the growth of the shares, tend to generate better earnings for their investors.

In summary, we, as traders, search the world for information that helps us form a valuation proposition on financial instruments we can trade. When the research we use delivers a value proposition that is significantly different from what is currently priced, a trading idea is born.

We can then strengthen our conviction in our trading idea by looking for supporting evidence to determine the degree of commitment we should have to the trading idea and what size move we can expect. We need to choose the trade construct that best reflects how we can take advantage of our information.

Trade construct (or trade design) is such a core element to our trade idea's overall success that the next several chapters are dedicated to it.

CHAPTER 10
Taking Your Idea and Designing a Trade

Designing trades is an interactive process. Some traders design their trades with a simplistic thought: "I think the security is going up or going down." When traders take this kind of basic approach, their trade construct often has no purpose but to simplistically represent their view without considering how the market may get there and the risks involved if there is random movement along the way.

Experienced traders know there may be several ways to express the same idea. Using my best-practices approach below, you will blend different objectives to construct the ultimate trade design.

Price Objective: The change from the current valuation to the new valuation.

Time Objective: How fast we expect the valuation change to occur.

Trade-Entry Objective: At what level is it most advantageous for us to enter the market?

In this chapter, I will focus on price and time objectives. Traders who design their trades with these objectives in mind will have a significant advantage over the rest of the pack because so many of the potential outcomes have been visualized by the trader and dealt with in advance.

Determining the Price and Time Objective

Let's imagine that the culmination of our research leads us to conclude that the US dollar will appreciate against the Japanese yen. Our idea comes from our extensive study of global trade flows. We find our view is unlikely to be altered by short-term news because global trading patterns have been established over the years and encompass billions of dollars of capital and financial investment. We also believe it will take approximately one year for the overall move to occur, given it will take several months of data to convince markets that a new paradigm in the price should be set.

The Price Objective and the Distribution of Potential Outcomes

When thinking of our price objective, we must understand that there is no right answer; any number of people looking at the same data might determine different possibilities about the change in the price. That is all right. In fact, it is more than all right—it is an advantage because most traders will pick some random objective and stick to that assumption come hell or high water. That is not trading—that's wishful thinking.

In reality, your price objective should be thought of as a probability distribution. Determining your probability distribution and the time frame for that distribution to come to fruition is as vital as generating the trade idea in the first place.

Probability Distribution

What do we mean when we talk about a probability distribution? A probability distribution is a measure of all possible outcomes for a given event.

A simple distribution can be constructed from rolling dice. If I throw a single die with dots (1 to 6) on each of its six sides, my distribution is the following:

1= 1/6 probability
2= 1/6 probability
3= 1/6 probability
4= 1/6 probability
5= 1/6 probability
6= 1/6 probability

The possible outcomes are 1 through 6; the probability is that each occurrence has an equal 1/6 likelihood of happening.

Many might be familiar with the casino game of craps, perhaps the most famous of all distributions in the gambling arena. In craps, we roll two dice together and add the totals. Now, see how the distribution changes when we roll two dice instead of just one.

2= 1/36 probability
3= 2/36
4= 3/36
5= 4/36
6= 5/36

7= 6/36

8= 5/36

9= 4/36

10= 3/36

11= 2/36

12= 1/36

Here, we see a vastly different situation concerning the distribution. In this case, results have quite different probable outcomes. If we make a bet on just one roll, which number would we choose? We would undoubtedly bet on number 7 since that is the outcome with the highest probability. But would we bet on number 7 as a sure thing? No, because the sum of the possibilities of all the other numbers combined is still much higher than the probability of the number 7 being rolled. Seven has the best odds of being rolled, but it is still not the most likely outcome!

Now, what if we wanted to make a bet with someone else about the roll of the two dice? We know the distribution; the number will be somewhere between 2 and 12. We also know the probabilities of each of those numbers being rolled. Thus, we would combine as many numbers as we could until the odds are in our favor. If we take 5, 6, 7, 8, 9, and 10 (instead of just betting on the number 7 alone), our payoff odds go from 1 out of 6 to 2 out of 3!

When we think of an objective for a change in a security's price, great traders think of distribution and the probability of the payoffs along that distribution. Our distribution must begin with our approximate entry point to solve for our potential returns.

How do we solve for our entry point? One tool is an analysis of historical data, often done visually by looking at historical charts of the security's price. For example, we can study the exchange rate between the US dollar and the Japanese yen. This historical analysis is a form of technical analysis.

Here are two examples of such a chart.

Chart 1
Daily Price Range of US Dollar vs. Japanese Yen, September 2012

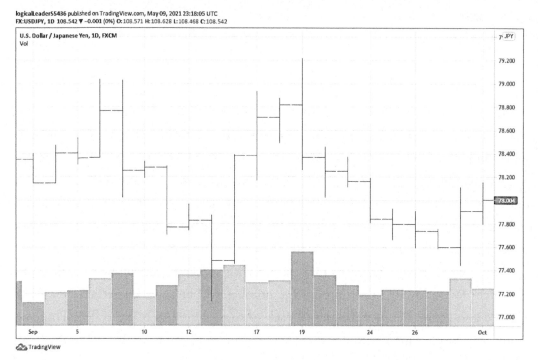

TradingView

Chart 1 is the dollar versus the yen's daily price range for September 2012. This chart will help us understand the likely price for our trade entry.

Looking at this chart, we can assume something as simple as the average over the previous month, which, in this case, is $78.16. We can also strive to enter the trade at the most advantageous price, which would be near the low of the past month, as happened on September 13th and September 28th. Note how using the low entry price for the past month versus using the average's entry price already affects our potential return by nearly 1.3% ($78.16/$77.13). We will discuss ways to achieve the best entry price in later chapters, but for now, our goal should be to consider a fair entry price to derive our payoff distribution.

Of course, this one-month chart tells us little about where the dollar-yen relationship has been over time. Thus, if we are thinking about a price objective over the next year, we need to match our historical data set with our timeframe objective. We need a set of samples long enough to show us some probabilities.

Here is a 20-year chart:

Chart 2
US Dollar vs. Japanese Yen, 1992-2012

Looking at Chart 2, we see the 20-year price movements. We can thus measure the 20-year low and the 20-year high for that period. Simplistically speaking, these measurements can help set the boundaries of our distribution.

We can also see where the dollar versus yen relationship was over the most recent few years. This particular time span is critical because it gives us a sense of where current investors (who are likely to still be in the market) value the exchange rate.

We can also look at areas where a trading range around the mean was established. Note that the range of $125 to $99 (the area within the grey space) generally held for 16 years around 112, which is the 20-year average for the dollar versus yen. The 1-year moving average of the yen's price to the dollar of 86 is shown in the grey Moving Average line.

Nonetheless, we are currently sitting at $77.96. We have recently had some rallies, notably in 2009 and 2010, which subsequently failed, and we ended at a lower price each time, down to the low of $75.35 reached on December 30th, 2011. This data tells us that in the short run, there will probably be sellers as the market rallies, as past speculators will be willing to bet capital that the market rally will fail again.

Overall, using a time horizon of historical data that fits our trade design's time objective helps us build a distribution of what our target could be. In the case of the US dollar versus the yen, we can visually see from the data that the low of $75.35 can be considered the bottom of our distribution in terms of downside risks. Several measures from moving averages ($86) to the long-term average ($112) or even the retracement back to the long-term resistance ($99.22) can all be considered as factors for our distribution probability of upside potential.

Fundamental Models

Another means of determining the distribution is the use of fundamental models. In currency trading, this might mean using models such as purchasing power parity or measuring GDP changes as a result of trade flows or capital accounts. In stocks, it might mean employing a bottom-up approach to future revenue streams and then applying projected future price/earnings (P/E) multiple. In commodities, it might mean measuring previous demand and supply shocks and deriving the percentage change those shocks caused in the price. In bonds, it might mean calculating the difference in the implied risk-free interest rate anticipated from a change in Federal Reserve policy and recalculating the expected bond price as a result of the rate change.

When the security we are interested in has an active options market, the trader can solve for the distribution by observing the prices on a set of options and solving (using an option-pricing model) to determine the market's implied distribution probability. For example, in currency trading, one can observe the price for a one-year maturing option given a 1%, 5%, or 10% move. This will give the trader an independent distribution of the probability of a move in the currency since option-market pricing is the sum of a large sample of traders' expectations.

Information from Other Market Participants

Beyond technical analysis and fundamental modeling, sometimes the probability distribution can be inferred by reading what other marketplace participants have to say. Financial reporters often write about anticipated price changes and the price objective expected by most traders in the market. By researching the trading views discussed in the media or on the web, you, the trader, can get an independent third-party projection of the distribution and compare it with your analysis.

Sometimes prominent officials who influence the security will render their own opinion on the future price distribution. Here is an excerpt from an article in *The Wall Street Journal* of December 23rd, 2012.

Global Currency Tensions Rise.
Japan's Abe Calls on Central Bank to
Resist Easing Moves by US and Europe

By Tatsuo Ito and

William Mallard

Updated Dec. 23, 2012, 8:25 p.m. ET TOKYO WSJ

TOKYO—Japan's incoming prime minister fired a volley into increasingly tense global currency markets, saying the country must defend itself against attempts by other governments to devalue their currencies by ensuring the yen weakens as well.

Mr. Abe on Sunday called on Japan's central bank to resist what he described as moves by the US and Europe to cheapen their currencies and noted that a yen level of around ¥90 to the dollar—it was at ¥84.38 in early Asian trading Monday, down from ¥84.26 late Friday—would support the profit of Japanese exporters. Tokyo markets were closed on Monday for a holiday.

Here is another example. This is from Bill Gross, who was head of Pimco, the largest bond manager in the world at that time, tweeting about bond prices:

(*WSJ* source) Gross, founder and co-chief investment officer of Pacific Investment Management Co. and manager of the world's biggest bond fund, made the comments on his Twitter account and in a subsequent interview with *The Wall Street Journal.*

Gross: The secular 30-yr bull market in bonds likely ended 4/29/2013. PIMCO can help you navigate a likely lower return 2 – 3% future.

PIMCO (@PIMCO) **May 10, 2013**

Finally, here is an article about hedge fund investor Carl Icahn talking about Yahoo:

> *In an open letter Thursday to Yahoo chairman Roy Bostock, the billionaire investor said he is launching a proxy fight seeking to replace the Internet company's entire 10-member board.*

> NEW YORK – *The following is the text of a letter from Carl Icahn to Yahoo's board of directors, announcing he plans to launch a proxy fight:*

> "Dear Mr. Bostock:

> It is clear to me that the board of directors of Yahoo has acted irrationally and lost the faith of shareholders and Microsoft. It is quite obvious that Microsoft's bid of $33 per share is a superior alternative to Yahoo's prospects on a standalone basis. I am perplexed by the board's actions. It is irresponsible to hide behind management's more than overly optimistic financial forecasts. It is unconscionable that you have not allowed your shareholders to choose to accept an offer that represented a 72% premium over Yahoo's closing price of $19.18 on the day before the initial Microsoft offer. I and many of your shareholders strongly believe that a combination between Yahoo and Microsoft would form a dynamic company and more importantly would be a force strong enough to compete with Google on the Internet."

To conclude, combining your models, the market's own implied distribution, third-party research, and predictions by market leaders can help you frame a reasonable distribution. Golfers and skydivers would love to hit a single spot when it is time to land, but they know that a range of places around the target area is a much safer way to make a living. So do great traders.

We have addressed two components: price objective and time objective. We learned the value of thinking in terms of distribution in forming a price objective, which gives a broader band for the trade to perform positively. We also learned that understanding and developing a time objective will allow us to design the trade to keep us in the game long enough to reach our price objective.

Trade Entry: An Important Part of Trade Design

A good trading idea with a bad entry price is no better than a flawed trading idea with a great entry price! The average trader stops thinking once he has generated his trading idea. He exhibits a high degree of pride in coming up with an idea and feels even more validated when he sees that someone from the Street is putting out research supporting his trading idea. Why worry about petty details like entry price and structuring the trade efficiently when his idea is sure to make money?

Let me tell you a story of one such trader. It was December 2004 when I was working as the head trader for a new hedge fund, Vinya Capital, and we were preparing to launch on January 1st, 2005. We had several assistant traders and our Chief Investment Officer working together as a team, and we had designed an excellent trade to initiate the fund. We planned to sell Brazilian bonds and buy Russian bonds. As a hedge of the deal, we decided on an FX trade: sell US dollars against the Brazilian real.

Our logic was that the market was too optimistic about Brazil relative to Russia, where the new Brazilian President Lulu was deemed to be increasing spending on wasteful programs while Russia was coming on strong as an emerging power. We hedged the bond trade with the FX trade because we felt there were still inflationary risks in Brazil that would be fought off with higher interest rates and stable currency.

We submitted our trade idea to a nationally known hedge fund consultant that ran a semi-annual contest with its clients on who had the best trade idea to help promote the fund. Each fund presented its concept, and the best ten ideas were nominated for the award. The consultant priced the trades on January 1st and the best performer on June 30th, 2005, was the contest winner.[23] It was a prestigious contest because the results would be published in many trade journals and leading papers, including *The Wall Street Journal*.

Good Trade Idea, Bad Entry Point

When we heard that we were selected as one of the top ten trade ideas of 2005, we were excited. As January 2nd neared, we were anxious to put the trade on with the firm's capital, but we were indifferent to the entry level. Why bother when we knew our idea was such a strong one? Brazilian bonds were on the move down. We wanted to catch that move and we jumped in at the market's opening on January 2nd to get started as quickly as possible.

Within a few days, the trade was going against us. Within a week, we were remarkably close to stopping out and wondering what was going wrong with a trade that was so well-designed. We began to frantically reassess our thought process and the market action that took place before our trade, and we soon realized what was

---

[23] https://www.drobny.com/assets/_control/content/files/Conference-Review-Barcelona-2004-8.pdf

wrong: we had not bothered to focus on trade entry and we had not studied the short-term market conditions very well either.

In retrospect, we learned two critical factors that were killing our trade. First, the volatility of Brazilian bonds was much higher than that of Russian bonds. Though we traded one bond against the other, it did not mean they would move at the same pace. Often, it took weeks for Russian bonds to catch up with the move of Brazilian bonds. Thus, entering the trade after a big move down in Brazilian bonds meant that we would lose money since Russian bonds would ultimately follow those of Brazil. As Russian bonds slowly sold off to catch up, we suffered more and more losses, being long Russian bonds.

Secondly, there was seasonality to how Brazil's bonds traded, similar to the famous "January effect" in US stocks. At the beginning of every year, Brazil's bonds tend to appreciate as short-term foreign investors make their once-a-year allocation to Brazilian markets. This flow worked against us since it took several weeks to buy local investments.

In sum, we were losing from poor entry. Brazilian bonds were rallying, and Russian bonds were not catching up in time because we did not focus on trade entry. After just ten business days, we had to close out our losing trade to avoid breaking the risk limits we had set as a fund with our investors.

Had we focused on our trade-entry objective by studying seasonality and price charts, and discussed flows with market participants, we would have known that almost any other time that month would have been a better entry point than January 2nd. The ultimate slap-in-the-face for our poor entry decision came in the mail six months later. It was a congratulatory letter from the hedge fund consultant that was running the trading contest. Our trade—Brazil bonds versus Russian bonds, hedged with the US dollar versus the Brazilian real—was the best performer over six months. We had won the contest, but had nothing to show for it!

Most traders fail to understand that trade entry goes hand in hand with trade design. They often find themselves shocked when market action causes them to stop out of a trade they had thought was such a good idea, only to see the market reverse course again and move back in the direction that their original plan had foretold. Traders underestimate the fact that a good trade idea with a weak entry point is incapable of handling random market volatility.

Imagine you have a bullish trade idea on one particular stock. Despite your bullishness, the market at that moment may be wrestling with bearish sentiment, bringing all stocks lower despite that you are bullish on one particular stock. For instance, the market may have concerns over decreased expectations in an industry sector and it may be willing to depress good stocks in the industry along with poor ones. There may be a substantial option trade going through, which will cause market makers to sell the stock as a hedge. There can be an entire confluence of adverse effects going on in the market at the time of your trade that may have unrelated but opposite effects from your trading objective.

Therefore, stepping back and assessing price action plus the current trading range, along with reading recent news flashes and researching seasonal factors—and looking for any indications of market distress—will go a long way toward helping your price entry avoid the pitfalls of immediate losses before your trade has sufficient time to work.

The Importance of Trade Design and Trade Entry: An Illustrative Example

Let us walk through an example of two different traders. Trader A is focused only on his ideas and is naïve about how critical trade entry is to trade design. Trader B understands the risk factors that go with trade entry.

Trader A has done unique research about a stock that has fallen out of favor lately: Cummins Inc., the engine maker, which trades under the symbol CMI. Trader A is convinced that CMI is about to grow earnings much faster than analysts predict as the market begins to reexamine the benefits of diesel fuel and looks for the global leaders who produce diesel engines. Trader A expects a 30% rise in CMI's stock over the next several months.

Chart 3
Price of Cummins Inc. Stock, October 4-October 5, 2012

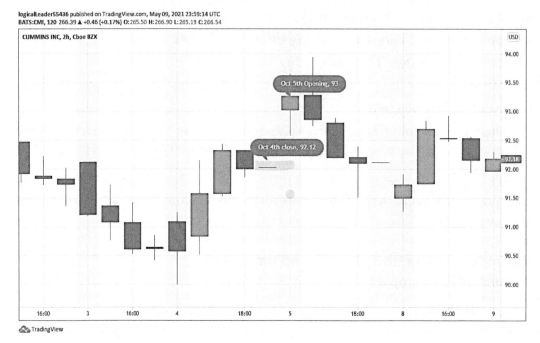

logicalLeader55436 published on TradingView.com, May 09, 2021 23:59:14 UTC
BATS:CMI, 120 266.39 ▲ +0.46 (+0.17%) O: 265.50 H: 266.90 L: 265.19 C: 266.54

Trader A is naïve to the risks of poor trade execution and decides to buy his stock at the market open. CMI closed the day before (on October 4th, 2012) at $92.12 a share. It opens the next day at $93 after an overnight rally in the general stock market that generally caused all stocks to open higher. "No matter," Trader A thinks, "the stock is on its way," and he buys the stock. He leaves two orders with his broker. The first order is to sell the stock at $117 a share for a 26% gain, and he leaves a stop order to close out the trade at $87.42, which would be a 6% loss. Trader A believes himself to be a disciplined trader because he puts in stop orders to limit his losses. He also puts in take-profit orders that are much bigger in gains than what he is willing to risk in losses. He then sits back and lets the market take its course.

Meanwhile, Trader B has independently come to the same conclusion as Trader A about the underlying fundamentals of Cummins. Yet, Trader B recognizes that additional research into trade entry and trade design is critical if she is to be able to stay in the trade and realize her trade objective. She studies the stock's most recent volatility and determines that the stock tends to move, on average, $2 a day. She also notes that the stock has been in a volatile $20 trading range for the past few months, having traded as high as $109 on May 9th, 2012, and as low as $82.20 on July 12, 2012.

Despite this volatility, there have been only a few noteworthy announcements with the stock to justify new highs or new lows. The stock trades with a 1.46 beta to the general stock market average, so it will tend to go up faster when the major indexes go up and go down quicker when the major indexes go down.

Trader B realizes that if she were to purchase the stock at around $93 a share, she could be down $2 as likely as she would be up $2 after just the first day. Within a few short days or a week, she could find the stock trading around $82 on nothing but beta movement with the general market (i.e., only due to the "noise" of the market). Let us review the entry points details on Chart 4 below. Note that Trader A and Trader B have the same entry point on the chart and the same entry dates approximately, but have different <u>trade designs</u>.

Chart 4
Price of Cummins Inc. Stock, May 2012-February 2013

Trader B realizes that she needs to design a trade that can best survive the "noise" for her to achieve her trading objective. She realizes that she has several choices of strategies and will choose the one that maximizes her gains with respect to the risk of losses she might take. She doesn't know whether she will ultimately make money on the trade, but she does know that by being an expert in trade design, she maximizes her probability of staying in the trade long enough to see if the market agrees with her premise.

To this end, Trader B looks at three different strategies: (1) buying the stock long, (2) buying call options on the stock, or (3) buying stock and buying put options as a hedge.[24] She determines that purchasing the stock is prohibitive because she does not want to take over a $6 loss on the trade. She knows there is enough volatility in the market to cause the stock to go down $6 without much reason.

Nor does she want to buy the stock and buy put options to limit losses because the put option's price is so high, she will only be protected if the stock drops $12 or more. Rather, she wants to be out of the trade after just a $6 loss.

But the price of the call is low because Cummins has been trading lower as of late. Trader B can buy the April 2013 expiration, 100 strike call for $4, allowing her to stay in the trade even if the stock goes down initially. Therefore, Trader B buys CMI April 100 calls for $4, giving up some of the gains she would have made by directly buying the stock like Trader A does. Yet, by purchasing the calls, she stays in the game if the stock were to sell off initially, which would cause Trader A to get stopped out.

Who Wins and Who Loses?

Sure enough, the stock continues in its trading range over the next few weeks. Trader A is stopped out on October 10th, 2012, when the market gap opens down to $86.50 from a previous close of $90.84. Not only is Trader A stopped out, but he also loses an extra 92 cents from his stop-loss order price because the market gapped through his level.

Meanwhile, Trader B, anticipating the general market noise that is commonplace, has only lost $1.70 on her option (versus Trader A's stop-out loss of $7.92) and is still alive when the market begins to sense two pieces of positive news: (1) Europe is starting to increase the sales of diesel cars, and (2) Cummins had done its homework and has ramped up production to meet higher demand and generate higher earnings. By early January, CMI has rallied from a low of $85 to a high of $115, and Trader B closes out her 100 calls for $19 for a profit of $15 a share!

The results: Trader A and Trader B both had similar ideas, similar timing, and related trade objectives. The only difference was their execution: putting thought

---

[24] Section IV, starting with Chapter 17, covers options in full detail. For now, a "call option" gives the buyer the right to buy the stock for a fixed amount of time at a fixed price. A "put option" gives the buyer the right to sell the stock for a fixed amount of time at a fixed price.

process behind trade design would allow Trader B to survive the longest until her trade became profitable. Focusing on proper trade-entry techniques is what often separates profitable traders from losers.

Enhancing trade entry can come from a variety of sources. Technical analysis can show in graphic form levels of support or resistance for good trade entry. Previous highs and lows tend to be revisited, often on the way to new highs and lows. Buying at new highs or selling at new lows can be great entry points because they confirm that the market must find compelling valuation to move into uncharted territory. Entering at the end of a big multi-standard-deviation day can also be a great entry point, as prices tend to explode when there is a new valuation premise not previously understood.

Great entry points include fighting the market makers for a few cents as well. It is tempting to simply cross the bid/offer spread when you are ready to act on your trade idea. However, often you are not disadvantaged to simply bid for your trade at the bid price, or try to sell at the offer price and allow another market participant to cross the spread to your benefit instead of the other way around. While no one can consistently buy at the bid price, consider you need not enter the trade either until you get the trade entry level you like.

Understanding how your order is presented to the marketplace is also critical to good trade entry. Many traders do not realize that there are over a dozen stock exchanges in the US where your order to buy or sell can be sent. Free commission brokers often send orders, particularly market orders, to exchanges that pay the broker a rebate (commission for the trade). This rebate comes out of the trader's pocket in terms of a bid-offer spread that is potentially wider than the best available price. This practice is legal because the order was sent to an exchange or legitimate market maker.[25]

Only limit orders can assure you of the entry price you seek. However, the drawback of a limit order is that the market (most likely a computer program) can read your order and use capital to move the market away from your limit order. Therefore, market participants see you are a willing buyer and decide to buy ahead of you in the hopes you will get frustrated and buy it at a higher price (once you come to understand your limit price is too low).

---

[25] US Securities and Exchange Commission, Investor Publications, "Trade Execution," January 16th, 2013

Trade design that incorporates your holding period, your price objective, and your trade-entry best practices will ultimately lead to your trade success. Getting into a trade at a price that is well thought out means the market will have to push further against your valuation proposition to get you stopped out of the trade. If your research is strong enough, market participants will feel less compelled to drive the market far enough away from your well-designed entry price to cause you to stop out.

CHAPTER 11

Determining Your Trade Size

If you ever ask a broker to buy you some stock, his first question to you will always be, "What size?" The size of your trade affects many aspects of your performance. Trading in a small size will lower the capital you have at risk but will also limit the amount of money you can make. If your trade size is too big, then you run the risk of being stopped out of your trade due to economic losses well before you have the opportunity to see if your valuation proposition was right.

Finding the balance between maximizing your potential gains and limiting your losses is a continuous process. As usual, there are no hard and fast rules—only best practices.

A corollary to the trade size then comes into play: do I start small and add to my winners, or do I try to take as large a position as possible when I initiate the trade?

To answer these questions, we have to make certain assumptions. First, we have to assume you are trying to act as a full-time professional, someone who is trading his or her capital or an institution's capital with the intent of achieving a professional return on that money. Later in the book, we will review the costs of trading associated with full-time trading. For now, suffice it to say that achieving a return on capital that not only covers your costs but also yields a return superior to what would have been achieved through a balanced passive portfolio is the minimum standard. In reality, the threshold for achievement can be much higher than our minimum standard if one is being benchmarked to other professionals trading the same style as you are. Superior returns can only be achieved by the proper mix of trade ideas, trade design, and sizing the trades appropriately.

Sizing Trades

The most consistent method for sizing trades is to solve backward, starting with what you would like your final performance for a year of trading to be, then working back to understand what that means for each trade's performance, and then solving for size.

When doing this exercise, you should account for (1) your trade volume, (2) your average winning performance compared to your average losing performance, and (3) the total number of trades you expect to make.

While all of this is an approximation, it creates objectives that can then be applied as a set of disciplines in your trade design. In other words, this exercise becomes a feedback loop for your trade design. Suppose the system does not meet your necessary and expected performance characteristics. In that case, you can redesign the trade size until it does, thus creating a self-fulfilling feedback loop.

Let us walk through an example. Imagine that I manage one million dollars in capital given to me by friends and family, as they've heard I am a good up-and-coming trader. To impress them and to outperform alternative investments, I want to achieve a 20% return so there is no doubt that my performance is superior. Working backward then, my one-year goal is to earn $200,000.

Next, I look at my strategy style to determine a trade count. My trading style is to generate original researched ideas on stocks and commodities that I believe provide a good value proposition, on average, over a six-month time horizon. The six-month period allows plenty of time for the market to see the same value proposition I have discovered earlier than most.

Also, my trading style is such that I tend to reassess my trades if they have either failed to perform after six months or have performed poorly and hit my pain threshold of 6% down from my trade entry. Furthermore, I tend to look for stocks and commodities that are at least 25% undervalued before I commit capital to them. I like to have an 18% trade profit objective to capture most of the movement towards my price objective. (I remember that having a profit objective closer to the mean of the expected distribution of returns is better market practice than always trying to achieve the maximum return.)

Thus, in general, my winners tend to make 18% of capital applied and my losers tend to lose 6%. I estimate that 40% of my trades are winners, 50% are losers, and 10% tend to end flat.

I believe I can produce about 30 trades every six months that meet my value proposition test from experience. We now have enough information to solve for the size we need per trade.

Look at the following table:

40% times 30 trades = 12 winning trades of 18% = 216%

50% times 30 trades = 15 losing trades of -6% = -90%

10% times 30 trades = 3 trades of 0% = 0%

If my trading unit is designated by the letter y, then we can arrange the following formula:

$(12 * 3y) - (15 * 1y) = \$200,000$

then $36y-15y=200,000$ or $21y= 200,000$, or $y= 200,000/21 = \$9,523$.

We are solving for y, with y = the amount per trade I am risking, using the table above as my distribution. I make 18% on winning trades. On losing trades, I lose 6%. I make three times more when I win than when I lose.

If I have 30 trades, I should be willing to risk \$9,523 on my losing trades while trying to make \$28,569 on my winning trades.

Now we have to do one final calculation: what capital applied will generate a \$28,569 gain on an 18% move?

$CA = 28,569/0.18 = \$158,716$. Thus, the capital applied must equal \$158,716.[26]

Limitations on the Number of Trades

One may ask: in theory, if my numbers above are correct, wouldn't we want to have an infinite number of trades on? After all, on average, every ten trades we have will perform in the following way:

Four trades up 18% for a total of   +72%

Five trades down 6% for a total of   -30%

One trade flat for a total of   0%

      Total Performance   +42%

While no trader will continue to perform if the net of his winners over losers is not positive, there are limitations that affect all traders regarding the number of trades he can have on.

---

[26] Note that 158,716 times 30 trades would equal 4,761,480 of total capital applied. This would mean the trader would have to use leverage to have all the trades on at the same time. Leverage can be achieved through the use of margin, options, and future contracts. We will discuss the pros and cons of leverage in Chapter 24.

First, each trade you have on requires capital. Capital has to be placed with an exchange or a bank allowing you to risk the trade. Capital needed on a particular trade can be as little as 3% of the principal (many futures contracts have a minimum capital requirement of just 3%) to as high as 50% of the total principal. (The US margin requirement for purchasing stock is currently 50%.)

In addition, you must have capital in reserve to cover losses beyond the initial margin requirement. When trades move against us, exchanges and banks ask us to post additional money, formerly known as "maintenance margin," to show we can pay for our losses. In all, we are constrained by our capital requirements when it comes to the number and sizes of our trades.

Secondly, there is degradation in the execution of strategies and identifying quality trade ideas. Most trading strategies become degraded with the more trades we apply to them. Furthermore, each time we try to find trade ideas that meet our quality standard, we degrade the pool of possible ideas until we can no longer easily find ideas that meet our quality standards.

If these are challenging concepts to grasp, think of your favorite singer and all the songs he or she has recorded. You probably have a list of your favorites from the artist. Still, as you listen to more and more of the artist's songs, the quality degrades, and you hear ones that just are not as beautifully written and sung as others. It is the same artist for each song, but the pool of ideas that the artist taps into degrades over time. In trading, too, if you continuously increase the number of trades, the quality of those trades will tend to degrade.

Third, the tools and the energy needed to manage your trades become exponentially more difficult as the number of transactions rises. Trades need to be managed in systematic ways. Managing stops and take-profit orders, assessing new information as it comes in, accounting, and risk reporting all grow exponentially as your trading volume increases. There is a human limit to what a person can manage.

Even if you have enough capital to add computing power to manage your trades continuously, the market environment needed for your trades to succeed is increasingly challenging to maintain. For example, as your trade count rises, there is a risk that the percentage of winners and losers you have at any one time might change due to one-off events such as natural disasters, economic shocks, trading errors, etc. If, suddenly, a large portion of trades become losers or unmanageable, you have a great chance of losing enough capital to put you out of the game for good.

Thus, if we are confident in our ability to trade profitably, we do not want one-off problems to cause a significant setback. We want to limit our trading volume to the minimum needed to achieve our goals and to avoid shrinking our pool of capital, ideas, or energy!

Finding the Appropriate Trade Size

There are many ways to iterate your trade's appropriate size as long as it is in proportion to your capital, your trading objectives, and, most importantly, your understanding of market volatility. When you lose money on a trade, the amount lost is the percentage of price movement from trade entry to trade exit times the amount of capital placed on the trade. One can lose the same amount of money from a large trade with a small move in price as from a large movement with a small amount of capital.

Good market practice dictates, then, that your trade size should be limited to the amount of capital that allows you to stay in your trade through what is known as average market volatility. Volatility is often measured in units called standard deviations. One standard deviation is the average movement that a stock typically moves (either up or down) away from its most recent price.

Traders need to study the volatility of the instruments they plan to trade within the trade design's timeframe. That is, daily volatility for short-term trades, weekly volatility for trades designed for a few weeks, etc. Take time to study extreme historical moments and see what a two- or even a three-standard-deviation move looks like no matter how unlikely you believe that will happen during your trade. Understand the choice you are making when sizing a trade: can you stay in it for a one-standard-deviation move? Can you stay in for a two-standard-deviation move? If the cost is too painful, you must consider reducing the trade size, regardless of other metrics one might use to choose an appropriate position.

You will learn in subsequent chapters to let winning trades run. Just because a trade makes your expected profit level does not mean you should close out the trade if the value proposition you perceive is still valid. One might ask, if a trade is performing well, should we add to the size of our trade to leverage our gains and take advantage of the trend?

While it is good market practice to add to winning trades and let them ride through our original take-profit level (if we believe there continues to be value), it does not change our initial sizing proposition. Finding the appropriate trade size does not mean we can afford to take a bigger size, using the premise that our winners will be bigger than our losers. Sizing trades is about probabilities, and probabilities pay off only if the sample size is large enough. If we have only executed a few transactions and all are winners, it does not mean that our track record will be perfect, and we pick whatever size we want. Nor if our first few trades are losers should it mean that we trade smaller than what is necessary to earn capital at a professional level. Size of trades is therefore a long-term exercise based on our trading plan. How much capital we trade, our trading style, our trade volume, our holding period, and our trade objective are all used to determine our trade size.

Trade management is just that—trade management. It is a separate market practice from sizing. We add size to winning trades when we receive confirmation that our value proposition is correct. Just because we added to a winning trade does not mean that we change our sizing calculation. We cut out of any trade when information comes to us that changes our investment thesis. We do not stay in trades when our view changes just because we sized the trade small enough so we can still afford to lose more money. Sizing trades properly does not mean we can afford losses. It means that we control our position to handle a series of losing trades that allow our winning trades to pay off.

In summary, sizing is an exercise done ex-ante—i.e., beforehand, based on expected results. We choose our size not knowing which trades will win or lose. Instead, we base size on a distribution of our expected results for the entire set of trades. We stop out, add to trades, and manage our size as we go through the lifecycle of an ongoing trade. That is, each trade performance ex-post (after the fact) may ultimately have a final trade size or a trade performance (in terms of percentage movement) that is different from our expected probabilities.

Altogether, trade sizing and trade management are independent forms of best market practices. Combining good trade sizing with ongoing trade management is a powerful toolset that leads to profitable trading performance.

SECTION III

ADVANCED CONCEPTS
OF FUNDAMENTAL MARKETS

CHAPTER 12

The Domino Effect: Your Trades Become Information

Trade execution is not a stagnant exercise. Traders must understand the nature of the marketplace and the balance that exists at any given price. When you plan a trade execution, you have to weigh how other participants will act (a) before you enter the market, (b) during the time you are in the market, and (c) when you plan to exit the market.

First, you have to understand why you entered the market. Was your idea researched in a way that provides you with an information edge? Then, your actions may have little effect on the market price until others discover the same information as you.

Alternatively, are you acting on news that everyone agrees might change an asset's value in the same way? In this case, are you working faster than others? Are you unaware that most participants have absorbed the "new" news more quickly and have adjusted the asset price as much as they need to already?

In a perverse way, you have to vet your idea with the marketplace, assessing how the market might react to the idea and how the market's reaction is likely to affect your concept.

Suppose we knew all the players who were trading a certain security—what motivates them, what their rule sets are for how they trade, how much capital they had, etc. In that case, you could study the ups and downs of that security in what we economists call a "closed system." In a closed system, we can solve how and why a security moved from one price to another. We can imagine that the market is balanced, and we know all the players who have a position long and short. We can also imagine that those players agree there is no reason to try to buy at above a specific price because the sellers have enough capital to push the price back down. The sellers think the same thing about the buyers, so they don't want to sell below a certain price.

The Effect of New Research: A Hypothetical

In our little test tube, we now introduce new research to one of the participants who is long the security. We will call her Buyer A. The research makes it clear to Buyer A that the stock is priced too high, given this new information. She knows that others will eventually receive the same analysis, and the other buyers will also determine that the security is overvalued.

Thus, Buyer A decides that she should sell not just because she thinks the information is enough to consider the current price too high but also because others with the same information will reach the same conclusion. Inaction on her part will not stop the security value from going against her as other buyers begin to sell their position. Therefore, Buyer A decides not only to sell all of her position but also decides to borrow additional securities and be a net seller now—i.e., she "goes short." She has concluded that the new information would be enough to overwhelm the buyers and that potential future information would not be enough to stop the price from going lower. Therefore, her best valuation assessment is that she can make a profit by being a seller instead of a buyer.

Since this is a closed system, no new capital can come in. When Buyer A becomes Seller A, the system is then out of balance. No longer does the current price represent neutrality between buyers and sellers. Instead, more investors are willing to sell at the current price than buy. This does not mean that there are more sellers than buyers, as you may hear from time to time from market commentators. It merely means that the price needs to adjust lower to entice buyers to take on aggressive sellers. The market needs to find a new equilibrium price to satisfy both buyers and sellers so that they stop trading.

Assume further that Buyer A (who now has become a net seller) had the new information earliest and sold first. Other buyers may initially try to support the market at just a little below the previous neutral price because they assume that, with nothing changing, a lower price seems like a bargain. Our Buyer A clears all her longs and can establish a short without moving the market very much because she has an Information Advantage. In contrast, others who lack that information are confidently willing to buy, thinking the market is still in equilibrium.

But soon, other market participants learn the same information that Buyer A traded on. Additionally, traders without the information also sell, only because the market is going down. In other words, no longer is the information the news—instead, it is the market going down that is the news! Now that the equilibrium has been broken, many buyers may no longer care even to find out what the new information was in the first place. Seeing the market go down is information enough!

Meanwhile, traders who were already short-sellers now comprehend the new information and realize that this information enhances their previously held view that the price should go down. They have more profit in their pocket because the price is already lower. They are motivated to add to their position even at a lower price. They make the same calculation that Buyer A had made earlier that the final clearing price will be lower still. Thus, sellers look to sell more and they must find buyers who will take the other side of the trade at a price.

The price continues to drop as the market tries to clear all these trades. The price of each trade becomes information in and of itself. And it is not just the price that becomes new information—the rate of change of the price is unique information too. If it is a slow pace, this rate of change may reflect trader uncertainty. But suppose the rate of change is more rapid. In that case, this may signal that traders are confident that the new information is valuable.

Finally, the market stops going down. Sellers no longer feel that the potential reward of selling at a lower price is worth the risk. Buyers no longer fear the current news, as everyone seems to know it. The new lower price at which the market clears is fair enough to the buyers that they are willing to take the risk that future good news could cause the market to rally from the new equilibrium trading level.

In our closed system, we learn that buyers' and sellers' actions become an information source. Without action, there is no price movement. The speed of the movement and the final change in price are direct results of the degree of motivation, fear, greed, panic, etc., of all the traders in our closed system. Since there are no statistics explicitly called motivation, fear, greed, or panic, we can only estimate the degree of these motivations through the amount of price change and the speed of that change.

The takeaway here is this: change in price and the speed of the change are information in themselves. Even in a closed system where we can identify all the buyers and sellers, price action tells us something about their motivation to buy or sell. Is it desperation, fearfulness, excitement, or greed that's out there? That can only be determined by the participants through price action.

What if the market is fearful? Often, a nervous market will move quickly through a series of bids on the way down, sometimes at a pace of four to five times what would be considered an average movement over the same period. The steeper the slope of the change, the faster buyers and sellers have to make critical decisions. Instead of making a leisurely decision about whether to buy, sell, or hold, a seller may have only minutes to decide what typically might have taken hours or days.

The Real World: Information and Open-Market Systems

We have just gone through an example of a closed system. We should realize, however, that almost all tradable markets today are open systems. Gone is the era of the specialist on the New York Stock Exchange or the concept of ten live cattle traders controlling the cattle-trading pit on the floor of the Chicago Mercantile Exchange. OPEC can hardly control the oil market anymore, nor does Cargill control the grains any longer.

Rather, the markets today are open systems. Traders worldwide with an Internet connection can play any market anywhere, and their motivations are diverse and difficult to discern. Information is instant but not equally absorbed by all participants. With data now nearly infinite, some items can be easily missed by market participants at the very time that others are using that information against them.

Thus, in an open system, information has to be evaluated not only on its own merits but also on the merits of what effects it can have on the overall system. In other words, how will information affect not only those groups of buyers and sellers who have already made their bets but also new entrants into a particular market whose participation may be predicated on entirely different sets of motivations than those of the original group of buyers and sellers?

In an open system, one must assess, for example, whether the information will force the price in a direction that may invite arbitrageurs. Or will it bring in new speculators who have been looking to buy the security on the cheap, regardless of one-off bits of information?

Or maybe the opposite is true. Perhaps the information is compelling enough to get traders off the sidelines. Perhaps they are now willing to get involved in a marketplace they previously saw as reasonably neutral. Still, with the introduction of this new information, they see ample opportunity to make a profit. This can mean a much greater movement than expected by the most recent price action because new capital is being deployed as the market scope is changing.

How can one build acceptable market practices around the price movement of the securities he trades? Let us look at a closed system and find some answers.

Imagine that you are playing Texas Hold'em in Las Vegas. When you assess your probability of winning with the hand you have, you value the likelihood of winning based not just on the cards you have but also on how others react to what you do. You win if you have the best hand or if everyone else folds before you do.

The same holds true for trading. If the information you trade on is ultimately proven not to be valuable, it can still lead to winning trades if other traders capitulate and trade in the same direction you do.

The value of a poker hand is essentially equal to the following formula:

$$VHt = \text{Cards Held} + \text{Cash Bet} + \text{Timing of Bets}$$
where VHt = Economic Value of the hand at time t.

In other words, the economic value of your hand at a given moment is a function of the actual cards you hold, the amount of cash that is bet, and the timing of the bets.

Information Has No Value Unless It Is Used

Having a good hand of cards is irrelevant if the hand is not used to make a bet. The same is true for information you hold about a security. That information is useless to you unless you take a real trading position to profit from it.

The second step in the valuation formula above is the amount of money placed on a bet or investment. No matter how sure we are about a hand or an investment in a security, we can only transmit that view one way—by putting capital to work. The amount put to work means different things to you than it does to the marketplace.

Suppose you place a large amount of money in a small poker game or an illiquid market. In that case, this money can cause dislocation regardless of the ultimate outcome. It can mean that everyone around you will fold and the path of how the cards would have played out if they were dealt is irrelevant in a poker game. Because of the large size of your bet and the resulting dislocation, you have already won the game.

In trading, a large amount of money can have the effect of moving the price far enough away from your entry point that it makes the trade profitable, even if it was the capital put to work that moved the market and not the information alone. For example, many traditional analysts believe that the Reddit phenomenon of 2021, causing previously weak stocks to rally dramatically (Gamestop and AMC theaters as the two best known), was caused simply by a group of traders applying an overwhelming amount of capital to these stocks. Better known as the "meme" movement, various hedge funds lost billions of dollars when they were forced to close short trades on stocks that small-time investors bought collectively by simply pooling their money together and egging each other on through chat rooms on famous financial websites.[27] On the other hand, if a large amount of money is deployed, the trader may find out that the traders on the other side are well-capitalized and confident in their view. This data point should be used as a signal to be on the lookout for additional information that confirms the value of your trade and to be alert that you are now exposed with a large bet of your capital (with a lot less to show for you than you expected).

A small bet in poker may allow the participant a chance for more significant action later, even though a smaller bet invites more players into the game who can also afford to stay in and see what future cards do for their prospects. Similarly, a smaller investment in the markets may allow the investor to enter the trade at his price without causing any dislocation. It may also allow for further capital to be deployed later at a time when the price is better or the Information Advantage is stronger. On the other hand, the small bet will be unlikely to move the market and will allow traders trading against you to stay in the market longer, looking for new information that supports their view.

Timing Is a Critical Signal

Finally, the bet's timing will usually have a significant effect on both the outcome for the investor and how it affects the judgments of those around him. For example, a player who goes all-in on Texas Hold'em after just two cards have been dealt sends a vastly different signal than if he makes a large bet after all the cards have been "flopped." The other players at the table will judge the timing and likely strength of his hand quite differently, even though the total amount he bets might be the same in each case.

The markets, too, pick up on the timing of investments. After all, the timing and size of a trade are the only information one receives about a trader's motivation in an open marketplace. A large investment made immediately following a surprising economic report will convince other investors that the trade is related to that information. At other times, an investment will be made and, subsequently, news that benefits the investment will follow. Investors watching this may assume, rightly or wrongly, that

---

[27] "Dumb Money is on GameStop, and It's Beating Wall Street at Its Own Game," *New York Times*, Matt Phillips and Taylor Lorenz, Feb 25, 2021.

the information was previously available somehow to the person who made the investment.

In summary, we have learned that valuations and new information are just part of what affects a security movement. How market participants react to other traders moving first on information is just as important. How they react reflects how the information is received. The reaction will differ in a closed market where the participants are limited as opposed to an open trading market where new participants enter all the time with various amounts of capital.

Overall, the capital committed to trades, the timing of trades, and the information that precedes and follows trades all affect the market's perception of value as much as the original information itself. One must make assumptions and constant assessments of what George Soros calls the "reaction function" of the marketplace. As much as we must draw conclusions about the valuation of the instruments we trade, we must also assess how new information and the collective trading that follows that information affect other participants—and how their reactions in turn will affect your positions.

CHAPTER 13

Tips from the Master

A t this point, let's take a break from the heavy dissertation and have some fun. This chapter will take a page out of the old-time classic trading books and offer you some tips.

I love a good tip as much as anyone, so I thought I would give you five of my favorites that can specifically help improve your trade design and risk management.

Tip #1. Average In and Get Carried Out!

One of the oldest stock investment tips around is the concept of dollar-cost averaging. This trading style requires you to allocate a certain amount of capital per trade and divide it by the price to tell you how many shares to buy. If the stock goes higher, you will make money regardless of the price at which you purchased the shares. But when the stock goes down, the theory is that you buy more stock at a lower price with the same amount of capital as before. Therefore, you will own a lot more shares numerically through dollar-cost averaging at a lower average price.

While it may be true that you will own more units at a better average price through dollar-cost averaging, it is hardly true that this is a good strategy. It differs little from doubling down at the roulette table every time you bet black instead of red until black finally comes up. It seems logical, and if you have unlimited resources, you will probably survive. Most traders have relatively limited resources and cannot survive a prolonged selloff when they are long, much less a selloff when they have bought more shares.

One of the critical problems with the practice of dollar-cost averaging is that it is a form of "anchoring." This issue, which appears in various forms in this book, is the critical challenge in being a professional trader. Look at every situation in which you trade and figure out if you are trading on the best information at hand or anchoring old information and old valuation thinking.

"Averaging in" is an excellent example of what looks like a sound strategy but is fraught with the risk that you are merely justifying your better average price to make up for the fact that you are probably ignoring new information, which is driving the price lower! "Why is the market moving against me?" should be your first question. If you do not know, shouldn't you get out while you only own a few shares and wait for the information to reveal itself to you?

This does not mean that I do not advocate buying lower once you have already purchased. No strategy in trading is absolute. There is no perfect stop level, take-profit level, entry-level, etc. I am willing on occasion to add to a losing position, but under the following general guidelines:

First—I will always leave about 25% of the capital I commit to the trade to add to the trade to make up for poor initial execution. Entering a trade has costs, including bid/offer spreads, market makers trying to guess what you are doing, and bad luck on your trade's timing. Once the initial transaction is booked, it is easy to see where you could have been more efficient with your execution. Often, the market will soon give you an opportunity to execute better, as we discussed in the earlier section about entering a trade.

Second—I assess new information as it arrives to determine if my trading premise still stands up to the trade value proposition. As traders become more adept at thinking of a trade, their reasoning soon gets further and further ahead of how other participants see the market. But often, the market does not react as fast. This presents a double-edged sword: on the one hand, it allows the shrewd trader to put on his trade at a fair price; but on the other hand, it may result in few positive results at the outset because other traders will not be acting in accordance with the way you see the market. Often, it takes time for the market to absorb new information in the same way as you do.

Thus, if the story remains compelling or becomes more convincing, I will look to add to the trade at a worse price, but with my eyes wide open. Adding to your position at a worse price always increases the trade's size and the potential pain of a more extensive loss per unit of movement. Adding to a trade will cause your stop-out level to move closer to your trading average than it would with a smaller position.

Third—If I am near my stop-out level and the information is still compelling, I will add to the trade even if it is only a few ticks away from stopping out. I find this strategy beneficial because the actual risk/reward ratio is quite good. Since you will be closing out this additional trade quickly, any further losses to your original position will be relatively small. Simultaneously, the opportunity to reverse course and provide a much greater reward is quite compelling.

Again, the point is not to throw good money after bad. If you know that the position is weak because new information has come to light, you should be stopping out anyway; why wait for more movement against you? Adding near your stop as a strategy is akin to the actions of a boat captain in a storm who knows the right approach is to steer into a big wave and take it head-on instead of turning the boat to the side. It may not save the boat, but it is merely the right thing to do when you believe that your trade is still appropriate.

Averaging in is a fallacy because of its appeal that you will own more when the market turns. Markets do not always turn but often continue lower for longer than you might believe possible, and just as often, they sit at the new lower level without bouncing. Thus, you lose the opportunity cost of having other trades be more productive for you by applying that capital to trade ideas that are working.

Let's suppose you sit and hold a trade with margin posted on some exchange or with a broker-dealer. In that case, you limit yourself from doing other trades. You are emotionally distracted by something that's <u>not</u> moving, which deters you from your primary purpose: capturing gains from trades that <u>are</u> moving!

Your job as a trader is to allocate your capital as efficiently as possible. Always have money ready to add to trades, but do not add to trades simply because they give you a better average price. You add because you have the capital to apply to a value proposition that remains as compelling as you initially thought. Even adding right before you stop out might still be the best use of your capital given the risk/reward. Remember, you should be considering the following when you add to losing trades: "This is a compelling value based on all the information I currently have." Your total position's lower price average is the mathematical benefit of adding to your position—not the reason you do it!

Tip #2. Leave Orders and Stops

One of the best uses of your time as a trader is to leave orders. Orders typically are of two kinds: taking-profit (limit orders) and stopping-out (stop orders).

In a take-profit order, you leave an order at a price you determine is an excellent level to close out a trade. As we have discussed, good traders think of their potential profit range as not just a single price but also as a possible set of prices under a normal distribution.

Often, it can be hard to come up with just one price that suits you to close out a winning trade. One way to resolve this difficulty is to simply leave a series of orders that have a profile similar to your distribution. For example, if you are short S&P futures contracts from $1,685, and you have a range of expectations from $1,610 down to $1,590 as your trading objective, you may want to leave small buy orders at $1,610 and $1,590 while leaving the bulk of your take-profit order at $1,600.

Other traders feel uncomfortable with the risk of getting their orders only partially closed out. They prefer leaving one large order so they know that they are either in or out. Either strategy works fine, but the key is to take advantage of the new era in trading where almost all products trade 24 hours a day. Thus, your chances of getting filled are two or three times greater because the market will have more instances of surprise news, gaps, and other events that can get your order filled at your level (but only if you leave an order).

Take-profit orders are interchangeable with limit orders. Typically, when we already have a position, we call the order we leave to close the trade a take-profit order. We designate the order this way so the exchange will look for an offsetting transaction in our book and reduce our total capital usage. Therefore, seeing the take-profit order reduces overall risk. While it sometimes happens automatically, there are many instances today where it does not; unless you notify the exchange, it will treat your long and short as two separate trades and charge a margin on both sides. When you want to work an order for a position you do not currently have, we call this a limit order.

When designing a trade idea, one must consider the possible entry price as a precondition for the trade to have value to you. Sometimes, by the time the analysis is done, the entry level needed to have adequate risk/reward on the trade is no longer available. Thus, leaving a limit order allows you the chance to focus on the entry level you want to achieve instead of feeling the need just to pay the current price.

Finally, since most traders don't leave orders and markets trade through their stop-loss limits, by definition, some of the fills you get from leaving take-profit or limit orders reflect the panic trading of others who are less disciplined.

Stop orders work in the opposite way. You leave orders to pay a worse price than the current price, knowing you will pay up and close out a short position that is moving against you if the market gets to the higher price. Thus, the word "stop" means "stop me from losing any further." Stop orders to sell lower than the current market price are used to close out long trades in a market that is dropping.

Stop orders are critical to risk management and capital preservation. One principle in this book that is truly an echo of all other trading books relates to the importance of stop orders. This importance is not merely because stop orders, which close you out of a losing trade, protect your capital, but because your heart and your mind won't let you be rational until a losing trade is closed out and you move on. That is to say, your emotions are ever-present. Even if you know that new information has come in to change the market's valuation about a stock from positive to negative, your heart will still secretly cheer for the stock to rally, prove everyone wrong, and save you the embarrassment of having to stop out of the trade.

In reality, all you should care about as of this moment is how you make money with all the current information that is in front of you. Trades based on information that has changed for the worse need to be reassessed. In theory, one can be quite intellectual and calculating in the middle of a losing trade, but in practice, this is quite hard to do. Consider a stop order less as a validation of flawed thinking and more as a best practice to make your trades as effective as possible on a continuous basis.

Stop orders need not mean you are closing a trade. Traders use stop orders to begin new trades, often using them at levels deemed a new break-out, such as new highs or lows.

There is a school of thought that the cost/benefit of stop orders weighs against them. One view is that these orders are only filled when the market is going against you. After all, why leave an order when you can close it out yourself at a better price the majority of the time?

One way I try to balance this debate between the benefit of stops and the problem with stops is to leave the stop order with a broker one price unit worse than my actual stop. I will then execute my stop order myself. Once executed, I will immediately cancel the stop order I have working. The difference between this and just leaving the stop order is that I control the trade's execution, so I can shop for the best price or get my exact price.

Typically, when you leave a stop order with someone else, they are incentivized just to get the execution done as fast as possible, regardless of slippage in price. By executing in a quick manner, your broker is usually pushing the market against you further than you would do on your own, and why not? After all, he is not getting paid for the execution price—he is getting paid for doing the execution! Yet if I forget, or if I am distracted or sleeping, and miss the chance to execute the stop order myself, at least the stop order is always working.

Stop orders also leave you susceptible to situations in which your order is almost filled. News comes out and the market gaps lower. In this case, your broker has a free option to fill you at the low range of the market gap even though he may have had the opportunity to sell on the way down. He is legally allowed to keep the difference, or at least not be responsible for the risk of this event occurring.

Even with these risks, I still advocate leaving stop orders. These crucial orders reflect your disciplined approach to managing your trades. Stop orders protect your capital and allow you to stay in the game, which is the essence of long-term trading success.

Tip #3. To Make a New High, You Have to Get to the Old High (To Make a New Low, You Have to Go Through the Old Low)

One of the conflicts between human nature and successful trading is thinking spatially. Like the rest of the human race, traders look at a picture and see the limits—not the space beyond them. When traders look at a chart, they see highs and lows, and most often think of the market as staying within the chart's boundaries.

For example, suppose you run an experiment asking people to look at a 10-year chart of oil prices and ask them to predict the price's potential range in the next year. In that case, just a few percent will name a price outside the bounds of the chart.

Many traders act quite simplistically. Their human nature tells them to sell at old highs and buy at old lows because someone else did the same thing before them and made good money, as the security eventually went back to the center of the trading range. But what they do not think about is that at that earlier moment, the market had broken an old high and made a new high before going lower.

Thus, the old high was once a new high at one time, and the person who sold the old high lost money. Eventually, some piece of news came along and reversed the price action. Still, the seller who successfully sold the high at that moment in time was likely acting on new information that had come along to change the market's course rather than taking a shot at selling an old high.

Often, when a market makes a new high or low, it will sit there for weeks or even months. This will create a series of closing prices around the new high or low, which, down the road, will look like a major resistance or support area, respectively, on a chart. Those traders who look to charts for ideas of support or resistance will often draw a line, using the high or the low as a starting point to create an array showing where the support or resistance is. The next time we get to this price range, mean-regression traders will be empowered to sell the old high or buy the old low because they have the additional confidence that a lot of trading went on within this range, creating major support or resistance levels.

Mean-regression traders and speculators are not the only ones who think selling old highs is a good idea. Traders who design models or algorithms based on historical data will also be tempted to sell at old highs and buy at old lows. The price history will always convince an analytical model that real value is most likely achieved by pushing the market back towards some regression-tested mean. This is particularly so in pairs trading, where the underlying thesis in a pair is that there is enough similar value between the securities in the long run that an ideal entry point for buying one and selling the other is at an extreme price differential, such as an old high or old low.

But a market's biggest change occurs at new highs and new lows. By definition, you cannot get there without going through the old high or low first. Reaching highs and lows are unique opportunities to trade and take advantage of large explosive moves. New highs are often achieved with gaps, followed by stop-out trading from those traders resisting new high lows. This can cause a short-term acceleration in price, a rise in the price of options as measured by their implied volatility, and often concludes with new theories about the security that had not been previously considered with much weight. This outcome can propel the market even further over time.

Gold breaking $700 an ounce in 2007 was a great example of this type of movement. Take a look at Chart 5 below. See how this chart could make a trader feel like gold will forever hold the $700 dollar high?

Chart 5
The Price of Gold, 1942-2009

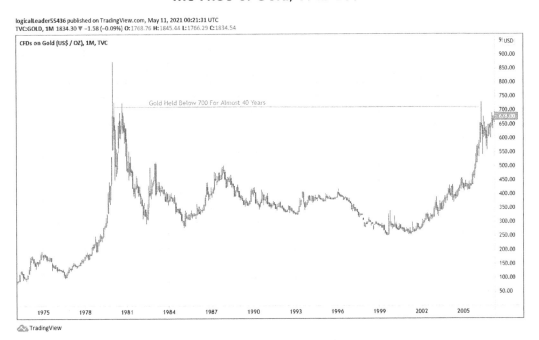

Now, let us look at prices several years later, after gold broke the long-term resistance level of $700.

Chart 6
The Price of Gold, 1970-2020

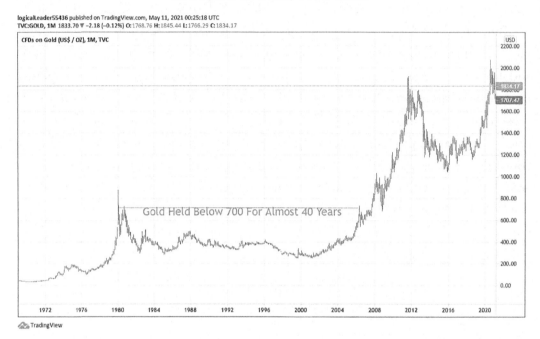

logicalLeader55436 published on TradingView.com, May 11, 2021 00:25:18 UTC
TVC:GOLD, 1M 1833.70 ▼ -2.18 (-0.12%) O: 1768.76 H: 1845.44 L: 1766.29 C: 1834.17

We got to the old high, and most traders began selling because it was the "resistance area" for almost 40 years. But one can never assume that any level is impenetrable; any level can be broken and lead to new highs if the fundamentals are right. Accelerating through old highs into new highs is a great mindset to trade because all the doubters who were proven wrong come with lots of capital to push even further into virgin territory.

So, too, the market thought that oil had a top of $41 a barrel, which had held for 30 years.

Chart 7
The Price of Oil, 1983-2004

But when we busted through $41 a barrel once and for all, our minds began to expand to the idea that there may be lots of room for the price to rise after all. Chart 8 shows that the old high now looks pretty insignificant in retrospect.

Chart 8
The Price of Oil, 1983-2014

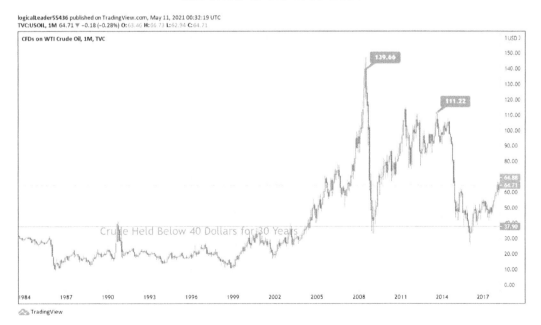

Let us consider Google's stock price as well. The market thought the $355 a share reached in 2007 was an aberration and an all-time high.

Chart 9
The Share Price of Google, 2004-2012

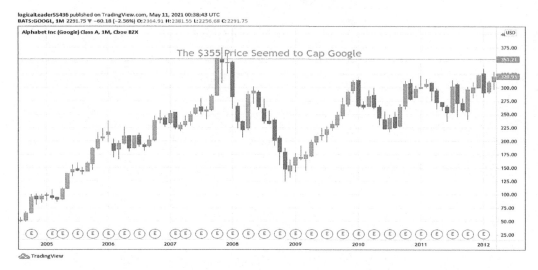

Chart 10
The Share Price of Google, 2004-2014

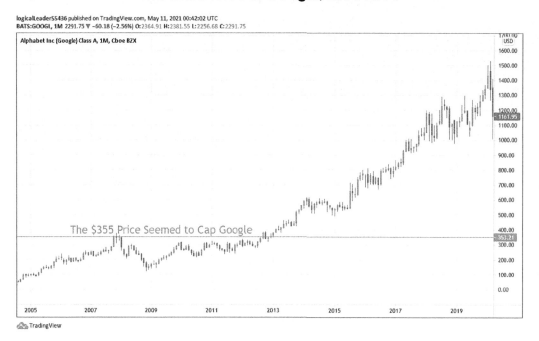

In all these cases, as the market approached the new high, volume was average and traders began to fight the break-out at the previous old high; when the break-out happened, volume jumped. New research began to surface to explain the new highs and pricing levels.

It's my oldest expression: whenever someone tells you we're at the high, and therefore that it's a bad time to buy, always remind him that you can't make a new high until you get to the old high!

Tip #4. Avoid the Chase

If you can only learn one thing from this book, make it this concept. It is key to your trading survival.

The emotional desire to be part of the pack is a siren's song that you will never learn to turn away from easily. It can call out to the best of traders daily. Beware: nothing is more dangerous than letting the fear of missing a trade that you wanted to do—but the pack got to first—guide what you do.

The more you trade, the more you will learn about the markets, and the more you will tune into why markets in any security go up or down. You will develop research techniques that are uniquely your own. You will identify under- and overvalued securities. You will notice that the timing of your discoveries of overvalued or undervalued securities is often not in sync with the marketplace. You may be bullish, but the rest of the market seems to disagree with your assessment and the security just sits there or even slowly declines.

As you follow the security, you may also identify market catalysts that create moments where everyone focuses on the same stock and pushes the price up. The triggers could be earnings announcements, economic data releases, corporate announcements, or data mining services with new insights. But for whatever reason, you had not put on your trade when the security took off. The change on the day flashes green for a big positive gain and your heart sinks because you missed it. You do not own any of this security.

And this is no ordinary security. Lots of things go up and down every day—and you could care less. But this one is personal; you have been watching this one closely. You've studied it. You've talked about it with your colleagues, your friends, your broker, and your boss. They deemed you the champion thought leader on this security and were impressed with your knowledge of the factors that drove it up or down.

But you do not own one unit of it! You missed the move, your heart is sinking, and you are sad—even though you do not have a position, somehow you feel like you have lost money.

Your brain kicks into action, quickly assessing how you can correct this error in judgment. It guides you to pick up the phone or move the mouse. It looks for any sign that the security will experience a momentary retracement from this explosion so you can get into the trade. Your senses are on high alert as you stare intently at the computer screen, looking for any sign of weakness, but it does not come. Instead, after a small pause, the security begins to trade even higher and at a faster pace than before. The screen shows the price changing quickly and the volume expanding to 3, 4, or 5 times the normal average. Other traders are quickly joining in the hunt for this security, but you are still out of the game.

Right at this moment, your heart is sending you a slew of emotions: sadness for not having been involved in this security earlier, embarrassment for not being involved when others touted you as the local expert on this security, indignation that the market took off before you decided it was time, and finally, the one thing that gets you to act hastily—jealousy.

Your body begins to feel a rage of jealousy that you are not in the trade where others are making money. After all, it's not just any trade, but the trade you knew so much about. Your brain may try to stop you, trying to use logic to tell you that this may be too high a price to pay. Yet, your heart may egg you on. It may say to you, "Hey, we now have confirmation that the market is excited about this security." It tells the brain to suggest a take-profit level that can be achieved if we buy it right now.

In the end, both your brain and your heart betray you. You push the button or make that phone call, and you are in the trade in an instant. You bought the security not at the price you had planned to enter but at the highest price of the day after a big rally. The security was up 4.5% on the day, and with all the volume going through, it looked to you as if it were going to go even higher, so you bought it. Within a few seconds, the market calms down and it pulls back to up 4% on the day, and you decide to buy again and average in your two purchases.

Two things begin to happen. First, your heart sends you a thank-you note; you have satisfied its insatiable desire to be part of the pack and not be left behind. You will be able to hold your head high if others ask if you are in the big trade and you can say with pride, "Yes, I'm in it." No one will ask what price you bought at; they will just look at you with admiration because you were as smart as you said and got yourself into the winning trade.

But the second thing that happens is more insidious. Your heart tells you to feel good. "Look at the performance of the security," it is saying. "It's up 4% in just the last few hours on this new set of news." Then, your brain goes to work. It begins to do some calculations, which do not seem right. The security is up 4% and the screen is green, showing a significant gain on the day from the previous close. Yet, when your brain calculates your profit on the trade, it comes up with a negative number! How can that be?

The security drops a bit more and is now only up 3.5% on the day. The brain quickly recalculates, and lo and behold, you are losing even more money than when you made the calculation just a few minutes earlier. "Wow," you think, "this really needs investigating!" And after a few minutes, your brain sends a signal to the heart. "You're an idiot," it tells the heart.

What went wrong?

Well, the heart, in its haste to have its desires met, completely ignored one of the critical elements of trading. The heart was anxious to be in the trade that it sent a signal to you that said, "Hey, the market's up 4%. I'm going to send you a feeling of satisfaction now that you have bought the stock that's equal to the feeling I would send you had you been in the trade from the beginning of the day."

The only problem is that you were *not* in it from the beginning of the day; instead, you bought at the height of the day, up 4.5%! In your haste to get involved, you bought at the absolute high of the day.

Your brain does the calculation that even though the stock is up 4% on the day, you are actually down money because your average price is up 4.25%. Thus, your heart sends a new signal, one of dread. It senses what your brain is reporting—*we have been tricked.* When the security pulls back to up 3.5% on the day and our recalculation shows you down even more, your heart sends a different signal: fear. Your brain is still scolding your heart for being stupid and forcing you to buy at a high price just to satisfy your greed.

Meanwhile, your heart is not listening. It is now scared that this rally could fail. When the market pulls back to unchanged on the day, everyone else will be even on the day, but you will be down 4.25%!

Now, instead of thinking about how much money you will make, your mind and heart are working feverishly to calculate the risks. Your heart sends fear signals while your brain sends you a P&L report with every change in the price. Upticks are greeted with a little relief and downticks are greeted with fear of ever-bigger losses.

Finally, your brain sends the order, "We need to stop out by selling our position if the market pulls back to up 2% on the day. Otherwise, the loss will be too big for our capital base." Now that your brain has given the order, there is nothing left for your heart to do but to be a cheerleader, hoping that the security will not fall that far. Your heart is hoping that the excitement of those first few minutes will return after just a small respite.

But alas, it is not to be! The market is beginning to calm down and long-term calculations about the real value of the security take hold. Sellers rush in, knowing the market will probably correct and the security will only go higher if there is more confirmation of good news in the future. As the market pulls back to up 2%, your brain gives the stop order. You close out the trade at a loss of 2.25%. Your heart sees the irony in all of this, as the market will finish the day up 2%. Everyone who was in the security the day before had a nice return of 2%, but you will finish the day down 2.25% and stopped out of the trade.

This scenario occurs every day in the marketplace. Sometimes, the scenario above plays out over a few minutes, or sometimes days, months, and even years! Without realizing it, many traders enter the market on almost every trade they do in this fashion. They do not even understand why it happens. They never get to the core of why they trade this way and therefore are unable to break the pattern. Essentially, a trader needs to understand and separate himself from the notion that the change in the market relates to the change in his own position.

We are built to be fans. We cheer on our favorite sports teams, and when they succeed, we feel like we have succeeded. While that emotional high for a winning sports team may lead to personal satisfaction, there is no place for getting emotional satisfaction from being in a trade at a poor entry level—that is, just to feel satisfied you are at least in the transaction. In reality, once we enter the trading ring, we should be involved only when our judgment and research tell us that our profit potential far exceeds our risk of loss.

In summary, there are no emotional victories. Owning a great security at a lousy price because you panicked to get in and ultimately lost money has no place in trading.

We are wired to put on trades for emotional instead of fundamental reasons. We need to override these core instincts or risk having our trading skills betrayed.

In overriding these instincts, start by avoiding buying or selling on emotion after big jumps. If you can overcome the desire to be part of the pack and focus on the discipline of entry and exit levels you choose through your research, you will be well-positioned to be a winning trader.

Tip #5. Do Not Design a Trade Because You Think the Market Will Believe Today's View Forever

Often, the market will anxiously await a seminal moment. Perhaps it is an important announcement from the Chairman of the Fed on the state of the economy. It could also be an earnings report on Bank of America that the market has been awaiting anxiously for months. It could be a report by the American Petroleum Institute (API) on the size of new oil reserves or gasoline production.

Whatever this moment is, it often causes a two-part state of events. In Part 1, the market tends to drift for a few days leading up to the news, with the drift often related to the impending story the market is about to hear. Sometimes, there is an important preliminary data point that in and of itself causes a big move, partially because traders were unprepared for any large movement until the day of the news release and partially because the market tends to be anxious, knowing there is still big news to come. Anxiety causes a rise in volatility priced into the options market. By the same token, higher volatility in option pricing often precedes volatile days because the seller of the option prices for larger-than-normal movements, given that the buyer is willing to pay a premium to protect himself from the news on the big day.

In Part 2, the big day comes, and the market is nervous. The news is often a more significant change than the consensus expected. When the information comes out, it has three effects:

- First, there is the "surprise effect," which accounts for a portion of the move in price following the announcement.

- Secondly, there is the more insidious part that a profitable trader must be ready for. In this phase, the market extends even further because now the mind thinks that this news is a defining event that will not be superseded by future information.

- Third, volatility drops in the options market, scaring traders even more because the options market no longer needs to price for shocks. Thus, the market affirms what the trader is thinking, "This is it, nothing is going to change!"

I have just described a form of anchoring, which we touched on in an earlier chapter. Typically, what happens to traders is that they now want to act as if this is the last piece of news we will get on the subject for such a long time that we can rationally design any trade that will perform in the same direction as the news!

This idea is also sometimes known as "irrational exuberance" (a term coined by Alan Greenspan, Chairman of the Fed at the time). It affects both good and bad traders who regret not catching the big move that is occurring right in front of their eyes.

Here are a few snippets of trader thoughts immediately after data events:

> *"If oil is now in short supply, I will do trades that take advantage of the news by buying oil even though the current price seems to have adjusted higher already."*

> *"If the Fed Chairman says he is not raising interest rates for the foreseeable future, I will buy US Treasury Bonds at any price, even if the Chairman says he reserves the right to change his mind if new data comes in."*

> *"If Bank of America beats expectations on earnings, I will buy their corporate bonds because they are forever done with credit issues."*

Why do we think this way?

First, we are disappointed that we are not part of the crowd that had it right, so we are dying to trade. Second, our instincts are to put on trades where the risk is low, and we justify the value by telling ourselves that no other news will come to knock down the market's current view. Third, the closer we are to information, the harder it is to play devil's advocate. We dare not question whether something could come along and shake our confidence, and we dare not even challenge the news on its merits.

For example, in May 2013, a strong jobs report caused the market to raise interest rates by 35 basis points in one day—nearly a record. Not only was the market reacting to the report, but it was also reacting to others who were anchoring that the data will never change again. In this case, the market did not even bother to critique the report itself, which, in actuality, showed that job creation was more part-time than full-time. Two weeks later, the very same information, when discussed by the Fed Chairman during congressional testimony, was taken as a sign of economic weakness, which caused the market to lower interest rates by 15 basis points!

The point of this discussion is not to encourage traders to countertrend big moves. Rather, it is to challenge you, as always, to think independently. Markets rarely close on the day at a point where they can only go higher or only go lower. They can continue a rally the next day no matter how intense the rally was the day before, and vice versa.

Do not countertrade for the sake of countertrading. However, understand that if a bullish oil report comes out, then there will be another API report on the oil contract just down the pike a month from now. Do you want to short oil for three months, or do you want to short it for two weeks, the latter being cheaper to do and through which you are less likely to get burned by new news? Overall, do you believe that the data is worth the move? If not, be prepared for the market to quietly reverse—most likely toward the end of the day or the next day when fewer traders means less support for extreme prices.

Remember, if the market sees potential for news to upset the apple cart, it will surely start to drift the other way, just in case. There is almost always a chance to get a better price and still money to be made from new news. You do not need to bet it all and hope that nothing changes. And in any case, news will come along that is fresher and more important (new information is usually more important than old data), and often sooner than you think. Changes in trading directions will occur if for no other reason than because those traders who have caught the move have no incentive to keep buying and have every incentive to take profit.

CHAPTER 14

Understanding the Principles of Other Market Participants

M any forms of trading styles interact in the market every day. All partici- pants are ultimately indifferent from whom they make their money. Yet, it is also true that others' trading styles are not necessarily in conflict with how you, as a trader, want to make money in the market. For example, a market- maker will put his capital to work in a tight-ranging market and provide you with an attractive offer for your buy-and-hold strategy.

While most traders consider themselves in direct competition with other traders who are executing on trade ideas generated by fundamental research, there are three primary forms of trading that are not based on starting with a trade idea. These forms are: (1) technical analysis, (2) algorithmic (or algo) trading, and (3) market making. Understanding the motivation of traders who use these styles can provide you with additional trade entry opportunities. In addition, knowing those traders will supply capital through bids and offers at key levels will help you better design trade entry and exit points.

While these three styles are quite well-known to the most experienced traders, there are subtle nuances worthy of your exploring to further enhance your trade designs.

Technical Analysis

Technical analysis is the study of changes in a security price, often presented on a chart and using historical pattern recognition to predict the security's future price movement. The prediction of where the price will go in theory is based solely on its previous price movements and the patterns that those movements form on the chart. These patterns are grouped into categories, with some being quite famous and com- mon, such as "head-and-shoulders" patterns. Others are so arcane and abstract that entire books are written on the subject. Modern technical traders will often deploy computers to help discern the pattern and even allow the computer to generate the trade order once the pattern is identified. The contemporary term for this enhanced style of technical analysis is "systematic trading."[28]

The Arguments in Favor of Technical Analysis

The historical arguments in favor of technical analysis consider three core reasons why it should work. The first is that all information that is known is ultimately incorporated in the price movement of a security. Therefore, the price movement should be the sum of all of the relevant information concerning the security. By extension, studying price action is more efficient than trying to learn all available fundamental information.

The second core argument is that patterns can be found in nature, particularly fractal or geometric patterns. For example, flowers under a microscope are nothing more than fractal patterns of growth. Thus, the theory goes: it is in our DNA as humans to trade in the form of patterns, back and forth. Even DNA is believed to be in fractal bundles![29] Thus, we should be able to identify human nature in the patterns of trading prices.

The third core argument for technical analysis is the most compelling—that with many traders following technical analysis, it becomes a self-fulfilling prophecy. Traders believe that other traders follow technical analysis, study it, and try to jump ahead of other traders when a clear pattern is formed.

One of the ancillary arguments for technical analysis is that traders believe that there is a certain amount of inside information that continuously affects pricing in securities trading, which can only be detected in the security's price action. For example, there may be an insider at a company who knows that sales of a new product are exploding and who buys the stock before the company's quarterly report is released to the public. Another example is when a bank trader sells a bond after learning from his friend at a credit-rating agency that the bond is about to be put on the watch list for possible downgrading.

Often, traders get research before publication because the researcher will test his ideas out on traders before publishing them to a broader audience. Finally, though not confidential, certain information is not released to all market participants at the same

---

[28] "Systematic Trading," Adam Singleton and Fabien Pavlowsky, Financial Risk Management 2008
[29] "A New Dimension for Genome Studies," Ann Trafton, *MIT News*, October 2009

time, and those traders who have it and act on it first have an advantage. For years, certain economic releases from private corporations were available for early release if you paid a fee.

All of this comes as no surprise to the technical analysis user; in fact, it only proves his point. Even if you wanted to trade only ideas based on your own research, you would not be able to come up with all the critical information you need to make an informed decision because some of that information is confidential or available to someone else first!

The technician says there is one place that the holder of valuable information cannot hide: the price, because to take advantage of information, one has to act, and to act means buying or selling. When you buy or sell, you leave a fingerprint in terms of the last price traded.

Now, says the technician, the odds tend to balance out because while I don't know what information you have to motivate you to trade, what I do know is that you were willing to pay a specific price to get your trade on. Let's suppose that price represents a significant rise from the price I saw yesterday. In that case, I know you must have enough confidence in your information to pay a premium. If others pay that premium, then a pattern will form that shows the market is breaking out of its current range.

The Downsides of Technical Analysis

Now that I have laid out the positive aspects of technical analysis, let me lay out the negative parts.

There is no ultimate, always-right trading pattern. There is enough price data available and computer power to prove that if a particular trading pattern had a positive, sustainable return, research would be published. Everyone in the market who is interested would know about it. Any average economics Ph.D. student can calculate an RSI (Relative Strength Index) or a moving average, take a database of historical pricing, and prove that the theory works or that it does not. (An RSI is a technical momentum indicator that compares the magnitude of recent gains to recent losses in an attempt to determine overbought and oversold conditions of an asset.) Since there has been no scientific proof of such a theory or pattern after all these years, it's silly to think you will be the lucky soul out of millions of traders to figure out the ultimate pattern that always works in practice.

The *"hard right edge."* Even if specific patterns exhibit a better winning than losing percentage over time, there is still the critical problem of knowing if that pattern is forming or not in real-time. In Alexander Elder's classic book, *Trading for a Living*[30] (sometimes simply known as the "Red Book"), Elder discusses technical analysis and the concept of the "hard right edge." He is referring to the fact that most patterns that are known to be reasonably predictive of either a rally or a selloff are only apparent after the pattern has completely formed. Often, it's too late at that point to put on a trade.

When you look at a typical technical chart in real time, the chart begins at the left and ends at the right with the last data point, with the chart's far right representing the current time. You have no other information than this. No matter how clear the chart looks at that point, you do not know, in real time, specific facts that ultimately decide what pattern you are looking at. That is the dilemma of the hard-right edge.

For example, let us look at Chart 11. It is a chart of Bristol Meyers stock price.

Chart 11
The Price of BMY Stock, January 1, 2019, to March 6, 2019

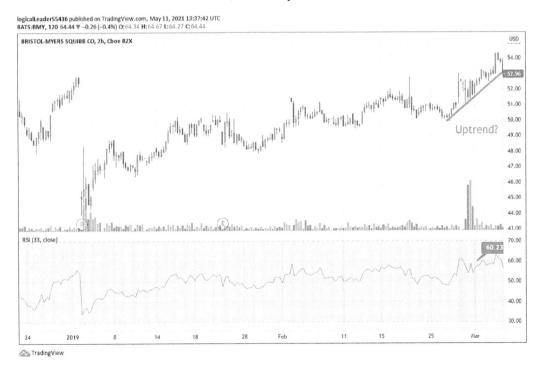

_____

[30] *Trading for a Living*, Dr. Alexander Elder, John Wiley and Sons, 1993.

This chart appears to show an upward break-out around March 4, 2019, with the RSI turning up past 60. This classic break-out in technical analysis jargon is usually the signal that an uptrend is beginning. But alas, you are out of information and you have to decide: do you buy, or do you wait for confirmation of the upward break-out?

If you wait and get confirmation, the security's price will be even higher later on. You will have to take the chance that this pattern is only a short-lived one and that you will be buying too high. But maybe it is just the beginning of a long-term upward trend and you are at the beginning of a break-out? It will not matter that you paid a higher price, given that it is a new long-term uptrend!

Chart 12 that follows shows that this was a false break-out. The RSI got to 63 and the price went from 53.61 to 54.18 before it turned lower, and had you traded, you would have followed a traditional pattern and lost money!

Chart 12
The Price of BMY Stock, January 2019 to May 2019

Fundamental information should always be considered. Fundamental information will still affect the market's direction. If a pattern is forming and new information supports the pattern, a technician will see that the technical analysis predicted the new information. In reality, the information was coming whether there was a pattern or not. And if the pattern is bullish and the news is bearish, you would bet your trading account that the market will still go down, no matter what the technical analysis says.

The lesson here is that depriving yourself of fundamental information is like having a toolbox with only flathead screwdrivers because they are easy to use, even though you know that there are plenty of situations where a Phillips head is needed!

Visuals, though alluring, can also be misleading. Humans prefer the visual to the non-visual. Charts are very visual. You can look at a chart and begin to imagine where you would buy and where you would sell to make a profit.

For example, see Charts 13 and 14 that follow. In Chart 13, I show six months of price action for the Corn Futures Contract. Notice that when I add the upward-sloping array in Chart 14, the trend becomes more transparent in your brain.

Chart 13
The Corn Futures Contract, December 2010 to June 2011

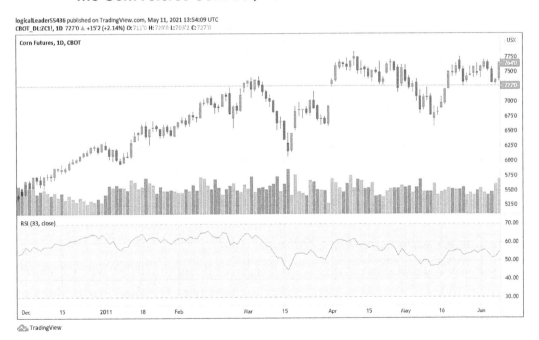

Now, let us look at the same chart with a trend channel drawn in.

Chart 14
The Corn Futures Contract, December 2010 to June 2011
(With Trend Channel)

This is why technical analysis is so alluring; it shows you the price action in a picture, and we love pictures. When we look at the picture with an upward-sloping chart and decide to buy, what we do not realize is that there is a reason why the price of corn was at a low; perhaps a crop report showed an oversupply. But looking at the chart gives the impression that the sellers were illogical and offered a buying opportunity for no reason. Drawings make us lose sight that fundamental information got the market to the lows and changing fundamentals—not the pictures—and good news got the market to rally back.

What Can We Conclude About Technical Analysis?

Technical analysis often gives the false sense of being predictive when it merely paints the story of how the fundamental news plays out. The danger is in thinking that the chart is driving the market instead of the market driving the chart! Once you start to believe you have a machine or a system that predicts markets, you are likely dooming yourself to failure because you lose your sensitivity to react to news and information that's really driving the price.

There are probably more books about technical analysis than there are trading books about how to do fundamental research. There is a reason for this. *Technical analysis is easy to understand while doing real homework and uncovering the fundamental background about a security is challenging.* Naturally, people often choose easy over hard. But since many people want the easy way out, a professional trader will need to respect the pattern followers of technical analysis and use technical analysis to help in their trading.

Technical Analysis Is Like Judo

I liken using technical analysis to the practices of judo. Judo is a martial art that involves two fighters, both wearing a heavy robe called a *Gi*, which simulates a real-world situation in which you will most likely be fighting with your clothes on (and weighing you down). The art of judo is essentially mastering the use of physics against your opponent. Thus, the lighter combatant has a chance against his heavier foe if he uses the heavier foe's weight against him.

For example, if the heavier person charges toward the lighter person, the lighter person who knows judo well will not put up his arms and try to stop the charge. He simply is not strong enough to stop it; however, much less force is needed to pull the charging man even closer to you, thus adding to his momentum and, at the ideal time, sticking your leg out and tripping the foe while pulling the charging man forward. Now, he is the weak one because he needs enough energy to stop both his charge and the additional force you are adding in the same direction, or he will fall forward over your leg and onto the ground.

Using technical analysis is similar in concept. For example, imagine that the market is charging forward, forming a well-known pattern that will lead all those who follow pattern recognition to declare that an uptrend has started and to throw buy orders into the market at higher and higher prices.

You believe the price is fundamentally too high, but you have studied the charts and know that many new buyers are coming in based on this new short-term pattern. Using their weight against them as a good judo fighter, you decide to step aside, knowing that the market will likely push higher. In addition, you realize that with the market looking bullish on the chart, you will get the opportunity to buy put options at a good price because, in the excitement of the short-term buying pattern that has emerged, buyers will pay more for calls than for puts. Thus, while fundamental information tells you to go short, knowing technical analysis might help you wait and get a much better price entry point.

Other Ways to Use Technical Analysis

I also like using technical analysis in other ways as well. First, technical analysis helps me project the size of potential moves. There are various techniques that use past movements to project the size of future moves. I like using these tools because it opens my mind to the possibilities of how far a market can move in a trend.

Look at Chart 15 below. It shows the prices of oil from March 2009 through December 2010. The market had been trying to sell off for months, only to rally back each time. In late December of 2010, fears of the global economic crisis began to diminish, and with it a belief that oil demand would increase significantly, along with global growth.

It seemed likely for oil to rally, but projecting how high was tricky. But by using a technical analysis technique for projecting a move, such as the "pitchfork"[31] pattern in this case, we can quickly get a handle on what a rally would look like. This is because the market tends to think in terms of percentage changes rather than absolute numeric changes. Technical analysis quickly normalizes changes in percentage terms and can project highs based on past moves.

This "pitchfork" tool suggests a possible range of $95 to $104 over the following four months of trading. Since this would be a new high for oil, technical analysis helps us visualize a price objective since historical data will not help us in this case.

---

[31] "Introduction to Pitchfork Analysis & Median Line Trading," Michael Boutros, Dailyfx.com, August 12th, 2019

Chart 15
The Price of Oil, May 2009 to December 2010
(With Pitchfork Technical Analysis Projection)

Now we can look at actual data in Chart 16 below and see how well the tool worked. The key to remember here is that the tool did not predict the price action; instead, it provided us with a sense of how far the market could move during a new break-out period where new price highs were being reached and there was no historical precedent to lean on concerning how far it might go.

As it turns out, the real price of oil went even higher than the range projected by the pitchfork model, but at least we had a tool to quantify what our expected range should be.

Chart 16
The Price of Oil, January 2009 to March 2011
(Showing Actual Price Movement from December 2010 to March 2011)

logicalLeader55436 published on TradingView.com, May 12, 2021 00:48:33 UTC
TVC:USOIL, 1D 65.41 ▼ −0.05 (−0.08%) O:65.46 H:65.63 L:65.40 C:65.41

TradingView

Algo Trading: Man Versus Machine

As with all aspects of trading, there are no definitive rules. If there were, the first one to publish them would eliminate the need for all other books to follow, not to mention that they would have invented a money machine!

Concerning algorithmic (algo) trading, there are ways for machines to perform better than people in terms of trading—and ways that people can beat machines. But remember, it is the trader's job to use his computer to the maximum benefit possible. A computer does nothing if it is unplugged. It comes to life only under human guidance, and even when the power is on, it waits for commands before it functions.

The Computer as Your Partner in Trading

Every trader uses his or her computer to some degree. It can be as simple as using it to read the newspaper and answer emails. Or it can be as complicated as having a Ph.D. in mathematics and programming an algorithm that runs throughout the day, managing thousands of trades.

A computer is an added value to your trading repertoire. When used correctly, it is your partner. When others use it against you, it can be your nemesis. In sum, you would no more abstain from using your computer than you would consider trading without the benefit of current news.

Computers never tire, which is probably the most valuable property a computer has when supporting its human partner. It never tires of watching orders for you at a price you designate and, if necessary, automatically executing those orders. It is happy to do endless comparative analyses and alert you when it sees a change in a relationship between a pair of securities it believes you will find valuable enough to trade. It will watch the market for you and send alerts to you, via any electronic means you prefer, about situations in the market you deem important.

Computers take in live data and calculate formulas to derive valuations. Those calculations help you compete against other professionals when determining the most efficient way to express a trade. Computers calculate your trading profits and losses, maintain your positions, and provide you with details about your risk at speeds much greater than you can do by hand.

For this section's purposes, let us deeply study the use of machines to generate buy and sell orders, along with the risks associated with this trading style.

Recent Issues with Algo Trading

While it is debatable which hedge fund is the greatest of all time, there is little debate that Renaissance Technologies is one of the premier funds in history that has been solely dedicated to algo trading. However, its founder, James Simons, would perhaps be the first to tell you that no algo trading system can think of every nuance. All systems expect humans to supervise the order flow, provide a sanity check over the process, and assess the trades to determine if the current market conditions are appropriate for automated trading.[32] In fact, due to a series of highly publicized auto-generated trading blowups, most exchanges require human supervision at all times, day and night, when an algo is used.

Beyond the supervisory role, there is an all-too-real liability role that the auto-trader has with regard to exchanges. This is because the exchanges hold the trader, not the machine, accountable for order flow that violates exchange rules or causes an

---

[32] *The Man Who Solved the Market*, Gregory Zuckerman, Penguin Random House, 2019

overflow of orders to flood the system. In the worst-case scenario, an errant order of large magnitude may occur that can cause a systemic short-term jump in the security price and result in large unplanned losses for the trader or even other exchange members.

Recent regulations have also turned against algos that depend on models that create a high volume of order generation, where many of the orders are ultimately canceled instead of traded. Often, models find value in trades only if they can buy slightly below the current price of one security while at the same time selling slightly above the current price of a different security. Buy and sell orders are thereby generated. As soon as the price of one of the two securities changes, the value proposition for the model might not look as rewarding and the machine will cancel the orders before they are filled.

Initially, the exchanges saw these algo-generated orders as a good thing, seemingly providing lots of liquidity and order flow to the system. Yet increasingly, exchanges and regulators see these types of orders as painting a false picture as to the actual liquidity available to trade at any given moment. Rules are now being implemented that limit the number of orders a single model can send to the exchange without executing a trade. In July 2013, Panther Trading LLC was fined and banned from trading for one year by the CFTC for creating order flow that was ultimately canceled before executing, even though doing so had been standard industry practice.[33]

Until recently, another practice that has been typical of algo models was generating a large amount of buy and sell orders for the same security. This practice makes it appear that there is a lot of volume intended to buy or sell a security when, in reality, the algo plans to cancel the order before any trades are executed. This is designed to trick the market into thinking there is a large buyer or seller, and it scares the market's participants into trading at a disadvantageous price. This practice is called "painting the tape." This term refers to the practice implemented years ago, when stock traders printed phony trades on the New York Stock Exchange, knowing the price would be broadcast on the ticker tape and sent out to the world (since the ticker tape was the only market data feed at the time).

---

[33] "High Frequency Trading Firm Panther Energy Fined in 'Spoofing' Case," Dina ElBoghdady, *Washington Post*, July 22nd, 2013

Attempting to trick traders is an illegal practice, and this is what Panther was accused of doing. However, the order flows of legal and illegal practices do look quite similar. It is the responsibility of the trader behind the computer to verify that his algos meet the legal standards that regulators have established. In addition, algo traders must not replicate the advantages that exchanges set up for their members, such as having the first chance to execute market orders; otherwise, membership value would be destroyed. Membership has its privileges, and there continues to be backlash against algo traders who try to skirt these rules. Therefore, we can expect stronger and stronger supervision by the exchanges to police algo traders who do not apply for membership.

Advancements with Algos

In recent years, new types of algorithmic trading have emerged that rely less on the pure speed of bids and offers. One such algo form is reading news using computer programs to search for keywords such as "surprise, unexpected, exceeded, negative," etc., and automatically acting on the securities they apply to without letting a human vet the story first.

Another new strategy involves factor models. A factor model seeks out factors about a stock or bond that the computer deems to be relevant or valuable, rather than understanding the complete fundamental view of the security. For example, factor models during the most recent coronavirus pandemic sought to sell the "factors" of travel and entertainment, given that people could no longer travel or go out, and sought to buy the "factors" of cleaning suppliers and streaming videos, both of which would be in high demand as people stayed home. Thus, the algo would look for stocks that have any of these criteria instead of looking at companies as a whole.

If you feel intimidated and think, "I'm not a computer wizard, I'm not sure I can compete against these computer gurus," take heart! Ultimately, many trading styles rely much more heavily on the human element than on a computer's fast calculating power. Let me give you some facts to support this proposition.

Twenty years ago, computerized trading of all kinds made up approximately 10% of the daily volume of stocks traded on the New York Stock Exchange. Today, that number is close to 60%. On the other hand, 20 years ago, there was $300 billion of capital dedicated to long-and-short fundamental trading on the US equity market. Today, that number is closer to $730 billion according to Barclay Hedge Database. All but a small fraction is traded based on slow-moving macro research.

Thus, today's market has as many, if not more, opportunities to trade on brain power than it has had at any time in its history. In fact, for the most part, the market has become somewhat bifurcated. Algo traders try to make money from retail customers who execute small orders on their E-Trade and Schwab accounts. They also take orders from other algo traders in the world of machine versus machine. But in doing all this, algo traders provide liquidity to the marketplace for fundamental traders who have a different perspective on where the value lies.

Market Making

Market makers and used car salesmen have a lot in common. I will leave it to the reader to decide if that analogy raises the class of used car salesmen or lowers the class of market makers!

Market makers essentially try to make money by "warehousing risk." That is, they will buy or sell a security from someone else, hold it for an unknown time—perhaps as little as a second or as long as a few days—until they find the opposite side of the trade. The market maker believes that if he essentially makes a well-thought-out bid/offer spread every time he trades, he will eventually make money on the total collection of trades, even if some of the trades lose money.

The market maker and the used car salesman both warehouse the risk they take on and hope that the infrastructure they build to hold their trades is profitable after covering all the costs associated with the business. The car salesman buys used cars and hopes to sell them at a profit. He has costs, including the mortgage on his property, repairmen to maintain the vehicles until a buyer is found, advertising, and salaries. He, therefore, has to price what he pays for the car very carefully. He has to pay enough that the seller will not go somewhere else to sell, yet buy low enough that he can cover his costs until he finds a buyer at a reasonable price.

A market maker does exactly the same thing. He creates a model to value the trade and creates a bid and an offer price around that model. If his bid is too high, he will not be able to sell profitably. The market maker must also cover his costs, including the cost of capital invested in making trades, his technology budget, and the salaries for himself along with anyone he hires. If his price is too low, he may not get enough trades to justify the business.

Market making is the core component of trading. Without market making, markets are nearly equal to any other form of commerce where trading takes place, such as real-estate speculation. In real estate, price transparency is limited. The time and place of bids and offers are uncertain and illiquid. Sellers cannot count on being able to liquidate at a moment's notice.

Market makers separate themselves from general commerce by providing a continuous price to buy or sell a security during a fixed set of daily trading hours. They provide facilities known as exchanges that help guarantee that the transaction will be honored and that the monies used to pay for securities are protected from theft. Because market makers provide such a crucial function by providing willing bids and offers continuously, exchanges offer their market makers special benefits. These benefits include lower fees to trade, the right to charge commissions to their clients, and the right to have priority in the order process. For example, market makers on the Chicago Mercantile Exchange get to move to the front of the line when placing a bid or offer in a futures contract if they, in return, make continuous markets in the same product.

Because market makers are trying to capture the bid/offer spread, they need lots of transactions to win over time. They will often be willing participants and counterparties to your trades even if you think you have an Information Advantage. This is because market makers still assume that for every trader who is right about buying or selling, there are more that are wrong. Guessing who is right and who is wrong is difficult and time-consuming. It is simply easier to make markets for everyone and assume that the law of large numbers will work in their favor and leave them profitable at the end of the year.

If we placed trading styles on a compass, idea-driven trading would be north, algo trading would be south, technical analysis would be west, and market making would be east. Since there is no rule saying that traders cannot blend styles, we can imagine on our compass, for example, northeast is a blend of idea-driven trading and market making. This style is the most common one at banks, where traders make markets and try to idea-trade for the bank's account. On the other side of the dial, southwest would be a combination of algo trading and technical analysis, where traders try to blend the best of both to generate trade signals.

In the end, we can imagine hundreds of combinations of the four styles. Understanding why others act in the marketplace helps eliminate our fear that they know something we do not. Even in a massive sell-off, there are buyers along the way, putting their capital at risk as they execute their trading styles. When we trade on our ideas, we need not look at the market digitally, meaning that our idea is either right or wrong. Rather, our idea on valuation is intermingled with the market maker's view on where he can buy or sell in the next few minutes. It is also intertwined with an algo trader looking to spread our trade against another security. Moreover, it is pitted against a trader using technical analysis, who believes that a trend line may justify taking the other side of the trade.

As professional traders, we embrace other styles, as they provide us with liquidity for our style. We study different styles to understand what insights they have about the market and add it to our knowledge reservoir. Understanding how and why others act in the market will help us form better trade ideas and better trade design.

CHAPTER 15

Bringing It All Together:
Sample Trades from Idea to Execution

In this chapter, I will give three examples of trades I executed personally. We will review the history from the birth of the idea, through trade design and trade management, and ultimately the closing out of the trade.

When you read about my trades, notice the imperfections in my process. Take heart that although you rarely have a complete information set to make a perfect decision, the other market participants do not have perfect information either. Most participants use simple rule sets or may have entered the market for purposes other than short-term trading gains. They may be long-term investors, corporate treasurers putting on hedges for their corporations, retail investors trying to diversify their portfolio, or mutual funds entering the market you are in to maintain an index of investments.

Most buyers and sellers will be less knowledgeable than you are as you do your fundamental work. They may have conducted the same trades as you, had they the time or the inclination to be as disciplined as you. Do not be discouraged by the feeling you are alone in your views or that your conclusions seem to be going against the tide. If you have done your homework and act with discipline, you will be fine in most cases. Just continue to work, listen, and manage your risk carefully—before, during, and yes, even after the trade.

Trade 1: September 2012: Buying US Dollar vs. Japanese Yen at 78

My interest in Japan began in 1994 when I joined Deutsche Bank as a foreign exchange trader. Before then, I had never traded any products outside the US in my career. Still, I was now thrown into a world where I had to quickly learn the economics of major overseas economies. I had to learn about Germany and its effect on the rest of Europe. I had to learn about the United Kingdom and its attempts to keep the British pound from weakening.

And I had to learn about Japan. Japan was the first major country in the world to cut interest rates to zero to try to foster growth and inflation when both were dropping to new lows every year. As a trader, I watched as Japanese citizens conserved their savings in yen and put it into bank savings accounts to grow their wealth instead of investing it because they expected to make less income year in and year out due to the continuous recession beleaguering the country.

Japan cut costs to the bare bone to make its products competitive on a global level, thereby preserving their positive trade balances. With high export growth, the currency began a nearly two-decade appreciation against the world's other major currencies. Japan was flooded with trade and investment surpluses as Japanese investments in the 1980s started to bear fruit in the booming 1990s and mid-2000s.

From 1994 to 2012, the Japanese currency appreciated from 172 yen to the dollar to a low of 75.9 yen per dollar, a change that hit in October of 2011. Japan was somewhat powerless to stop the yen's appreciation because politically, they had an agreement with the Federal Reserve and the European Central Bank to not intervene in the financial markets.

Chart 17
Japanese Yen vs. US Exchange Rate, 1987 to February 2014

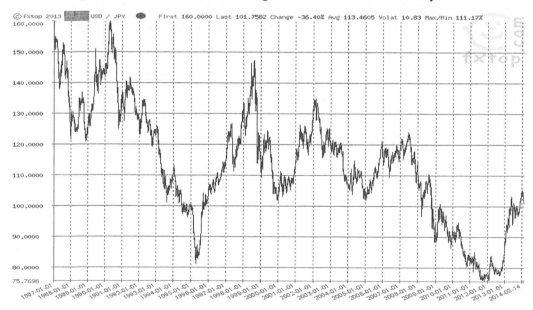

Following the financial crisis of 2008, the European Union, the US, and Japan, who had the three largest trading currencies, agreed to avoid intervention as much as possible to promote the idea of free capital flows. However, the rest of Asia was not listening. Most of Asia had gone through a nasty currency crisis in 1998. Therefore, Asia (excluding Japan) set a course to accumulate reserve currencies, keeping their currencies as weak as possible to help their trade balances and save capital for future economic crises. As a result, no matter how far the yen appreciated, Asian central banks continued to accumulate yen.

From time to time, Japanese authorities would intervene to slow the yen's appreciation. At times, Japan would buy yen with such quantities that they could depreciate the currency from 5% to 10% in days. But within a few weeks and months, the market resumed its course and the yen appreciated to 76 yen per dollar in 2011, where it was sitting when I arrived in town.

On March 11th, 2011, Japan had a great earthquake followed by a tsunami, which significantly damaged many northern prefectures (regions) and caused several nuclear power plants to be damaged and leak radiation. In June of 2011, I was working for Bank of America. They asked me to move to Japan to be the head of their Interest Rate Trading and Foreign Exchange group for that country to help boost morale for the bank's traders. I arrived in late July, only 120 days after the earthquake. Tokyo was only 238 kilometers from the quake's epicenter and was still feeling aftershocks every day (aftershocks as big as earthquakes for everyone else in the world).

Overall, morale was low, and yet there was unanimity among the Japanese to do what was needed to help the country. Each weekend, thousands of volunteers went up to Sendi and other damaged cities to help clean up, using nothing but their hands and shovels. In Tokyo, all businesses were asked to keep their offices at temperatures of 80 degrees in the summertime to conserve energy, and that they did. Relief donations reached billions of dollars. In light of these unifying efforts, seeds were being sown for what was later to become known as "Abenomics."

A country that had been burdened with a prolonged postwar recession, low growth, and deflation was now also facing the world's most significant disaster rebuild, causing an even greater economic slowdown. Over the next few months, I studied the financial conditions and anecdotes of business in Japan. The one observation that struck me most was Narita Airport.

Narita Airport is Tokyo's busiest airport and historically one of the busiest in all of Asia. In fact, it had gotten so much air traffic that city planners built an even larger airport closer to the city. Yet, to preserve jobs, planners still had more flights come in and out of Narita than at their new airport, Haneda.

One day, while waiting for my flight to take off, I noticed a sign that seemed strange to me: "All transportation from Narita to Tokyo ends at 10 p.m." I was a little puzzled by this because there were many forms of transportation from the airport—buses, trains, and taxis. Why would all of them be unavailable after 10 p.m.? And then it dawned on me: no flights were scheduled to arrive after 8 p.m. anymore. No one was coming into Japan! No tourists, no businesspeople, no one. Imagine if LAX or JFK shut down at 10 p.m. every night. How much of a recession must the US be experiencing to cause that much of a shutdown?

As it turned out, a lot of what plagued Japan was human creation. And like most countries in the world, Japan's problems were easily identifiable, but the suggested policies to fix them were much more politically challenging to implement.

The ineffectual nature of the government was laid out for all to see. The Democratic Party of Japan (DPJ) had managed to take away power from the Liberal Democratic Party (LDP) in the previous election for the first time in 50 years. The LDP, determined to take power back, realized it was their own lack of leadership that had caused their downfall. The LDP knew they needed to find a unifying leader to simultaneously deal with the nuclear mess and the tsunami cleanup while also finding a way out of the recession.

They found their leader from the past: Shinzo Abe, who had been prime minister in 2006. Still, he had been considered boring and ineffectual, like many LDP prime ministers before him. But Abe was willing to take a chance if the people would give him a mandate. He would promote growth and inflation at any cost to revitalize a stagnant economy.

I left Tokyo in March of 2012, and by the summer of 2012, I was back in New York trading for a hedge fund. I began to read the LDP party's policy plans, and it was clear to me, given my observations of how united Japan was for a change, that the LDP would win regional and general elections.

Shinzo Abe knew from his own experiences leading Japan that he had no choice but to go all in on policy this time. Most days, Tokyo's stores were empty; Japanese consumers would only window–shop, rarely buying. The only tourists were Chinese, who had the one currency stronger than the Japanese yen and could afford to visit. The airports were empty. Corporations were paralyzed, not knowing if they should commit capital to their own country or not.

To understand this, I had not read an analyst's report from a fancy brokerage shop; rather, I had observed all this from my personal experiences. I saw how low morale in the country was and how willing the citizens were to sign up for a plan of action.

When Abe's campaign began in earnest in August of 2012, many traders back in New York took little notice. I, however, had already conceived of my trading idea. My own experiences had led me to believe that Japan had to weaken the yen as part of its overall policy to regain growth. A weaker yen would bring in tourists, allow exporters to compete in the world marketplace, and might even cause prices to rise at home.

I also knew if I could secure an entry level at around 78 yen to the dollar, I would be significantly protected against the downside risks, since the government had intervened over the previous two years to sell the currency each time it strengthened to 76 yen per dollar.

Next, I had to develop my price objective and my distribution of possible outcomes. I realized that for Japan to achieve mild growth, it needed to have conditions similar to its last growth cycle, which was from 2005 through 2007. During that time, the currency had averaged around 105 yen per dollar, a 35% differential over the 78 yen per dollar I was considering! Realizing that countries would protest such a substantial change in the currency, not least of which the US, I looked at the average depreciation change of major countries over the previous ten years and calculated that 10% moves were quite common for one year. A 10% increase got me to 86, so I set my trading objective for a range between 86 and 105, with a take-profit level of 94, slightly below the midpoint of the range.

My next step was to design a trade and size it correctly. I realized that despite the strength of the currency over the past five years, investors still need to hedge against even further appreciation of the currency. As I discussed in previous chapters, other traders with other trading styles often provide you with liquidity and the opportunity to execute your strategy.

Since there was demand for call options on yen, I could design a trade where I buy put options on yen at a strike price of 82 and pay for those selling calls to those interested investors with a strike price of 72! Demand was that strong that I could actually buy an option that was 4% out of the money and pay for it entirely with proceeds from an option I sold that was 7% out of the money. This type of trade is called a "Risk Reversal" and often avails itself when the implied volatility in the options price is different than what you, the trader, perceive as fair value.

Now having my trade design, I was left to ponder my trade size before execution. I managed $500 million of capital at the time. I wanted my trades to provide an average of 5% returns on that capital, knowing that some trades would be losers that I would exit after a 2% loss.

Since my goal was to make 5% or $25 million, and knowing that my minimum price objective was 86 (up from 78), I knew I had to make $6 million for each one-point move in the exchange rate from my strike price of 82. I sized my trade accordingly and bought options on $500 million worth of US dollars.

Chart 18
Yen to US Exchange Rate, January 2010 to February 2014

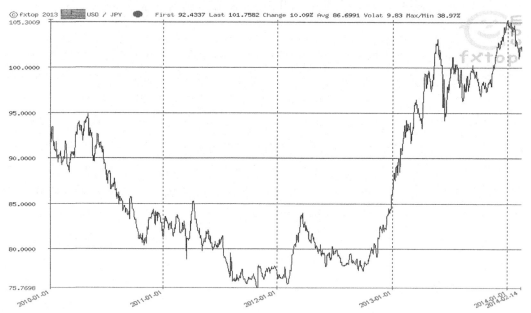

By December 30th, 2012, the trade had reached my initial objective of 86. But the story had not changed, as Abe had been elected prime minister in a landslide. He had honed his policy speeches to be even more direct about his goals to create inflation.

I decided to run my position further, funding new yen put options through closing out my 72-yen calls and reselling yen calls at 79, knowing now that Japan did not believe the currency would go below 80 or risk the policies being considered a failure.

In the end, I closed out my position at 93.5 after the currency depreciated to beyond 95 and then fell back, setting off my trailing stops to protect my gains. As one can see from the chart above, the rally continued long after I exited the trade. I believed in my valuation premise, accepted my exit point, and did not regret that the market continued on without me. Only in hindsight do we know the perfect entry and exit point. Though, in retrospect, my trading discipline took me out of the trade too early, my trading research and trade design got me into the trade before others and allowed me to maximize my returns during the trade.

Trade 2: Buying Facebook, January 2013, at $23 a Share

In September of 2012, Facebook went public at $38 a share. Soon, the company became a poster child for greed and poor execution of an IPO. Here was this world-famous company, the IPO of which had been anticipated for years and who had hired almost every major investment bank on Wall Street to help lead its share issuance. As the time drew near to go public, the company was swayed to continuously raise the issue price on what was perceived to be good demand for the stock. In short, Facebook wanted to launch at the richest market valuation possible to solidify its place as the leading social media company in the world.

Within hours of its launch, the stock began to trade lower, from $38 down to $36, and within a few days, it was down to $28. The stock began to sink further in the weeks and months after that, until it hit $16 a share on November 10th, 2012. The company had been so focused on its initial valuation that it had spent little time explaining to investors how it would make money in the future.

The market assumed Facebook was a two-trick pony: a place where influencers and game designers could run ads on Facebook's website. To many, it seemed like a limited marketplace with growth not nearly fast enough to justify such a high stock price. In the media, pundits took pleasure in downplaying the stock since many famous investors had fought to buy the stock pre-IPO in private transactions.

Like others, I watched the stock drop. I wondered if I could bring any perspective to the valuation argument, given that many analysts in the US were already watching the stock. I knew if I were to find value in a place where everyone else was looking, the perspective would have to be uniquely my own!

Chart 19
The Price & Volume of Facebook Stock, IPO to February 2014

I began by researching the main views of the analysts on how the company was valued. The majority of them gave Facebook credit for the growth it had achieved on the web in advertising and game sales. Most derived a growth model on those two revenue streams and then added a bonus kicker from some mobile growth as their value proposition.

Most analysts assumed that as ads were run, people would stay on Facebook less and less. For that reason, video ads were significantly discounted as an opportunity. In addition, the analysts felt that Facebook would have limited success on the mobile app because the experience of reading Facebook pages took up so much of the available space there was little room for paid ads.

Using these projections on how future revenue would play out, most analysts felt that the Facebook stock was only ultimately worth between $23 and $25 a share over the following year. If one were realistic about its prospects, the IPO had been too aggressively priced at $38 a share.

Given this set of assumptions as a starting point, I looked into my own experiences to determine if I agreed with the premises. As a philosophy minor in college, I learned that you had to attack the assumptions when making a rebuttal to an argument. If you grant your counterpart that his assumptions are correct and indisputable, then you have already lost the argument because the conclusion falls out from what is accepted as "facts."

In the case of Facebook, I had learned from personal experience, traveling throughout the world, that most of Facebook's user growth was coming from outside the US. Though China had entrepreneurs with enough capital to take on Facebook, many smaller countries did not, and Facebook quickly became the preeminent way for people worldwide to connect. What better way to level the playing field of knowledge, culture, family life, etc., than having a Facebook page that did not discriminate from one's being a wealthy person living on the Upper West Side of Manhattan or a poor child from Romania?

I quickly calculated that international users' growth would dominate Facebook's development for years to come, and that user growth would be more than double that of the analysts' expectations. In addition, with few alternative ways to connect to the world, I predicted that time on the site per user would rise as opposed to fall, as many analysts were expecting.

Another critical issue for Facebook would be how "sticky" their users would be once the users were confronted with ads intermingled with their personal information on their Facebook page. In contrast to the common belief that users' time on the site would drop as people got frustrated with ads, I thought that time on the site would actually rise!

My reasoning for this is as follows. First, there was no alternative to the site for most people, so if you individually protest the ads by temporarily leaving the site, you will soon feel you were missing out on what everyone else was doing (popularly known as "FOMO"). Unless everyone leaves the site en masse, you will sooner or later be back with your tail between your legs, catching up on what you missed. This time, you will stay longer, knowing that ads are just a part of life in return for such a free, elegant service.

Second, even as new competitors popped up from time to time, Facebook had already shown the smarts that had evaded America Online (AOL) and ultimately killed its business. (In my view, AOL was the first social-based Internet service conglomerate, even though in those days, its business model was for users to pay a fee for its Internet Service Provider function).[34] AOL refused to use its large capital base to buy competitors, thinking it could out-compete all newcomers through internal design improvements. In contrast, Facebook realized that social trends and tastes change, particularly around the youth set that was the heart and soul of Facebook. It

---

[34] "The Rise And Fall of AOL," CNBC, Video, August 15th, 2019

had already bought Instagram with the capital it raised from its IPO. Instagram, which was a fast-rising competitor of Facebook, would now be a synergistic asset!

Finally, there was the question of mobile. To me, mobile was an advantage, not a disadvantage. For those users dedicated to Facebook, reading and updating in real-time was a vast improvement. Thus, seeing ads on mobile was a small price to pay to catch up instantly on the mobile device. If anything, more ads could go on the mobile app than on the web-based site. In any case, Facebook was at no more of a disadvantage than any other publisher. Whatever market share there was to gain in mobile, Facebook would get their share.

Therefore, armed with my assumptions instead of the street's assumptions, I began to apply my stock's financial model. In my model, the number of users, powered by international acceptance, would grow to over 1.5 billion accounts by 2018. It turned out that I missed that number by a mere 1 billion! In addition, I projected a 50% annual growth in revenue from all sources for at least five years. I also assumed that costs would not grow at the same rate as in the past because most of the company's build-out stage was behind them, so the company could benefit from economies of scale and grow their income and cash. After five years, I applied a low 25 price-to-earnings ratio to the stock and still derived a stock price of around $42 a share versus $18. That translated to an annualized growth rate of about 30% for the stock price, which was double the S&P average.

In review, I had applied my unique perspective to the analysis of the stock. I had used my personal experiences of how people outside the US viewed the site in order to garner insight that others might have missed. My analysis depended on assumptions on how *humans* would react to the site and how *human investors* would react to those results. As covered earlier, my edge was understanding human nature, as I was not privy to all the detailed data that street analysts often receive from the company, its competitors, and industry databases. Nonetheless, as traders, we look for tipping points, and I felt confident that the street was not considering my arguments for the tipping point in the stock.

I had scant time to determine a good trade entry. For one thing, the stock had its IPO in May of 2012 and the price action had been generally down since the first few days of the IPO, hitting a low of $17.73 in early September. Within days, that stock had bounced back to about $20 and was trending around the low $20s through October and early November.

With no real sense of what the trading range could be, it was difficult to determine what an appropriate option strike should be or a time horizon to get there. Would the market revitalize their interest in a few days, a few months, or a few years? It was difficult for me to assess. Yet, what was not difficult to determine was that the stock low was 50% below the IPO price. My experience had always been that any company with growth prospects tends to find support in its stock price when it gets to be at a 50% discount from its IPO price.

I reasoned that many investment bankers spent long nights trying to price the IPO correctly. Though they do miss quite often, a 50% discount was usually the worst they get wrong. While I was not confident in my time horizon, I was confident in my downside risk. If I entered around $23 a share, my downside was limited to approximately $19 a share, or one-half of the $38 IPO price. As a trader, when you are uncertain of the timing but confident in your downside valuation, it is usually okay to just buy the underlying stock and trade with a stop below your worst-case valuation expectation.

Finally, I had to set my price target. Again, I looked to the IPO valuation. Usually, markets tend to retrace back to their IPO level if the company is performing to expectations. Also, since my model's valuation was $42, I was able to come up with my distribution: $38 low, $42 high, with a mid-expectation of $40 a share.

In mid-November, I entered the trade at $23 with a stop of $17.72, just below the year's low point. With a take-profit of $40 a share, I had a risk/reward of about 3 to 1, an excellent ratio.

The stock's performance was disappointing at first. It rallied quickly to over $31 a share, only to fall back to near $23 by June of 2013. I had been right to avoid options, as the market spent eight months assessing the stock valuation—this, in the face of a reasonably large rally in the stock market in a general sense.

Yet, in mid-July of 2013, Facebook announced its earnings for the quarter ending in June 2013. To the shock of many, but not to me, almost every metric I had assumed to kick in began to bear fruit. Mobile ads were up huge. International users continued to grow significantly, and, most importantly, there was significant growth in the average time spent by all the users. Even Facebook itself had predicted that user time would go down and observed it was surprisingly wrong on that count!

Within four weeks of that announcement, the stock approached $40. I took profit on one-third of my position, as I felt that current momentum was overwhelming my valuation proposition. Now, note that my valuation proposition did not change—just my management of the trade.

I then moved my trailing stop up to $38, which was my minimum valuation, and left an order to sell another one-third of my position at $42, my full valuation calculation. Soon, that order was filled, and again, I raised my stop to $40 and left an order to sell at $45. That order was filled just three days later, and my exit was complete.

The stock continued to rally, and some may say that I traded poorly. They may say I should have raised my stop without leaving a specific sell order. After all, don't the best trades end in tears? As it turned out, to my detriment, I had violated a best practice strategy. If I left a rising trailing stop, my average exit would have been closer to $45 a share.

Even in times of great success, we have to battle our minds and our hearts. My mind and heart wanted to prove to the world that I not only knew where the bottom of Facebook was but where the top was as well. Great traders must constantly fight emotion and instead channel their energies to finding new trades and let the stop orders do their job.

Trade 3: Shorting Oil, June 2013

By June of 2013, everyone, it seemed, knew the developing oil story of the US. Once the world's leader in oil production through traditional wells, production had dwindled from 9 million barrels a day to below 6 million from 1972 to 2010. That was twenty-eight years of stagnant production on our shores; as someone opened a few new wells, some older wells went offline.

A history of accidents, often due to storms on the Gulf Coast, had limited offshore drilling licenses. The infamous Exxon Valdez spill off the coast of Alaska had forever tainted California's appetite for oil drilling at the risk of hurting their beautiful shorelines.

The result was a limited supply of crude oil and its byproducts against a background of the ever-growing demand for oil worldwide. Since the early 1970s, when the Arab oil boycott of the US caused oil prices to skyrocket along with significant gasoline shortages for the first time in American history, Americans had made efforts to conserve oil and consume it efficiently as possible. By the late 2000s, growth for gasoline demand had ground to a near halt, as the growing number of cars on the road was more than offset by their fuel efficiency and lower miles driven.

Oil comes in many forms. Different countries produce different grades, meaning that the oil in Saudi Arabia has a different structure than Texas oil, such as more sulfur and less carbon. To refine oil into gasoline, various processes are needed to refine one grade of oil versus another. Thus, each grade is given a name, so buyers know which type of oil they are getting.

The two most actively traded grades are Brent Crude, produced in parts of Europe and the Middle East, and West Texas Intermediate (better known as WTI), produced right here in the US. To protect the country from future oil shocks by hostile nations, Congress passed a law in 1974 that made it illegal to export American oil. The idea was to keep local production here at home to reduce the risk that a pricing war would erupt and cause a spike in domestic oil prices. Knowing it was illegal to export WTI, most refineries in the US are set up only to refine WTI into gasoline.

As 2010 turned into 2011, new drilling techniques began to unlock vast oil fields in Texas and South Dakota that were long assumed to be unusable. Areas that held oil dispersed in pockets between the rocks underground had been ignored in place of fields where oil sat in large pools straight down. But with these new techniques, which essentially involved drilling sideways instead of straight down, vast new oil reserves could be unlocked and were unlocked quickly. As a result, from January of 2011 to June of 2013, US oil production, which had been unchanged for two decades, rose 50%!

As we have learned, there was little place for the WTI to go since it was illegal to export the crude to other markets, even if there was less demand for it here. In addition, these same techniques worked in Canadian fields, which were even more significant than in the US. That oil could only run north to south—i.e., from Canada down to the US for refining. There are no pipelines yet running to the west coast in Canada due to similar environmental fears that there might be an accidental spill. Thus, with refineries at near-record capacity by June of 2013, it seemed inevitable that the price of oil would decline.

While there were many oil analysts with more experience, I had several unique information flows I thought could be the tipping point. For one, at my hedge fund, I sat next to a full-time oil analyst who provided our team with weekly stats on where the excesses of oil and gasoline were in the system. Second, we had additional research on how much more capacity was coming online and we could calculate that the potential for oversupply was rising. Third, our political consultants had let us know that the Keystone pipeline, a potential new way for Canada to move oil through the United States and on to ports where oil could be exported, was bogged down in Congress and not likely to be passed as soon as many market participants had been expecting. Thus, Canadian oil could only really be sold to the US market.

Further supporting my confidence was great price entry. I had already sold oil once in April and repurchased it in May. The market had rallied back in June from $92 a barrel to $99 a barrel. The entry level seemed ideal since our projections had the valuation of WTI oil closer to $85.

I formed a range for my objective: $90 to $85, with a goal of $87. Since oil is a fast-moving commodity, and since the supply build-up was happening in real-time, it seemed that options would be the ideal way to construct the trade. Besides, oil often rallies when there are problems in the Middle East. In the summer of 2013, fighting continued all over the area, so it would be highly risky to structure the trade by being short oil without protection from an option.

Since oil prices were frequently volatile, each option tended to be priced high because oil could quickly move up or down. However, when volatility is high, it's usually a good trade to buy a spread, meaning to buy a put option and sell another put option with the same maturity but with a lower strike price. The benefit of this strategy is that the cost of the option is significantly reduced by selling another option. The drawback is that if oil were to drop precipitously, the profit on the spread would be limited compared to just owning a put by itself. In my case, owning the spread suited me because I had no expectations of a drop larger than my range.

I entered the trade on June 14th, buying the October 94 puts and selling the October 87 puts, a spread trade that cost $1.35 per option. Since the spread was $7, my potential gain over my cost was $5.65 for over a 4-to-1 risk-reward. July to October was not a lot of time, just three months. But the oil story changes so quickly that I felt if the current facts did not drive oil down, new facts would come along to change the entire story all the same.

Chart 20
The Price of WTI Crude, December 2012 to December 2013

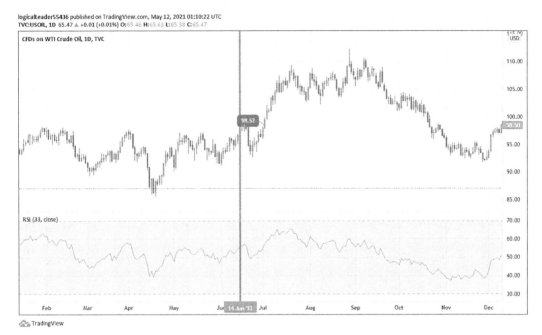

I bought my put spread with oil trading around $98.52 a barrel, as denoted by the grey line in Chart 20 above. It seemed my analysis was spot on, as oil dropped within days to $96.

However, things went wrong very quickly from there. Oil began a two-month rally, going from $96 to $110. My option spread started to drop in value as the market went from $3 above my strike price to $16 above my strike. The cause was no mystery. Once again, tensions in various Arab oil-producing states had caused supply shocks. Developments in Egypt and sanctions against Iran, Sudan, and Libya all caused large amounts of Brent Crude to come offline. And while Brent Crude produced by these countries should have little influence on WTI production, it still caused WTI to rally in sympathy. Whether I agreed with the market or not, I had to manage my risk with the hand I was dealt.

I had a choice: modify my trade and take advantage of the fact that the market would likely drop from this point, or cut my losses since I was uncertain how long the panic would last. I chose to cut my trade, knowing even if the market reversed, it was unlikely now to reach my target before the put expired. Besides, the market was even more volatile than before, so it would be difficult to switch from a put back to just shorting the contract without any options protecting me. Finally, as I'd expected, new information had come along to affect the balance in the market. My research data on surpluses was now getting old while new information that had come in was affecting the market more. I lost my information edge; to go short now would only be guessing.

In the end, I closed out the option spread at 35 cents, losing $1 for each put spread that I had bought. The market ultimately did decline below $100 a barrel, but not before my options had expired worthless. It was time to move on to a new trade and accept the losses as the ordinary course of how trading works.

CHAPTER 16
Taking Profit

I f you made it to this chapter, you have tough skin. It has probably been a challenging ride for you. Many trading myths have been dispelled along the way, and a lot of learning and hard work has been put in its place. I have shot holes in the hope that there is some great system out there—be it technical analysis, a research method that continually guarantees profitable ideas, or an algo system—that will last forever. When you have navigated the road less traveled—the one that takes hard work—that instead of ignoring the risks which lurk behind every corner, you are ready to embrace those risks and incorporate them into your thinking.

When you have followed that path, the reward is within your grasp. Your trades are well thought out and well-designed. You are using your capital wisely and your positions are performing well. The market is moving smoothly, making movements that match your prior assessments. News matches your expectations. You are protecting your downside with a trailing stop.

But now you realize there is one final challenge: how do I determine what my take-profit level is? How do I know when I have maximized my profit? Look at all the hard work that got me to this point, and now I am not sure how to proceed!

"The Best Trades End in Tears"

Throughout this book, I have strived to promote best practices over a hard-cast rule. Take-profit strategies are no different.

The first best practice of taking profits is trailing stop orders that follow behind your trade while attempting to let the market run. One of my best analogies to explain this concept is the idea that "your best trades always end in tears." "What the hell does that mean?" you ask. "The best trades end in tears?"

To understand this statement, let's look at the history of a famous trader from Chicago, Richard Dennis. Mr. Dennis preceded my career in Chicago by about eleven years, but boy, did he make those eleven years count!

Dennis and the traders he trained became known as the "Turtles."[35] Turtle traders and their disciples still walk the halls of trading firms today, forty years later. Their core philosophy is simple: mentally prepare for lots of losing trades and a few exceptionally large winning trades. As we have seen in earlier sections, there is no way to make a large winning trade without assuming considerable risk at some point in the trade.

No option can keep you protected until the last second and then bestow you with a large windfall. In reality, you have to have your full allotment of capital on the line, and you have to stay with that allotment as the market moves your way.

Richard Dennis was one of the first to understand that not only do you need to have your maximum bet and let your capital ride as the market moves your way, but you need to get out of the way and let it run when all the stars are in alignment and there is no information contradictory to your core view.

To make a large profit in any given year, Richard knew you only need a few large trades to pay for the hundreds of smaller winning and losing trades that will inevitably occur in the search for a breakout trade. Dennis, who started with a few thousand dollars as an 18-year-old, went on to make hundreds of millions of dollars over his 30-year career.

Soon, he learned one more lesson concerning large trades: it is better to let the market run and keep trailing stops than to get in the way of a large trending trade. Thus, by definition, you will always be closing out your trade at a worse price than the absolute top of the market, simply because you do not know where the top of a market trend is until after the fact.

The top of the market will come and go. Eventually, the market will stall or trend lower, and you will begin to lose money compared to the moment of your largest gain. Soon, you will lose enough money that you are stopped out of your trade.

And here comes the "tears" part of Dennis's lesson. Since you will always have had more money in your account at one point before the market turns against you, instead of being happy, you will feel like crying because you lost money at the very end of the trade.

In reality, if you had tried to pick a level to get out of, what would have been the result? Would you have anchored your expectations to a chart and failed to imagine

---

[35] "The Amazing Life of Richard Dennis and the Turtle Traders," editor, traderlife.co.uk, 2018

how far the market could go if you were right? Would you have gotten nervous because you set a goal of how much the trade should make and taken a profit too early because the trade hit some objective in your mind?

When you finally do get stopped out, you will feel pain. Still, you will also feel vindicated that you let the trade run its course to the maximum of your staying power—by using best practices.

Understanding How Your Trade Is Designed

Taking profit using trailing stops is a fundamental practice of a great trader. But a second important aspect of taking profit is to understand how your trade is designed.

In previous chapters, I have explained that you should have a profit objective at the initiation of your trade and a take-profit zone defined as a distribution. Trailing stops do not contradict this concept. Rather, trailing stops are another form of limit order once your trade hits the take-profit zone. They allow you to maximize returns while maintaining your discipline around capital management and taking profit objectives.

Typically, I may leave a series of take-profit orders around my distribution of expected gains. However, if there is an opportunity to modify a take-profit to a trailing stop, particularly if the market is moving quickly and profitably in my favor, then I will exercise this strategy.

Often, trending markets are driven by new information that supports and enhances the strength of your valuation thesis. Switching to trailing stops allows the market to set the ultimate new valuation. As Richard Dennis and the Turtles found out, the market usually knows better.

A second best-practice methodology is to understand what the take-profit should be when trades have a maximum payout level by design. For example, many option trades have a maximum payout as a function of time and price. A call spread (long a low strike call and short a higher strike call) has a near-maximum payout based on price as a function of time.

Let's say we have a call spread in Home Depot stock. We own the $70 call, and we are short the $75 call; the stock is trading at $73. If there are thirty days to go until expiration, the call spread's maximum payout may be reached when the stock hits $77. If the stock goes even higher (to $79, for example), the extra profit will be relatively small versus the risk that the stock goes back down.

Traders often leave options they have sold short to expire worthless when the market moves away from the strike price, not understanding that the risk associated with the market reversing direction and making the option valuable again is greater than the remaining premium left to collect before the option expires.

Therefore, modeling each trade's payout, particularly if any part of the trade involves options, is essential. When you reach a maximum payout level, you are prepared to leave orders, take profit, and close out the trade.

Finally, a third best-practice method involves trades where the marginal return for any additional price movement may be significantly worse in terms of risk/reward versus merely closing out the trade. One example is holding successful trades into news events where the reward of additional gains is entirely unknown or beyond the scope of your original valuation. Smart bond traders will often exit a successful trade after prices go higher if there is a risk that a pending economic announcement could have a surprisingly negative effect on bond prices with little potential additional gain before the report.

Avoiding Unnecessary Losses

Taking profit is not always about the culmination of a great trading idea. Another best practice is to have the discipline to avoid unnecessary losses from a trade idea that initially performed well but is now heading for failure.

We often put on a trade after doing meticulous research and initially see the trade move profitably. Yet, whether due to poor trade entry or new information that affects the valuation, the winning trade begins to reverse. Many traders will let a trade go from positive gains to "negative gains" because they feel the trade has not had sufficient time to work. They think that a small increase that turns to a loss is still an active trade that can ultimately go positive again, as long as the overall stop-loss has not been triggered.

Great traders know that this type of trade should usually be closed out before it goes from a gain to a loss. Usually, for a well-researched and well-designed trade to initially go positive and then reverse almost always means that more recent data is influencing the market and the trade needs to be reconsidered. *Closing winning trades out while they are still profitable is critical to capital preservation. We need to take profit on these small winners to compensate for the portion of our trades that will never go positive and are sure to be stopped out for a loss.*

Note that this best-practice recommendation is different from always having a trailing stop. Let's imagine that we buy an oil futures contract at $95 a barrel, expecting a 10% appreciation to $104.50. When we design the trade, we set a stop-loss to sell the contract at $92.15 for a 3% loss.

The trade begins to work as we expect, and the market moves up to $96.85 after two weeks of trading. Soon, however, the market stalls and starts to go lower each day.

After three days, the price of our oil contract is back to $96.10. If we simply do nothing but raise our trailing stop to a level equal to the total percentage gain we had on the trade, our stop would only be increased from $92.15 to $94. Therefore, we are still at risk of getting out at a loss.

Using a basic formula for trailing stops will not protect your capital if you are trying to preserve a winning trade. Instead, by raising the stop to a simplistic minimum gain such as 0.5% (equating to $95.47), we preserve capital and give ourselves room to assess the new information that clearly changed the market's view of the valuation proposition compared to your original thought.

Taking profits appears easy and fun. We imagine we will feel vindicated that our trade supposition and design beat the market on top of feeling financially satiated, at least for the time being.

In reality, a great trader knows that taking profit is the final step of a disciplined process. It is a process that began with a well-thought-out trading idea, morphed into a trade design that maximized the idea's potential, and ultimately culminated with you, the trader, running through a series of best practices:

- Managing the risk while the trade was on.

- Setting a distribution to take profits.

- Figuring out which method of take-profit is best suited to the market conditions presented.

Let's return to the surfing analogy in Chapter 1. A great surfer does not plan how he will get off the board at the end of a great ride. Rather, he uses his physical skills and training to choose the best exit, given the surf conditions presented to him. His goal is to have a long ride on top of the wave and exit as close to shore as possible. He knows if the wave is acting unexpectedly, dumping out safely is a much more disciplined approach; there will be many more waves to ride in the future.

Taking profit employs the same thought process. We know what our goal is—to maximize our profit and ride the trade as long as possible. We also know that what we would like to happen has no bearing on the fact that we will use our best market practices to assess the market conditions thrown at us. It is best practice to make the disciplined decision on when to cut out, knowing there are many more trades to follow if we preserve our capital when conditions are uncertain.

Section IV

OPTIONS BASICS: LEARNING IN A NEW WAY

CHAPTER 17

Understanding Basic Option Theory

earning the value of options trading is one of the most critical factors in becoming a successful trader. Options trading is a much-misunderstood practice, even for most professionals.

There is a perception that trading options is the ultimate panacea for risk management. Many trading books tell stories about how the great traders figure out what the next big move is in some asset—say, a stock price—and they buy options to take advantage of that idea, limiting their losses while obtaining the opportunity for potentially unlimited gains.

This idea of limited losses with the potential for unlimited gains has driven many a trader's dream. Who would not want that?

On the other hand, options sound exotic and are, in some ways, intimidating to the novice user. There is a certain degree of arrogance in the trading world separating options traders from other traders because some consider options traders to be "smarter" than other traders. After all, the price of an option has to be derived using a mathematical model.

The original option-pricing model is called the Black Scholes model, named after Fischer Black and Myron Scholes, two University of Chicago professors credited with inventing the most commonly used option-pricing formula in 1973. Since that model does not solve perfectly for all financial instruments, many modified versions of option models have been developed over the years that involve relatively high levels of mathematical sophistication.

In reality, for centuries, options were priced without models. Traders who wanted to make a bet on markets have bought options from willing sellers throughout history. The oldest recorded option bet dates back to the sixth century BC, when Aristotle reported that his colleague, the Greek philosopher Thales, had predicted that there would be a big olive harvest and secured the right to use olive presses for a fee.[36] Thales knew that if the harvest were poor, he would lose nothing more than the fee he paid. But when the crop turned out to be exceptionally large that year, and demand for olive presses rose dramatically, Thales sold back the right to use the presses at a handsome profit!

Centuries later, rice traders in Japan would buy and sell options to better help the Shogun Dynasty manage their finances. Jesse Livermore, the most famous speculator in American history, thrived on buying and selling options on stocks in the early 1900s.

Options trading has existed with or without sophisticated models because the price of an option is intuitive. Humans move the prices in markets, and humans are capable of mentally determining the probability of prices moving up or down in the future.

In the next few chapters, I will demystify options trading and show you that the basics of pricing an option are quite logical and straightforward. In addition, I will debunk the concept that options have limited losses and unlimited gains because that viewpoint is much too simplistic to be of any value to you as a trader when evaluating whether or not to use options. Finally, I will review why using options will improve your trading and show you what risks you manage when you trade options.

What Is an Option?

Let us begin with the definition of an option. An option provides the right, but not the obligation, to purchase a security at a predetermined price within a predetermined time frame.

A typical option has five essential characteristics: (1) the security on which we are basing the option (called the underlying); (2) the price of the option; (3) the strike price of the option; (4) the maturity of the option; and (5) the direction of the option (also known as a put or a call).

The buyer of the option pays a fee upfront, also known as the option premium. In return for paying this fee, the option buyer has the right, but not the obligation, to buy a security at the strike price up to the time the option expires, often called the maturity date.

---

[36] "Thales—The World's First Option Trader?" David Foulke, alphaarchitect.com, November 29th, 2013

A Simple Option Example

Here is a simple example to see what each of these points means.

Imagine it is June 1ˢᵗ, 2013, and an option buyer wishes to buy the right to pay $26 a share for Facebook on or before December 1ˢᵗ, 2013. The seller of the option sets the option price (called the option premium) at $3.25, and a trade is made.

The buyer now owns a call option—the right to buy Facebook shares at any time between June 1ˢᵗ and December 1ˢᵗ at $26. We say the buyer is "long" the right to buy.

The seller keeps the $3.25 premium, but in return, must stand ready to sell shares to the buyer at $26 a share, no matter how high the stock price goes. We say the seller is "short" the right to buy.

Chart 21
The Price of Facebook Stock, March 2013 to December 2013

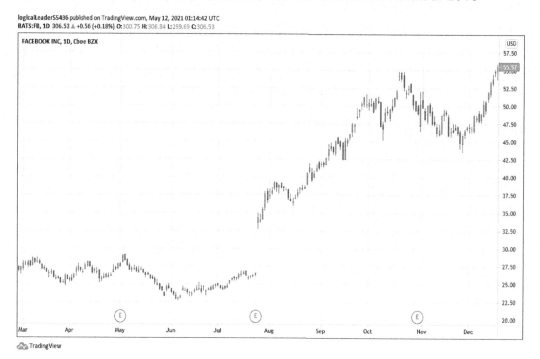

logicalLeader55436 published on TradingView.com, May 12, 2021 01:14:42 UTC
BATS:FB, 1D 306.53 ▲ +0.56 (+0.18%) O: 300.75 H: 306.84 L: 299.69 C: 306.53

Lo and behold, Facebook stock begins to rally, and by October 16ᵗʰ, 2013, the stock trades at $50 a share (Chart 21). The buyer's option for $3.25 a share is now worth $24.25, and he would like to take profit on his trade. When he sells the option to close out his trade, he will have no more risk in Facebook's price and will have made a profit of $21!

Now you may be thinking, "Wow, what an idiot the seller of the option is! She sold the option for $3.25 and the option went to $24.25. She lost over seven times the premium! Isn't that a terrible risk/reward type of payoff? I can only make $3.25 if I am right, but I stand to lose as much as $24.25 or more if I am wrong?"

Fear not for the seller. If she is a professional trader, she most likely hedged the trade by buying Facebook stock as it rallied. Remember, options are always based on an underlying security—in this case, Facebook stock. The amount of stock the seller would need to buy as a hedge for the option she sold is called the "delta" of the option. In general, if the seller purchased enough stock along the way as Facebook rallied, the profit she made on the stock purchases would offset the losses she had on the option.

At the limit, if options were free, we would always use an option to express our trading view of a specific security rather than only buying or selling the security outright. The reason is that our loss on the trade of an option is limited to the purchase price of the option. At the same time, our gain is equal to the security price movement over and above the strike price, no matter how far it goes over!

But there is one small problem: no one will sell us an option for free. The seller only wants to sell that option at a price she believes will leave her a small profit after she has covered all the costs and risks associated with hedging the option.

Already we see a hint as to how we price an option. *An option price ultimately derives from an agreed-upon bet between two humans regarding the potential future value of the option.* In other words, the seller believes she will receive enough of a premium to pay her costs of hedging. The buyer believes the option's price is low enough to justify expressing his trade in option form rather than just buying or selling the underlying security.

Pricing Options in Your Head

As we have already noted, options have been priced for centuries before the Black Scholes model was widely distributed in 1973. For centuries, traders priced options in their heads. Therefore, as your guide to the fundamental understanding of markets, there is no better training on being a great trader than teaching you how to price options in your head!

In pricing options, the point is not to replace using models. After all, the granularity of a model and the speed at which a computer works are critical to trading success.

But by understanding how to price the option using logic, you will make better decisions about the value of using options and reduce your fear of them.

It might come as some solace to the reader who is not heavily mathematically inclined that there is no perfect solution to the price of an option. Many of the factors that go into pricing an option using a model are not constant. For example, the basic Black Scholes model assumes that dividends paid on stocks and interest rates both remain constant during the life of the option, when these two factors change all the time.

All the best models generate an estimated price and tend to solve well only for certain controlled situations. For example, a model may solve with great accuracy an option that is At the Money (close to the current stock price). Still, the same equation will not derive a consistent price for an option far from the last trade price (Out of the Money). For the novice trader, a pricing model provided to you on most computerized trading platforms will be quite sufficient for deriving the cost of an option you would consider trading. However, by learning to price an option in your head, you will understand the computer model's variables and better understand when an option provides an added benefit to your trading.

Options in the Everyday World

First, relax your minds when it comes to the notion that options are complicated. In truth, all of us sell options every day! When we tell our child, "Always come to me if you need help with your homework," we have sold an option. However, we do not actually set aside an hour each day sitting in a room waiting for our child to arrive. Rather, we go about our day's business and take the risk that our child will not ask us for help most of the time and that we will not have to stop what we planned to do. Also, the "fee" we receive for writing this option is our child's love and admiration that we are always there to help!

We tell our neighbors, "Call us if you need help." But again, we do not sit around idly waiting for our neighbors to call us. We take the risk that we can drop what we are doing and help our neighbors at whatever cost that entails. In return, we receive the "fee" of trust and reciprocity from our neighbors that they would do the same for us! In human interaction, we make calculations all the time about the cost and benefits of the options we buy and sell.

Now let us look at a business option far from the world of trading securities—the dreaded commute to work. Many of us take a train to work each day. When the train runs smoothly, it is a pleasant experience, knowing you can sit back, relax, or read while the engineer takes you to work faster than you could ever drive by car.

But alas, trains have their problems, particularly in bad weather. Invariably, a few times a year, the trains are delayed or even fail to work at all. Delays often happen at the peak of winter when storms cause delays on the tracks or in the summer when the heat causes transformers to blow out. During those days, you are often surprised when you arrive at the train station only to find that you cannot get to work, and you find yourself needing an alternate plan on how to get to work.

When you do not go to work, a great deal of income is lost. You are willing to pay quite a sum of money to find alternative transportation. In this example, next to the train station is a taxi company that has ten taxi cabs on call that are first come, first served. The charge to drive passengers to the city usually is $50. Everyone knows that the charge goes as high as $100 or more on bad-weather days because it takes longer to make the trip. Even at $100 for the trip, there are often not enough cabs for everyone who wants to take one on bad weather days.

After several years, it dawns on you: "What if I buy an option from the owner of the taxi company to have a taxi waiting for me on a bad weather day of my choice?" Brilliant, you think, and you go to the owner and the parameters of the option are set as follows:

Time to Maturity = 6 months (October 1st, 2013, through April 1st, 2014)

Underlying Security = the cost of a taxi ride to the city

Strike Price = $100 fare

Direction = "Call," or the right to buy the ride at $100 regardless of the real price

Price of the Option = $20

Each side decided the risks associated with the option and agreed that the rewards outweighed the risks. Thus, a deal is struck. For you, as the buyer, you risk the fact that the weather might not be bad after all and the trains will successfully run all winter. In that case, you would not need a taxi and your $20 cost of the option would be wasted. Or even if the weather is terrible, the risk is when you get to the taxi stand, there are enough taxis for everyone who wants one for $80. In this case, you will not need to exercise your option because although you need a taxi, you do not want to pay $100 when you need only pay $80!

The taxi owner, as the option seller, is risking that when the weather gets bad, he will reserve a taxi for you that goes unused. In addition, he risks that the weather would be so bad that he could normally charge $150, but because of the agreed–upon option, he has to let you use the cab for $100.

However, despite the risks, each side decided that the deal was better than doing nothing. The taxi owner got $20 and decided that chances were small he would need to charge more than $100 for a ride to the city in any case. You decided that knowing you can get to work and not lose income on a bad-weather day is worth the loss of $20 if you did not exercise the option.

Both the buyer and the seller decided about the volatility of the weather. The buyer believed he could not manage the risk and decided to hedge against bad weather. The taxi owner decided he could handle the risk and sold the hedge to the buyer for a fee. Notice how neither party was naïve about the weather's potential volatility but mutually agreed on the price of the risk. The real value of that decision is not known until we go through time, but at the time of the transaction, the price was fair.

More on the Taxi-Ride Option

To continue with the taxi example, let's consider some more scenarios that might follow.

In the first case, word spreads that the taxi company sells options on the right to a cab ride in bad weather. Others take an interest, and soon demand grows for these options and the owner of the taxi company has to decide what to do. He wants to accommodate the new buyers, but he cannot sell options on all his cabs. Thus, he must raise the price to a level that only the buyers who want the option the most are accommodated. Yet, regardless of price, the taxi company only has a limited number of options to sell so he can fulfill his obligations and manage his risk.

The owner can either raise the price of the option of a $100 cab ride to $50 so only a few more people will buy it, or he can raise the strike price from $100 to $125 and continue to sell the option for $20. As we can see, in either case, demand—not actual problems with the weather—has driven the price of the option up! That is, the anticipation of future events, particularly if more people anticipate the same risk, drives the price of options.

Now, imagine that bad weather is forecast for December 20th, 2013, right in the middle of the option period. Instead of lousy weather being anticipated, bad weather is actually coming. The phone at the taxi company begins to ring again, as more people want to buy options for cab rides. But these callers are surprised to find out how high the price for an option is, and only a few agree to buy options—and the price stays the same.

Thus, at a specific price, we learn that buyers of options no longer benefit from hedging their risk, even if volatility is coming or is already here. Meanwhile, our taxi owner is licking his chops. Bad weather is coming, and he has sold options at reasonable prices that he expects to be exercised. He decides to get greedy and invites more cabs than average to work the day of the storm, figuring he will have lots of demand. In essence, he over-hedges his risk, reasoning that the demand for taxis can only go one way—up!

As predicted, the storm hits, the trains do not run, and the taxi owner awaits his windfall. But much to the cab owner's surprise and dismay, the options' high price has convinced most of his potential customers that there probably will not be enough cabs available at a reasonable price. That is, the commuters hedged their risk based on the price information available through the options that were sold and made alternative plans.

On the day of the storm, only a few customers show up to take a taxi. The fare quickly drops to $80, as the increased number of taxi drivers want to get some work. In the end, the option buyers do not exercise their options.

The taxi owner is now screwed—having hired extra cabs that did not get used—and still exposed to future storms since no one has exercised their options! In addition, option prices for future cab rides go down as the buyers readjust their expectations on how many cabs will be available in future storms.

When buyers learn about the price of an option, they determine if the risk can be managed more efficiently by other means, such as, in this case, by planning not to go to the station at all! Even if the event is volatile, if new supply is made available, the option's price can just as easily go down as it can go up.

Finally, it is not uncertainty itself that makes an option price go up or down—it is our belief in whether we can manage the uncertainty that drives the price. Seeing that the taxi owner could quickly bring in more cabs during a storm allowed the option buyers to lower the price they would pay for the right to reserve cabs for future storms.

Here, we are learning that a variety of factors drives the price of options. The critical factor is one's belief that the inherent risks can be effectively managed for less than the option's cost. If it cannot, we will look to buy options.

The uncertainty about the future price movements of our underlying security is called volatility. When we use a model to price an option, we quantify the term "volatility" into a number that is roughly equivalent to our expectation about the potential percentage change in the price of the underlying security.

Options in the Financial Market

Now, turn your attention to pricing options in the financial market. Let us challenge our minds to derive the price so we better understand what drives option pricing.

If our mind were programmed to run a Black Scholes formula, we would ask for five inputs: (1) the strike price (we use the letter k = strike price); (2) the current risk-free interest rate (we use the letter r =risk-free rate); (3) the current price of the security (p = price); (4) the time length of the option (we use t to represent time length); and, of course, (5) volatility, represented as v. However, instead of solving the equation in our mind, we would blend these five inputs into a single probability expectation.

Here is an example. Imagine we are asked to price a call option on two different stocks. The first is IBM and the second is Tesla. On November 8th, 2013, after a wild day in the market, Tesla closed around $139.77 a share and IBM closed around $180 a share. You are asked to price a call option in each stock, with a strike price of $200.

Chart 22 shows the prices of IBM and Tesla for six months leading up to November 7th.

Chart 22
The Price of Tesla and IBM, June 2013 to November 8, 2013

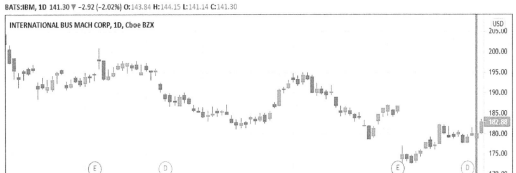

By doing some basic research—like checking the historical price action over the last few weeks, months, and years—you learn some interesting things. First, IBM is an old historic company with relatively small daily changes in its price, except on earnings-reporting days. You also note that IBM has never traded higher than $216 a share. Tesla, meanwhile, is a newer company with lots of significant price movements each day. Its 52-week range was a wild $29.84 to $194 a share. Clearly, Tesla is more volatile than IBM.

Even though IBM closed 30% higher than Tesla on November 7th, we can understand that there is more risk that Tesla could rally higher than IBM over six months. It also has a greater chance to sell off faster!

We can think of volatility risk as the absolute value of potential change, whether up or down. Not only will $200 calls on Tesla cost more than $200 calls on IBM, but 100 puts will also cost more on Tesla than on IBM. We care about the risk of absolute movement. In fact, $200 June 21st, 2014, calls on Tesla cost $8, while $200 IBM calls cost only 25 cents! Tesla is such a volatile stock that the market does not know where it will go next. A $100 strike price on June 21st, 2014, expiring puts on Tesla also cost $8, while $100 IBM puts cost only 15 cents!

The charge for a call option on Tesla is based on the fair probability that at expiration, the stock is equally as likely to be over $200 a share as it is to be under $200. If we did not price the odds of that event correctly, we would not find a buyer or seller to take the other side of the transaction. Thus, the market often derives what is fair, and then the quants come along, take that option price, and solve backward for what the volatility value should be!

Jump Risk and Swing Risk

There are two other essential aspects to volatility we need to incorporate into our thinking.

We noted earlier that we care about the absolute value of a security's potential movement when determining the value of the option. We also care about two other types of movements: "jump risk" and "swing risk" (the second is what I like to call "noise risk").

When a security has jump risk, it tends to gap from one price to another, usually off a news event (earnings reports, economic releases, corporate announcements) with minimal trading between the original price and the price to which the asset jumps. Jumping risk is difficult for the seller of the option to hedge because, as the asset's price moves, the amount needed to hedge the option (called the "delta" of the option) is changing rapidly. This is called "gamma risk."

For example, Google is a fairly steady stock with lots of volume available to trade at each price point during the day. But on earnings-reporting days, Google is famous for having jump risk. Chart 23 shows the stock price of Google from 2018 to early 2020, indicating the dates of ten quarterly earnings announcements during that time. Each announcement is shown on the bottom of the chart with a grey "E."

If you look closely, you can see the jumps at each report. This makes the option quite difficult to hedge for the seller.

Chart 23
The Price of Google Stock, 2018 through 2020
(Showing E for Earnings Announcements)

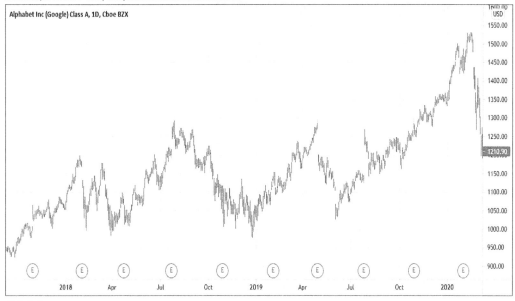

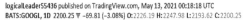

The seller of an option would be hard-pressed to adjust his risk during these large gap movements. Therefore, he needs to incorporate jump risk in the price of an option. As the buyer of the option, you must decide if its cost, with the jump risk charge embedded in it, is worth it to hedge your risk against a bad earnings announcement.

When a security has swing (or noise) risk, it means the price tends to move up and down around its mean without following through in one direction or the other. Typically, larger stocks, stock indices, bonds, and commodities all tend to have some amount of noise.

On Chart 24, we look at two securities that follow this pattern. On top is the price of Oracle stock, and on the bottom chart, we show the price of the British pound from 2010 to 2012. Notice how both Oracle and the pound tended to keep coming back to their long-term average price but still have lots of noise, as shown by the many times each tends to trade 5% above and below the mean.

Chart 24
The Price of Oracle Stock (top) and the British Pound
vs. US Dollar Exchange Rate (bottom), 2010 to 2012

The seller has to charge for this noise because he will continuously be putting on hedges that will be losers, selling the asset as it goes down 5%, only to repurchase it as it returns to its average price—and in the opposite direction, buying the same when it goes up 5%, only to lose on the hedge when the asset goes back down again. The buyer has to decide if the charge for the noise embedded in the option's price is worth the cost, or does he want to avoid the cost and manage the underlying security himself?

From this analysis, we can see that the three major aspects of volatility are: (1) absolute movement, (2) jump risk, and (3) swing risk. The seller logically considers all three aspects to price the option. The buyer must consider all three aspects when deciding if an option represents a better way to manage his risk versus merely buying or selling the underlying security.

Though movement is the critical component in the option's price, it is worth discussing the other inputs as well for completeness of thought. We care about the *interest rate* because we have a choice of how we manage our cash. If we buy an option instead of buying a stock, we have money left over that could be invested in a bank account. If interest rates are high, the seller of the option will charge more because he has to buy stock as a hedge of the option while you get to leave your money in the bank!

We care about the *dividend rate* of a stock or the coupon of a bond because, typically, the buyer of the option does not receive it while they hold the option, but the seller of the option, who buys the underlying as a hedge, does get this benefit. Thus, the option's price is adjusted downward in proportion to the value of the dividend or coupon payment.

The value of the option is typically greater the longer amount of time the option is in existence. A one-week option will be worth less than a one-year option because there will be more time with the one-year option for movement to occur—both absolute and noise movement.

Finally, an option strike that is close to the current price of a stock will cost more than a farther-out strike. For example, the $200 strike price six-month call on Tesla will cost more than the $210 call, while in turn, the $220 call will cost even less, assuming that all the options have the same maturity date. The closer strike, being lower in price (for a call), will more likely have intrinsic value than a strike price that is further away (or higher). (Intrinsic value is exactly equal to the amount the strike price of a call option is below the stock's market price.)

It is important to note that the difference in the price of an option between these three strikes is not a linear interpolation. The $200 call costs $3, the $210 call costs $1.50 and the $220 call costs $0.70. Notice how the difference between the $200 and $210 calls was 150 cents, but the difference between the $210 and $220 call was only 80 cents. Option prices begin to approach zero as the probability of an option being valuable before expiration is low. Nonetheless, sellers of options do not want to give them away, essentially for free. However, on a pure statistical calculation, the odds of getting as high as $220 before expiration are very low.

The option seller will not sell the option at the theoretical option price (in this case, 25 cents). The seller deems the economic incentive to risk that the option will end in the money is not worth a 25-cent fee; he wants more, regardless of the model. When an option seller wants more than the model predicts, the model's volatility assumption has to change since it is the only moving variable; the rest are fixed. To get the option price to solve for the 70 cents, we must make the volatility assumption higher in value.

When we force volatility value in a model higher to fit the price we observe in the marketplace, we call that "skew" effect. If the volatility is higher than we expect, we say the option has a positive skew. When it's lower, we say the option has a negative skew. Suppose a set of options on the same underlying security have ever-increasing volatilities. In that case, as we move further and further away from the current stock price, we say there is a "smile" on the option surface. If we plotted the volatility prices on a graph, it would look like a smile!

Look at Table 1 of option prices for IBM as of the close of business on February 21st, 2014. IBM closed that day at $182.79. The table here is for five different IBM calls that expire on June 21st, 2014. There were approximately 120 days left before expiration. The last column, labeled IVM, is the Implied Volatility Model price. The market makers trade options in price and then solve for IVM. Notice how IVM rises as the option strike goes higher. The market makers demand a better price to take the risk.

Table 1
Prices of IBM Call Options Expiring June 21, 2014
(Close of Business, February 21, 2014)

Symbol & Strike	Last	Change	% Change	High	Low	Bid	Ask	IVM
IBM Jun 21, 2014 190.00	3.65	-0.25	-6.10	4.35	3.65	3.60	3.70	15.85
IBM Jun 21, 2014 195.00	2.36	-0.02	-0.80	2.80	2.36	2.21	2.27	15.85
IBM Jun 21, 2014 200.00	1.37	-0.20	-12.74	1.50	1.37	1.30	1.36	15.95
IBM Jun 21, 2014 205.00	0.83	-0.07	-7.78	0.83	0.83	0.74	0.80	16.1
IBM Jun 21, 2014 210.00	0.44	-0.08	-15.38	0.52	0.44	0.42	0.46	16.5

Logic Trumps the Models

Once again, logic trumps the models. Sellers will not give options away cheaply, even if a static model tells them it is a good idea! Rather, option sellers demand a premium in the same way you would on the following bet: imagine I told you the odds of a Super Bowl game ending with a score of 16 to 15 are statistically one million to one. Would you give someone one-million-to-one odds? Would you risk losing $1 million to make one dollar just because that is what the statistics say? Probably not, even though the model says it is a fair bet.

It is the same with options. Sellers do not like to sell big-payoff bets cheaply just because the model says it is correct.[37]

As we have seen in this chapter, option pricing is a game of logic based on the factors that go into the price movement of a security. While the past is some indication, it does not incorporate all possible future movements. If it did, models would work perfectly. In fact, if the past were a guarantee of the future, all trading would be easy and profitable. Since future expectations are an integral component of option pricing, you must assess the possibilities to use options correctly.

I have spent this chapter getting you to understand how important the mind and logic is to understanding options. However, just as you would use your car instead of taking a skateboard to work, you should use your computer models to make the final calculations faster and more accurately. Therefore, a model is an excellent tool for calculating hedge ratios and understanding how the price will change over time once we have solved for the volatility we want to use. Models are also excellent for testing various stock moves scenarios, serving as an essential component in a professional trader's tool chest.

---

[37] Sometimes sellers do give away low-priced options close to a model price in the hope of collecting the premium without having to do any hedging. The common expression around this phenomenon is called "selling tails", with "tail" coming from a term meaning the extreme end of a probability distribution where, mathematically, there is a low risk of the option paying off. Many option buyers like to look for cheap tails because they like the risk/reward parameters of low-priced options, even if they pay off infrequently.

CHAPTER 18

The Myth of Unlimited Gains:
Dissecting the Real Benefits of Options

One of the myths of options trading is that when you are the buyer of an option, your losses are limited, but your gains are unlimited. This expression is so simplistic that it borders on misleading. Let us review an options payout structure in more detail to understand what options can and cannot do for your trading performance.

For efficiency, I will limit this discussion to buying calls on a stock versus buying just the stock. Still, the logic applies to buying puts versus shorting stocks or buying options in any asset class. We will study calls on Facebook versus merely buying the stock outright.

First off, there is not one single option to buy. Instead, there are a series of options to choose from: different maturities and different strikes. We will compare six options, each maturing in three months, ranging from a 10% delta to a 97% delta option. (Delta is the percentage the option movement replicates the stock price. An option that has a 50% delta moves in price half as much as the stock price.)

Below is Table 2, which shows the six call options for Facebook. The lower the delta, the lower the option's price because the option is further and further away from the current stock price.

Table 2
Facebook Options with 90 Days to Go, February 1, 2013

Facebook Options		Facebook Price = 30 dollars a share		
Strike	Price	Option Type	Days to Maturity	Delta
35	$1.00	Call	90	10%
32.5	$2.00	Call	90	28%
30	$3.20	Call	90	50%
27.5	$5.00	Call	90	66%
25	$7.50	Call	90	90%
22.5	$9.70	Call	90	97%

We should observe that if each option delta is different, it cannot be that all options give you unlimited upside and limited downside. What options really do is give you varying degrees of payoffs for various degrees of risk of loss.

For example, look at the 22.5 strike priced at $9.70 with 90 days to go. That option has a delta of 97%, meaning the price will go up and down 97% as much as owning stock in Facebook—not much of a change in your risk profile, is it? On the other hand, the 10% delta option with the $35 strike only costs $1. But we need Facebook to go above $35 a share to make any money before 90 days have passed, or the option will expire worthlessly. Thus, with low-delta options, we trade a low cost for a more difficult path for the stock to travel before making any money.

Option Terminology*. Let's take a moment to discuss option terminology. An option strike that is significantly above the current price of the security is called an Out of the Money option. One that is close to the price of the security is called an At the Money option. One where the strike price is actually below the price of the stock is called an In the Money Option. Note, however, that these terms are not formalized by any official standard measure. For example, an option with a delta of 0.55 could be called an At the Money by one trader and an In the Money option by another trader: the terminology is used on a best-efforts basis.*

However, when you ask a dealer for a price on an option, you may say, for example, "Give me the At the Money, three-month call on the price of oil." In this case, the market maker will derive where the oil price for delivery three months from now is currently trading and quote you a 50-delta option exactly! In other instances, you may ask for an Out of the Money option. That same dealer may assume you want a quote for a 25-delta option, or he may ask you, "How far out of the money do you want?" A Way Out of the Money option is usually a 10-delta option.

Now, look at Table 3, 60 days later. The price of Facebook has dropped to $25 a share, or $5 from the $30 price.

Table 3
Facebook Options with 30 Days to Go

Facebook Options		Facebook Price = 25 dollars a share		
Strike	Price	Option Type	Days to Maturity	Delta
35	$0.10	Call	30	2%
32.5	$0.45	Call	30	10%
30	$0.80	Call	30	25%
27.5	$1.00	Call	30	37%
25	$1.80	Call	30	50%
22.5	$4.40	Call	30	88%

We can make some further observations here. Not all the options performed better than buying the stock. The 25 and 22.5 strikes lost more than five dollars! That's because options change price based on three factors: (1) the movement of the stock (to reiterate, in option terms, this is known as the gamma); (2) the change in time to maturity (known as theta); and (3) the change in the volatility assumption (known as vega). In the case of the 25 and 22.5 strikes, the options lost money from the $5 change in the price of the stock (gamma) and from time decay as 60 days have passed (theta).

Overall, there is no guarantee that options give you limited downside and unlimited upside. Options simply give you additional ways to manage your risk. As we can see, the remaining options all lose less than the $5 that the stock moved down.

Option Terminology. *Option Decay is an expression meaning that all else being equal, the option's value will slowly decline over time until it is ultimately intrinsic value (the exact difference between the strike price and the stock price) or zero at the date of the option's expiration. The option does not decay in a linear manner—i.e., it does not decay by an equal amount each day. Instead, it decays exponentially faster as a percentage of the total value of the remaining premium as time expires.*

Why does the option decay slowly at first and then pick up speed at the end? Simply because the more time there is left in an option, the more time for an event to occur to reverse its course and go back up. In addition, as an option approaches its maturity date, it becomes easier to hedge. That is because there is less time for the option to move up and down. For example, if Facebook stock is at $30 and we own the $35 call on that stock with 30 days to *go, there is still some time for news to come out and perhaps allow the stock to go above our strike price. But with three days to go, almost no information can get the stock price to go high enough to make the option worth it.*

Now, examine if you had bought the 10-delta, three-month call option on Facebook for $1. To your detriment, the stock price went down over the following two months, which caused you to lose almost all the value of your option premium (90 cents). But that is not the same loss you would have experienced had you bought 100 shares; in that case, you would have lost $5.

But now, there are 30 days to go and you are in the business of trading to make money. Yes, your loss was limited, but now we must strategize our next move. Always remember that there is an opportunity cost to doing nothing. Here, the option has depreciated to 10 cents and the strike is now $10 away from the current stock price. We must assess the new probability of where the stock will go and whether this option will slowly decay away to zero, even if Facebook's price may be on the move up again!

Once an option you own is way Out of the Money, it provides no additional benefit to you. In fact, at some point, doing nothing costs you money—the decay of the remaining option price, plus the opportunity costs of not moving on to a more profitable trade strategy, both are costs to you as a trader.

Thus, the loss-limiting profile of options has in and of itself a limited benefit over owning the stock outright. A worthless option must be replaced with the stock again or another option to profit going forward from that point.

When Options Are Less Attractive than Owning the Stock

Now, we will examine some issues that make options less attractive than owning the security outright.

The first is time. The option has a time limit before it expires, so it only protects you during this period.

Second, the option only protects you over a specific movement in the price of the stock. For example, assume that the initial move of an asset you are holding is a surprise to you. Perhaps you expected a stock to rally and it declines. The option will perform better than the stock, but at some point, it is to your benefit to close out your option. That is because if the stock begins to rally back after a selloff, you will not benefit if there is not enough time for the stock to cross back over your strike price. That is, your option is decaying and will expire worthless even as the stock rallies back.

In Table 4, where we consider Facebook at the time of expiration, we can see the six different payoff scenarios from the point where Facebook rallies back to $30 a share.

Table 4
Facebook Goes Back to $30 at Option Maturity

Facebook Options		Facebook Price = 30 dollars a share		
Strike	Price	Option Type	Days to Maturity	Delta
35	-	Call	0	0%
32.5	-	Call	0	0%
30	-	Call	0	0%
27.5	$2.50	Call	0	100%
25	$5.00	Call	0	100%
22.5	$7.50	Call	0	100%

Notice that from the point of one month to go before expiration until expiration, owning the stock from the $25 price going forward performed better than owning any of the options! Even if the stock rallied to a level above the strike price, the stock performed better because the time clock on the life of the option expired. While the remaining delta of some of the options gave us some money on the rally back, we still lost some value from theta. At expiration, all that is left of the option's value is its "moneyness" or "intrinsic value."

Option Terminology. The "moneyness" of an option represents the amount of an option's value that is based solely on the stock price being higher than the strike price. For example, if Facebook is at $35 and I have a $30 strike price option that is valued at $6, we would say that the moneyness of the option is $5. The rest is the excess value of the option for the time value remaining. At expiration, there is no time left, and the value of the option is its moneyness alone. In this case, the option would be worth $5.

If the strike price is above the stock price at expiration, the option has zero moneyness, and the option is worthless.

In our examples of Facebook options, I demonstrated a worst-case situation. In any market where the start and the end price are the same, options will perform less well than owning the asset. I used this example for a reason: to demonstrate that no rule of thumb works in all cases. Low-delta options or high-delta options can perform just as poorly, given specific market paths.

Continuing with a real-world example, imagine we bought the 50-delta call over purchasing the stock. We were nervous about how the stock would perform and we wanted to protect ourselves from Facebook falling for a while, and $30 a share might be a poor entry point to buy the stock outright.

Initially, that strategy was prudent. But the question remains: does an option protect us more than owning the stock outright? And the answer depends on how we would trade in the real world.

Had we bought 100 shares of Facebook at $30 instead of buying the option to control 100 shares at a strike price of $30, would we have acted the same way? Most likely not. Since we are learning to be a professional trader, we would use all the other skillsets we have acquired. We would not trade in a vacuum. We might have cut our losses as the stock dropped or stopped out of the trade altogether.

Suppose we had extremely low trading costs and excellent trading discipline. In that case, we could mimic the option's performance very closely by merely trading the stock!

For example, let's buy 100 shares of Facebook stock at $30 instead of buying the option. We could immediately start selling those shares if the stock goes down. If we are efficient, we can sell enough shares that by the time the stock gets to $25, we have lost no more money than had we owned the option.

Look at Table 5 for a simple example of this.

Table 5
Professionals Can Manage Option Risk by Adjusting Shares Owned*

Comparing long 100 shares of Facebook to being long 30 Strike Price Call on 200 Options						
Facebook Price	# of Options	Delta	# of Shares	Option Price	Option Loss	Stock Loss
$30	200	50%	100	$3.20	–	
$29	200	42%	86	$2.70	$ (100.00)	$ (100.00)
$28	200	36%	72	$2.28	$ (188.00)	$ (186.00)
$27.5	200	28%	56	$2.00	$ (240.00)	$ (242.00)

*Note we buy two options, controlling 200 shares to give us the same delta as 100 shares of stock alone.

In the example in the table, we execute three sales at each one-dollar price point on the way down. We are no worse off by buying the stock than we were with the $30 call options! Any strike purchased can be replicated by buying or selling shares as the stock moves up or down.

Finally, let's consider the concept of unlimited gains. We see from the five tables in this chapter that as the stock's price moves up or down, the delta of the option changes. As the stock's price moves higher and higher, the delta on an option will begin to approach 100%. In other words, the option price will start to replicate the stock price change one for one. At this point, it matters little what you paid for the option or what the original delta was at the time. Once the option performance matches the performance of the security one for one, your mindset of managing the option is identical to your mindset of managing the stock. They are interchangeable. You can switch from owning the stock to buying a call option that is deep in the money anytime you choose. Your performance will be the same, and your unlimited upside is the same whether you own the security or the option.

The concept that the option gain is unlimited exists only because the stock keeps going higher, not because the option makes it any easier to hold the position. Your mind, heart, bank account, and stop-loss rules will all need to be deployed equally once the option reaches a delta of nearly 100% of the security. Thus, the option's value only occurs within the framework of when the option gives you a risk/return performance that is different from owning the stock outright.

This is a critical point about options. Options are simply a calculated guess as to the value of the underlying security's perceived path—nothing more and nothing less. As we learned in the last chapter, the seller of the option prices how volatile he thinks the underlying security path will be. As the buyer of an option, the only value to you is that you believe the stock's predicted path is more volatile than what you can manage on your own. In short, it is not preordained that every option offers better risk/reward than managing the security volatility yourself!

Consider two stocks with the same price and compare their option value. On February 19th, 2013, IBM and Netflix were both trading at $198 a share. However, the three-month $200 call on IBM was priced at $9 while the three-month $200 Netflix call was priced at $25! Note that all the inputs into the option calculation to derive these two prices are precisely the same except one, the volatility assumption.

Option Terminology. We use the term "volatility assumption" instead of simply "volatility" because the input is an assumption. It is not known for sure. We can calculate the rest of the terms precisely.

Chart 25
Prices of IBM and Netflix Stock, February 2013 to July 2013

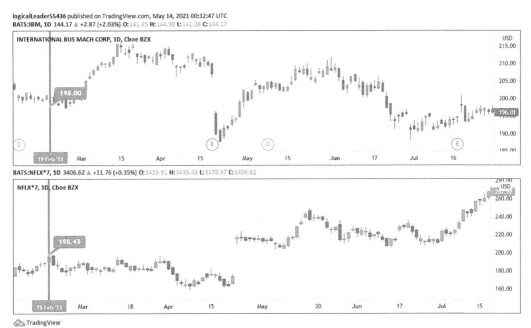

Even from a cursory glance, we can see from Chart 25 that Netflix is a much more volatile stock than IBM. It goes up $10 one day, then down $20 the next. IBM is a much older and more established company with little mystery about how it makes its money.

Note on the chart that the Y-axis for IBM goes from $185 to $225, while the Y-axis for Netflix goes from $160 to $280 over the very same period. IBM's price tends to move up and down by only a few dollars each day. Thus, as the seller, which option is easier to replicate through the buying and selling of shares? It is IBM, of course, because it moves much more slowly. The option seller is willing to sell the IBM option much more cheaply than the option on Netflix.

Unlimited Upside with Options?

What is missing in the premise of "unlimited upside" is the idea that somehow you are making money differently than if you had bought the security instead. Once the option approaches a delta of nearly 100%, you are making or losing money in the very same manner as if you owned the security—there is no difference at all! All the gains, losses, and all the emotions of making money and perhaps losing money, if the price action reverses, are identical. Therefore, your risk management skills, the harnessing of your emotions, your thought processes, your capital preservation skills, and your willingness to take in new information all need to be the same.

In conclusion, options trading is not, by definition, a less risky alternative to trading the underlying. It would be less risky if the price of the option were zero. But there is a trade-off for using options, as we have seen. The critical parameters of an option—limited loss with potentially unlimited gain over a fixed time—are replicable by the seller of the option by buying and selling the underlying security. Were that not the case, the seller would not be willing to sell you the option.

There must be other decision metrics for using an option than merely the general concept of limited loss and potentially unlimited gain. We have shown that the sweet spot of options is most often in their initial ranges immediately after their purchase when dramatic, unexpected price movements can cause significant losses if one only owns the security. However, knowing when the option's value no longer improves your risk/reward profile than holding the underlying stock is the skillset that a great trader needs to acquire.

CHAPTER 19

How to Use Options in Your Trading

The real value of options is more complicated than merely that they provide unlimited gains and limited losses. From Chapter 18, we have seen that the profits and losses from options can be replicated by buying and selling shares. The gains and losses of options very much depend on how we manage them. Options possess many characteristics that enhance our risk management, and the study of these characteristics is critical to improving our profitable trading potential.

In this chapter, we will cover some of the key reasons to use options: (1) leverage, (2) "jump risk," (3) the uncertainty of volatility, (4) the value of staying power, and (5) designing strategies unavailable through buying or selling the underlying instrument alone.[38]

Leverage

The most common reason for using an option is for leverage. Leverage is a critical component of professional trading, and I have dedicated an entire chapter to it. For now, let us understand leverage in the context of an option.

All exchange-traded options and most Over the Counter (OTC) options offer two kinds of leverage. The first type of leverage is the more obvious one: the amount of capital controlled by an option compared to the amount of capital controlled by buying the underlying security.

Here are examples in three different asset classes: foreign exchange, stocks, and commodities. In each case, when we buy the asset, we are looking at controlling $1 million of value in the underlying asset. Different assets trade on various exchanges with varying requirements of margin. Nonetheless, when we compare each asset with its corresponding option, we can see in all cases that it takes less capital using an option to control $1 million than it does just buying the underlying asset.

---

[38] This list is nice subset—but a subset nonetheless—of the power of options. Please take your options and study as far as your mind will let you. There is now a 40-year history of options literature and many of these writings will enhance your utilization.

Chart 26
Leveraging Your Capital

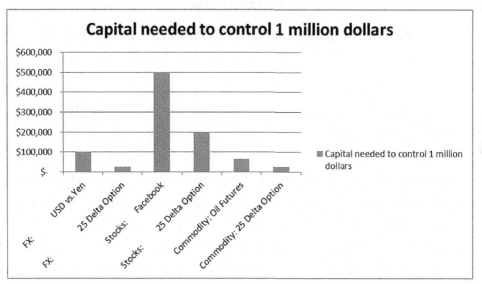

From Chart 26, we can see that in all cases, options offer at least double the leverage measured by the amount of capital one controls in the underlying security. The exchanges offer the extra leverage to entice traders to use the product and because the risk to the trade is usually limited to the premium spent on the option.

Of course, we know the buyer's capital risk is limited to the option's price in any case, so giving them leverage is not a significant issue. However, even if you are a seller of the option, your overall risk is not that the security will instantly be worth nothing or go up exponentially. Instead, your risk is most likely to be some percentage change that can be managed with less capital than what is needed to pay for the entire security's principal amount. Thus, as a trader, you may want to use an option to control more of an asset than you can afford by buying or selling the security alone.

The second type of leverage is much more subtle and not as easily understood. The buyer of a low-delta option has embedded leverage because he can avoid margin calls and stay in a trade regardless of where the security goes.

Now, imagine a stock trading for $100 a share. If I only have $1 million in cash in my trading account, I would only be able to buy 20,000 shares and control $2 million in stock! But if I buy a $200 call option for 10 cents on a stock that is trading at $100, I can control 100,000 options—or, put another way, $10 million worth of stock! (Each option allows the buyer to control 100 shares of stock.) This is powerful leverage. If the stock begins to rally, your gains and the dollar amount of stock you control grow exponentially as the option delta rises.

Let's suppose I am a seller of the option and there is some risk that the price can go up. In that case, the exchange may limit me to only be able to sell 50,000 options or even less, depending on their margining system.

As we discussed in previous chapters, whether you trade with an exchange or a private counterparty, you will have to put up a variation margin (additional funds into your account) if you are a seller of an option. However, if you are a purchaser of an option, you never have to put up any additional capital than what you initially paid for the option. This means if your confidence is high and you wish to stay in a trade when it moves against you, you do not have to reach into your pocket to put in more capital.

But getting leverage is not an advantage in and of itself. The key to using leverage is based on your belief in the value of the trade. If you have high conviction on a trade—i.e., if you are confident in a way that is well above your average confidence level—you'll want to raise your leverage so the returns on that trade will be greater than your average trade.

In blackjack, card counters will often raise their bets to 20 times their normal bet limit when they believe the odds are more in their favor. In trading, it is the same way; you should increase your leverage when your research or beliefs give you confidence that additional capital is justified. Using an option gives you a way to raise your leverage beyond what can be achieved by trading the underlying instrument. The greater your conviction, the greater your potential return because you can get more and more leverage with the same premium through higher strike, lower price options.

But more leverage does not necessarily equal higher profit. The more leverage you are using, the more you are betting on a specific price path. For example, say you buy a $200 option on a $100 strike price. You must have supreme confidence in the stock's direction because the stock can't just go up a little bit; for you to be right, it has to double, and then some, for you to have a winning trade. If it goes down first, even a little, the cost of your leverage may be lethal to your trade because there may not be enough time for the stock to achieve your price objective.

On the other hand, the more confidence you have that the stock's path will quickly move higher, the cheaper the option will be because you can hone your option purchase in terms of time to maturity and strikes chosen.

For example, look at Table 6.

Table 6
Calls on Yen vs. US Dollar Exchange Rate Going from Spot 98 to 103

Calls on USDJPY with Current Spot Rate of 98 USDJPY going to 103 USDJPY					
Strike	Maturity	Cost of Option	Leverage per MM	Value in 2 months	% Gain
100	180 days	$30,000	33.3 X	$50,000	83%
101	90 days	$10,000	100 X	$35,000	350%

Suppose you are somewhat confident that the US dollar will rise against the Japanese yen from its current spot level of 98 yen to the dollar, but you are unsure of the timeframe. In that case, you may choose a six-month-maturity US dollar call at a strike price of 100 yen to the dollar. This will cost you 3% of the total capital you wish to risk on the trade ($1,000,000 x 0.03 = $30,000). Your leverage will be 33 to 1.

If, however, you have more confidence about the move—for example, you expect the move to happen within two months—and you expect the dollar to be worth 103 yen, you can purchase a shorter maturity with a higher strike and spend much less. In this example, the 101-strike price on the US dollar call for just three months maturity is only 1% of your capital and your leverage goes up to 100 to 1! You can manage three times the amount of capital as before since you are confident of the timing and the path. In this case, your profit was more significant ($25,000 versus $20,000) because you had more leverage even though you risked much less capital ($10,000 versus $30,000). More leverage does not mean more capital at risk, but it does mean you are more confident about the timing and path of where your asset is going.

Jump Risk

Jump risk is a more straightforward way of discussing volatility. With jump risk (also known as "gap risk"), you are concerned about your underlying security jumping without being able to hedge or make a trade.

Recall the volatile Netflix stock. On April 22nd, 2013, the stock closed at $174.23 a share. Fifteen minutes after the close, the company announced its earnings report. The stock immediately rose, trading at $215 a share with no trading taking place between $175 and $215. That is, the stock "jumped" to $215.

Chart 27
Netflix Jumps on April 22nd, 2013

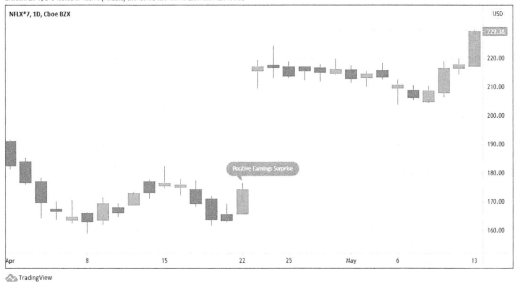

If you were long the stock, this is quite a rewarding event. However, if you were short the stock, you might be upset that you had no opportunity to close out your trade up from $175 to $215. Even if you left a stop order to buy back the stock at $200 a share, your order would not be filled until $215, which is where the stock opened the next day. Thus, you may be willing to buy a put option on Netflix rather than shorting the stock because you don't believe you can manage the jump risk and want to limit your risk from poor execution of hedging and stop losses.

This jump risk is theoretically embedded in the price of the options on Netflix. The seller of the option makes his own opinion of the jump risk, derives a suitable volatility parameter for it, and includes that risk in his model's price, which produces the ultimate cost of the option.

You, however, as the buyer of the option, are not forced to agree with this assumption. You may believe there may be several of these jump events over the life of the option and that the seller of the option is pricing this risk too cheaply. In that case, you may not even have a view of the final price or value of the option. You may have a view that the dealer of the option has assumed too little jump risk. You may buy the option only based on the belief that others will also see that the option understates the jump risk and that the option's price will go higher on its own. This is called buying volatility.

Thus, as a professional trader, you can make money not just on the final outcome of the security's price, but you can also make money on the degree of volatility of that security.

The Value of Staying Power

An option is a two-sided cost/benefit asset. When nothing is happening, it loses money compared with a long or short stock position, which sits idle. That is because an option has a limited maturity. The time value of the option is a vital component of any option-pricing model.

For example, think of an option on the price of gold. Imagine that it is July 27th, 2013, and the option expires 20 days later on August 16th. Gold is trading at $1,310 an ounce and the option's strike price is $1,325. The market assumes that gold will go up and down about $10 a day. Our goal is to make $40 if the price gets to $1,350 and limit our loss to $25 dollars if the price goes to $1,285.

We compare buying gold to buying a gold option, using an option model to analyze our potential results. The volatility metric used in this model will be 18% annualized. Our computer model then replicates hundreds of paths that could theoretically take place over the next 20 days. Some of those paths are straight down towards $1,200, making the option quickly worthless. Other paths have gold going quickly through $1,325 and up to $1,400. Those paths show the $1,325 strike gaining value quickly! Then there are even more paths in which the price goes up and down, hovering close to $1,325 but not trading above it as the days pass.

In all, while volatility determines the size of each path, the number of paths in total is a function of the number of days to maturity. One can easily imagine, then, as each day passes without a significant price change, paths are eliminated. With fewer paths, there are simply fewer opportunities for the option's price to be higher than the strike price. Thus, no change in the price causes "time decay," or we can use the more technical term in that a day's "theta" is lost. While time decay is a negative aspect of holding an option, the benefit of an option over a long or short position is the ability to have staying power.

Option Holders' Staying Power Benefit from Market Surprises

An option allows the holder to see more of the market because losses are limited to the option's cost. This is critical because markets surprise all the time.

An option takes surprises into account. Remember the paths we discussed earlier? Some of the many possible paths include surprising changes to the direction of the trend that seemed firmly in place. Thus, when one purchases an option, he has pre-paid for the surprises and strange reversals of fortune that often happen in the live markets.

Let us return to our gold example. The date is now August 3rd; seven days have passed, and the price of gold has rallied, as we expected, to $1,320. The market is now only $5 away from our strike price and the value of the option has gone from $10 to $14. The option has made less money than holding gold on its own ($4 versus $10). This is because the option strike price is still above gold's value. Therefore, the price of the option moves a smaller overall percentage higher than the total price change.

Using a model, we can derive the price change estimate in advance, 40% of the total change, by observing the model's delta calculation. We are moving in the right direction to make the option valuable, but we are less profitable than had we bought gold with cash.

The next day, news of a central bank selling some gold reserves unexpectedly drives the price down to $1,305. If we were just long gold (either cash or futures), we would have lost $15 in one day. The option price, however, drops back to $8 (see Table 7). Note that the option is valued lower now on August 4th than on July 27th, when gold was $1,310.

Partially, the price of gold is five dollars lower than when we bought the option. The remaining loss is due to time fading away each day as we move closer to the option's maturity. The power of time decay is working against us. With only thirteen days left and fewer paths to get us higher than $1,325, the option's price would decline even without gold's price moving.

Table 7
Price of a $1,325 Call Option on Gold vs. Buying Gold at $1,300 as Time and Price Change

Price of a 1,325 Call Option on Gold vs. Buying Gold at 1,300 as Time and Price Change					
Date	Gold Price	Days to Maturity	Price of Option	Gain/Loss Gold	Gain/Loss Option
July 27	1,310	20	$10	0	–
August 3	1,320	13	$14	10	$4
August 4	1,305	12	$8	-5	-$2
August 5	1,295	11	$5	-15	-$5
August 6	1,285	10	$4	-25	-$6

But now, the power of the option kicks in and staying power begins to show its mettle. Gold drops again the next day, August 5th, this time on a rumor that another central bank is also selling gold. The price of gold opens lower at $1,295. If we were merely long gold, we would be down another $10 an ounce.

We have to consider stopping out since we are now down $15, and if the rumor turns out to be accurate and gold goes down further to $1,285, we will have to stop out based on our own money management rules. At that point, we will be down $25 on a trade on which we were trying to make $40. If we hit this point, our rules say, "get out."

On the other hand, if we are holding an option, we do a different calculation. We bought the option for $10. But now, at $1,295 and with ten days to go, the option price is down to $5. Note that compared to the previous closing price of $8, we have only lost $3 on this last $10 drop.

Chart 28
Price of Gold, July 2013 to August 2013

logicalLeader55436 published on TradingView.com, May 14, 2021 00:45:08 UTC
TVC:GOLD, D 1824.87 ▼ −1.25 (−0.07%) O: 1826.13 H: 1827.22 L: 1824.09 C: 1824.81

CFDs on Gold (US$ / OZ), 1D, TVC

Gold Closes at 1284 on August 6th. Call Option keeps us in the game!

This is because the option is bound by zero. We've already learned that no one would sell an option for close to zero no matter how improbable that gold will rally from here. Thus, our option still holds some value.

In fact, by using a model, we can determine in advance approximately what the value will be at $1,285. The option will still be worth $3. Overall, if gold drops from $1,305 to $1,285—a $20 drop—the loss on the option will only be $5! And even better, its maximum loss after that is $3 from now until expiration on August 16th.

While it is less likely that the option will pay off, the loss protection is real—a $7 loss versus a $25 loss is quite a difference. The value of the option's staying power is visible when we consider that these large drops in price have a limited effect on our ability to stay with our trading thesis.

Those of you familiar with the rules of blackjack know all too well the advantage the dealer has by making you go first when it comes to deciding to hit or stick. If you choose to hit on a hand of 12 or greater, you risk going over 21 and losing to the dealer, even though the dealer might ultimately draw cards that put him over 21 as well. Thus, by going over first, you are out before additional information comes along that helps you make an informed decision.

The odds in blackjack are 56/44 in favor of the dealer if you play strictly by the house rules using the best set of blackjack principles. If you could see the dealer's bottom card before you decided what to do, the odds would move to 52/48, still in the dealer's favor. If you and the dealer agreed that if you both go over 21, the hand is a draw instead of the dealer winning automatically, then the odds would be 50/50. The value of staying power is critical in both blackjack and trading.

Now let's go back to that gold rumor. The market opens at $1,295, and rumors abound of a second central bank selling. That rumor makes sense to you because if one central bank is selling, others want to sell before the price goes down.

As in the blackjack example above, you have to decide with less information than you would like. Do I hold to my original stop price of $1,285, or do I get out now, knowing that the market could drop fast if the rumor is true and I will quickly be out of the trade? Why suffer the extra $10 loss?

Or worse, what if the price of gold slowly drops a dollar every 20 minutes while the market waits for the rumor to be confirmed? If the rumor is confirmed, the risk is for the price to "jump" downward from $1,290 to $1,280. Not only will gold go to our stop price, but we have "jump risk" that it will go right through our stop loss before we have a chance to stop out! Thus, we have to assess the rumor and the choice to stop out early in case the story is proven to be true. We also have to evaluate the "jump risk" if the rumor is confirmed. Many scenarios can weigh on us when considering closing out a trade at a loss. The rules of stopping out are never perfectly black and white.

On the other hand, the option buys us lots of time. No matter what we do, we cannot lose more than $5—the option's value at the close on August 5th. In addition, even if the stock drifts down to $1,285 if the rumor is confirmed, there is still the possibility that other factors will rally the market back. The option gives us multiple chances to come back. If we wait for better information, we can survive jump risk much better with an option. We can salvage something for our option because of the zero limit.

The Greater the Expected Volatility, the Higher the Option Value

There is an additional value to an option, which often comes into play during a larger-than-expected move or during a bout of unexpected new information. The option's value can rise as traders' price in that the expected paths of the underlying instrument will be more volatile. As traders use a higher input for the volatility calculation, the option now has more value for the same price.

Let us return to our gold example once again. Gold has dropped to $1,290 as we await confirmation or denial that a second central bank sells gold. Based on yesterday's closing price of $8 for our $1,325 option when spot gold was trading at $1,305, we can assume that our option pricing model's volatility input is 17%.

Now we are at $1,285, and we decide to check on our option price with a market maker. Based on the same 17% volatility rate from yesterday, we would reasonably expect the option's price to now be at $3. To our pleasant surprise, the market on the option is $3.75 bid to $4.25 offered or a mid-price of $4. When we solve the current volatility, we find that it has now gone up to 20%, so we have stayed in the trade and even lost less money than expected.

When the market gets edgy about short-term news, the price of volatility rises. Why? Because the buyer and the seller know the short-term forces that pushed the price of gold down quickly could easily be dispelled by just a headline denying the rumor. The volatility assumption in the pricing model must rise to solve for the actual pricing of the option. A 20% volatility input solves for the new $4 price we are observing for the $1,325 gold call.

Of course, the flip side of this situation is that if you try to buy options to replace your asset during a volatile time, you will have to pay more! A buyer attempting to buy a gold option at the height of uncertainty will have to pay the higher price generated by the higher volatility input. If the news fades away, the volatility input may decline again back to some long-term level, and the option could lose money even if the market moves up a bit.

For example, a buyer who comes in during the highly volatile moment of our gold example might pay $5.25 to buy the $1,325 option when the spot is at $1,290. Along comes a news flash that there is no truth to the rumor that a second central bank is selling gold, and gold begins to rally back to $1,295, where it closes that day. The market decides the fire drill is over and assumes that gold will act normally going forward, with trading ranges of only a few dollars a day.

When the new buyer of options goes to check his price, he is surprised to see that although spot gold was at $1,290 when he bought his option and now it's at $1,295, his option's price has gone down slightly! The price declines to $4.75 because the market makers return to lower volatility in their pricing model.

To return to our earlier surfing metaphor, markets are like waves in the ocean, going from calm and steady to unpredictable and large, then back to calm and steady. These waves are a common phenomenon in both nature and markets. We cannot make the market focus on long-term fundamentals when it wants to focus on short-term news stories, and vice versa. When the market focuses on long-term fundamentals, it will surprisingly ignore short-term news flashes and stories.

Options have a place in our risk management toolbox for their ability to shield us from short-term events that may cause gap changes in the price of our security without necessarily affecting our long-term expectations. They also have a place when we perceive it challenging to manage our trading stops, perhaps due to higher volatility.

Expressing Trades Uniquely through Options

There are specific trades that can only be expressed through options. This is because the trade design is meant to take advantage of changes in the option's value that cannot be replicated by the stock's price going up or down.

One example we have already seen in the preceding chapters is this: if expectations rise that a security will have more extensive and more unpredictable price movement than in the recent past, the price of the volatility in the security will rise. Remember when the cost of reserving a taxi went up as commuters anticipated storms, or when the price of gold options went up when the market got nervous about future central bank selling? Only through being long an option can we monetize this view of the marketplace because rising volatility is only reflected in option pricing, not in the underlying security itself.

A second example is the value of time or the lack thereof. Traders who believe the market will be less volatile than what is priced into an option will sell an option, expecting that as time passes and nothing happens, they will collect the option premium without any associated hedging costs.

In Chapter 17, we learned the taxi owner was willing to sell options on taxi rides because he felt he could manage the risk even if there were winter storms. Let's suppose a trader feels she can manage her hedges through an anticipated volatile period. In that case, she is said to be a seller of "gamma." Gamma refers to the measurement of how much a hedge of the option changes as the price of the underlying security moves. A seller of gamma is considering the current implied price of volatility and deciding that it is too high, given his expected costs of hedging the risk.

Whether we think we can manage the expected volatility or believe volatility will be higher than anticipated, options offer a way to have a payoff distribution that is different from owning the underlying security. This structure allows traders to maximize the payoff of their trading view by incorporating options into their trade design.

When we buy a new car, a thoughtful purchaser will take the options that make sense for her and not waste money on extras that will go unused throughout the car's life. Using financial options in your trading has the same benefits: you can design the trade in a more tailored fashion and focus on the exact returns in terms of the direction, time, and leverage you are trying to achieve.

In this chapter, we have learned how options can enhance your trading, particularly if you have a view that extends beyond buy or sell. In many cases, we have also learned that options mimic the actual performance of holding the stock's underlying position. A profitable trader can mimic an option's benefits only by readjusting their stock holdings as the market moves.

Moreover, we've seen that not every situation is ideal for an options trade to replace a simple stock position. A model will help you compare the cost of the option and the added benefits it may bring as the trade progresses over time. Options, used wisely, are valuable tools and worthy of consideration when constructing your trade design.

SECTION V

THE HIDDEN COSTS OF TRADING

CHAPTER 20

Dealing with the Bid/Offer Spread and Slippage

Most novice traders assume the bid/offer spread is a given in the marketplace and spend little or no time thinking of how to mitigate the risks involved. Besides, many books assume slippage between your expected execution and your actual execution is simply due to volatile markets or using market orders instead of limit orders. In both instances, you would be wise to study the risks associated with both concepts in order to maximize your potential return on your trades.

The width of the bid/offer spread immediately affects your profit potential while slippage is most often caused by market makers taking advantage of your poor trade execution.

I will spend this chapter looking at these two risks: the risks of the bid/offer spread and the risks of slippage, both of which are two large hidden costs of trading.

Distinguishing Between Bid/Offer and Slippage

We can start with a way to distinguish between the bid/offer spread and slippage to attack each issue with our best-practice methodologies.

For the sake of argument, we can define the bid/offer spread as something that is independent of you. The bid/offer is something that is equally shown to all comers—the price anyone can trade at if they want to transact in size no larger than the posted bid or offer amounts.

Let's look at Table 8 for an example using Facebook.

Table 8
Sample Bid-Offer Screen

Bid/Offer Screen for Facebook			
Bid Size	Bid Price	Offer Price	Offer Size
2,000	25.34	25.36	3,200

Bid Offer Screen for Facebook, After Trader Bid for 1,500 shares			
Bid Size	Bid Price	Offer Price	Offer Size
3,500	25.34	25.36	3,200

Table 8 shows that the bid/offer spread on Facebook stock is 2 cents wide with 2,000 shares on the bid and 3,200 shares on the offer. In the second half of the table, we see that a trader has come in to bid for 1,500 shares at $25.34, raising the bid size from 2,000 to 3,500. Note how the trader is trying to save 2 cents a share by joining the bid instead of lifting the offer. If he is successful, he will have reduced his transaction cost from the bid/offer spread by $30 (1,500 times 2 cents).

On the other hand, slippage is the change in the bid/offer spread that you, the trader, either knowingly or unknowingly, affect by your actions when you attempt to execute a trade.

Now, in Table 9, let's look at the same bid/offer spread after a trader comes in and bids for 50,000 shares instead of 1,500 shares.

Table 9
Demonstrating Slippage

Bid Offer Screen for Facebook			
Bid Size	Bid Price	Offer Price	Offer Size
2,000	25.34	25.36	3,200

Bid Offer Screen for Facebook, After Trader Bid for 50,000 Shares			
Bid Size	Bid Price	Offer Price	Offer Size
52,000	25.34	25.38	55,000

The market now sees that a much larger buy order is in the system. The sellers move their offer higher by 2 cents to account for the additional risk of the large buyer. At the higher price of $25.38, the market will now offer 55,000 shares, or enough to fill the buyer. If the buyer has to pay $25.38, he will have paid 2 additional cents in slippage for surprising the market with a large order.

Thus, the first misnomer here that we need to correct is that slippage is caused by higher-than-expected volatility. Higher volatility is a cause for the bid/offer spread to widen but everyone is equally hurt by higher volatility; it is not a unique problem that you caused.

Slippage is a cost from your actions in the market. In the previous example, the trader caused the wider bid/offer spread by signaling his intent to buy a large number of shares. That is called slippage because the trader uniquely causes a wider spread. When this trader goes away, the bid/offer spread will most likely return to 2 cents.

Expectations of Low Volatility

Many traders design trades for a smooth, low-volatile ride from the beginning of their trade until they exit. Yet, history has shown that volatility returns again and again.

It is human nature to not foresee uncertainty. We believe that calm markets will remain calm. Yet, in this century alone, we have had several stock crashes—the Internet bubble of 2000, terrorism sell-off from 9/11, a financial crisis from 2008 to 2012, and, most recently, a sell-off due to the coronavirus pandemic.

When we are in these volatile times, our human nature leads us to believe that volatile markets will remain volatile. However, before the 2020 COVID-19 incident, volatility in markets hit an all-time low in most asset classes.

There are many theories as to why this is the case. One theory I like is that when things are calm and the markets are strong, we underestimate optimism and attribute rallies in assets to a better understanding of current conditions than previously thought. The market feels as if everyone around us has perfect knowledge. Even though we cannot find value at inflated asset prices based on our own analytics, we assume that others do, so we get optimistic and we buy as well.

But as it turns out, others are assuming that when we buy, we are the ones with perfect knowledge, so that it is alright if they buy on optimism as well! Eventually, as a group, we are overconfident and overoptimistic instead of cautious.

The result of this overconfidence is that when markets start to go down and get volatile, we panic because we did not really invest with a valuation proposition; we were just optimistic. When we discover that others were also optimistic instead of acting as informed investors, it causes us to panic even more. This cycle ends when price movements go far enough that even basic research will reveal that there is value to be had, and purchasers begin to come to the market out of knowledge instead of optimism. And the cycle starts once again.

Expecting Calm Markets Is a Fallacy

Most traders design their trade with the expectation they will always be getting out in calm markets, where they can expect a tight bid/offer spread. But since bid/offer prices are quoted by humans (or machines controlled by humans), the spread will widen dramatically in times of higher volatility.

When times are scary, market makers are more interested in protecting their capital than providing a consistently tight spread. Traders who follow good market practices know to expect wider bids/offers from time to time and account for that hidden cost when assessing the risk versus reward of making the trade.

Most traders assume that the bid/offer is some defaulted divine right that will always be there when they need a fair price. Traders look at today's automated marketplace and figure that a computer now provides the liquidity that humans need and the markets are always efficient. But in reality, humans make markets for other humans. The machines are just there for our convenience.

A disciplined trader can draw an analogy between the conventional view on automated markets and the Cuban Missile Crisis. Cuba is 95 miles from Florida, and it has been 50 years since the missile crisis, when Soviets deployed ballistic missiles to Cuba that almost resulted in nuclear war for the US. However, we still have troops standing on the wall at Guantanamo Bay, watching the Cubans to make sure that they do not repeat any attempt to arm themselves against the US.

I have been trading for 30 years, and I still study every bid/offer spread in the markets I trade in because I know it is not a machine that makes the price. Every price is ordered to be there by a human of some kind.

When a market maker tells his machine to make a bid/offer spread, and one side or the other gets hit, it is a human who gets that position on his books and that position sways his future thinking. If he senses trouble, he simply turns off his machine and moves to the sideline. This starts a chain reaction that may be unnoticed for quite a long time. Still, if enough pressure is put on the market, all market makers will reduce liquidity and the bid/offer itself will disappear!

This scenario is not ancient history. We do not even need to consider the 2020 pandemic or the 2008 financial crisis and crash as examples. Instead, let us go back to June of 2013, when markets of all kinds began to crash: bond markets, stock markets, credit markets, municipal markets, and emerging markets. No model could predict that they would all simultaneously be in trouble because finance theory tells us that investors will run to other markets for security when some markets are in trouble. Traders at market-making firms saw losses coming at them like a freight train, as hundreds of customers called each day asking banks to bid for all kinds of financial instruments. And for a few days in June, the answer was the same to all: "no bid." That incident in the marketplace would come to be known as the "Taper Tantrum."[39]

Part of the reason was the perfect storm of the Fed threatening to reduce liquidity at the very same time that banks were being told to cut down the use of their leverage by bank regulators. In a crisis, there is always a reason for why there is no bid/offer. This reason does not help you as a trader, but it may somehow make you feel that at least it is not personal. As I said earlier in this chapter, bid/offer hidden costs affect everyone equally.

Best Practices for Managing the Bid/Offer Spread

What are the best practices for managing the bid/offer spread from what you observe as average liquidity?

First, continuously monitor the markets you trade or plan to trade, looking for anomalies in the bid/offer spread. Is it wider at night or during off-market hours? Is it wider before economic or corporate announcements? Are there articles or stories about volatile periods, gaps, or traders making complaints about illiquidity? It takes discipline to look at markets in which you do not have a current position. Knowing how those markets work, regardless of whether you are trading at the moment or not, will provide you with valuable insights.

Second, look at your trade objective and determine the hard limit price you expect to achieve to match the return you are trying to achieve. Does your limit entry price reflect the current price? Suppose the current price is below your planned limit

---

[39] "Four Lessons from the Taper Tantrum," John L. Bellows, Western Asset, August 1st, 2017

price. In that case, you may be witnessing an opportunity to buy at an advantageous price. Barring any short-term surprising bad news, you should consider buying at or near the offer price. If the price is already higher than your expected entry price, study the range of the day in the price. Is the market volatile enough that you can work the price at the bid or even lower to improve your expected return?

Generally, the market for most traders is liquid enough that attempting to work a price in the middle of the bid-offer for a few minutes, or even a few seconds, allows price improvement without tipping a market maker to move the price higher against you. Market makers care most about dealing with market orders, which call for immediate action. This allows you, working the price in the middle of the spread, to become the quasi-market maker to see if someone else will trade on your price. Remember two critical points about this strategy: first, you will likely see the benefit over time; do not measure your success of improving your trading by how you do on any one trade execution. Instead, review over many trades if you have improved your executions. Second, individualize your expectation for each asset you trade. A slow-moving stock may only allow you to improve your price by a few cents. A volatile asset may allow you to work a bid (offer) even lower (higher) than the initial bid/offer. As the market churns through market orders, you can achieve improvement.

Slippage Through Showing the Market Your Intention

Slippage takes place in many forms. I will discuss the most common examples of slippage in this chapter, and it will be your job to hunt for them in the markets in which you trade. By identifying slippage points, you can reconfigure your trading strategy to incorporate the risks and costs associated with slippage, and make your trading much more efficient.

The most common form of slippage is showing the market the direction you want to trade and allowing the market to adjust the bid/offer spread against you on the idea that either: (1) you will not notice or (2) you simply have no choice but to pay a worse price for no other reason than because you revealed your intention.

As a trader, how do you signal your intention? The most common way to show your intent is to tell the counterparty what you want to do before you do it. Sounds obvious, right? But many traders tell their counterparty their intention either vocally or electronically. These traders are then surprised to see the market moving against them before transacting.

For example, you might tell your futures broker that you are looking for the size of the bid on August wheat futures. Just by hearing your question, the broker tips off the traders in the pit on what you are looking to do. These traders will gladly give you a bid for the size you need, but only after they have first shifted the bid/offer spread downward!

Even if you do not volunteer your direction, the market maker can infer it from the type of trader you are. If they know you to be a bank trader, they may move the market lower if they believe that banks, in general, are selling. If the market makers hear that the account is a large hedge fund, they may move the spread, fearing that the fund will hit the bid for large size.

Electronically, you can signal your intention by joining the offer when you intend to sell. When you do so, every buyer can see that the offer side has grown and be leery about showing as aggressive a bid. Unfortunately, the electronic marketplace now provides electronic descriptors of the trader who enters the order. Thus, the market makers using a program to read the order book know whether the order is from a market maker, a member of the exchange, or a customer of an FCM. Using historical data patterns is enough to tell the market maker whether it's safe to keep the current bid/offer spread or shift it before you even decide to trade.

Slippage Through Front-Running

Slippage can also take the form of front-running trading. Often, market makers will provide you with a small bid or offer when you ask for a quote, just to learn whether you see enough value in trading. They know the size they show you is too small to hurt them if they are wrong. But the value of the information is critical because they can learn what direction is perceived to be more valuable at the moment. They can then copy the trade idea and front-run you by: (1) executing the same trade in front of you before you can get your full size off, or (2) removing their price and leaving you to pay a higher price with a different market maker.

Slippage can also be caused by attempts by the trader to do greater-than-average size. All markets have an expectation as to the size of the average trade. For markets to be fast and efficient, bids/offers are posted for a standard-size trade. As a trader, you need to know what a standard size is, as it varies from one instrument to another.

How to Minimize Slippage

There are several steps most great traders take to alleviate slippage.

The first step is to estimate what size you can trade, given a particular bid/offer spread. This pre-trade analysis will help form an objective for your entry level and will allow you to assess in a calm manner what execution you can expect when you "go live"—here, "go live" means the moment in time when you are very likely to trade. By having a plan on your execution price, you can quickly determine if you are likely to lose money due to slippage and which steps you can take to mitigate that loss.

The second step is choosing the most efficient way of executing the trade using all available means at your disposal. For example, the options market may be two basis points wide on the bid/offer compared to a one-basis-point bid/offer spread on the futures market. But you may determine that by the time you can get off the size you need on your order, you will have moved the bid/offer spread three basis points in total, making the options market a better deal in the end. On the other hand, you may choose to do a series of trades, all at standard-size amounts, so the bid/offer spread is as tight as possible.

The third step to avoiding slippage is to use your study of the markets to ask for prices at the ideal time for the market maker. For example, I often make my foreign exchange trades in the early morning, when dealers can access London and New York for liquidity. On the other hand, I will trade bonds in the early afternoon, when all the economic data for the day has been released. The dealers are not worried that new headlines will come along and hurt them.

Fourth, use methods to prevent the dealer from reading which way you want to trade. One way to do this on an electronic platform is to offer your size on the machine and then cancel the order after a minute or so if you do not get filled. Market makers who were leaning on that order to buy in case the market goes up will tend to bid more aggressively if you cancel your order and then return it to the market a few minutes later, lest they miss the offer a second time. By being unclear as to your intentions with the market makers, they will provide you with a fair bid/offer to not lean too far one way or the other. When dealing with a human, ask for prices in a professional and nondescript way every time, always asking for a bid and an offer instead of just the one side of the market you need to trade.

In summary, many traders do not even bother to calculate the hidden costs of bids/offers and slippage. It is not glamorous or enjoyable to study bid/offer spreads.

But it is an essential part of the best practices of great traders. Understanding the value of bid/offer spreads gives your trade an edge over the competition. After all, when you cross the bid–offer spread, you are already down money on your trade idea.

CHAPTER 21

The Costs of Doing Business

There are costs to trading. Understanding your expenses is a critical component of being a profitable trader. And know this: no two traders have the same fees, even two traders sitting side by side at Goldman Sachs or Pimco. Every person has a different cost structure.

This chapter goes into great detail about costs. I cannot cover all the industry costs in one chapter. Doing your homework on this subject is essential. One of the great books on this subject for those who want a detailed understanding of all that goes into the back office to process your trades is *After the Trade Is Made* by David M. Weiss.

The Major Costs of Trading

Every business has costs to overcome before there is a profit. Trading has many hidden fees that it pays to hunt them down and expose them. Here is a taste of the costs involved, in no particular order. Do not let these costs scare you. The best traders can manage them efficiently.

- The cost of your salary
- The cost of the room where you work
- The cost of your computer and any software that helps you
- The cost of data
- The cost of any exchange membership, association, or license you need
- The cost of the commissions you pay
- The cost of the bid/offer spread (covered in the previous chapter)
- The cost to borrow on margin (covered in another chapter)
- The cost to clear your trades
- The cost of compensating anyone who works directly for you
- The cost of taxes on profitable trades
- The costs of professional services (e.g., lawyers, accountants)
- The cost of raising money

Wow, that is a lot of statements that begin with the words "The cost(s) of"! And all of them apply to almost every trade you do. But we can work through this list, understand these costs, measure them, and manage them.

Accepting the World as It Is

I have a saying I tell traders who work for me (and I tell it to myself too): "As a trader, you have to accept the world as it is and not as you want it to be." That statement applies to many aspects of trading, including understanding that your cost structure must be dealt with for you to become a profitable trader over time.

This may seem obvious, but as we recall from the early chapters of this book, the heart plays tricks on the mind. The heart wants you to feel successful even if your mind tells you that the math does not add up.

You can see this most commonly in a casino. Most players walk into a beautiful casino, with waiters offering free drinks and pit bosses providing complimentary food and hotel rooms, and still believe they have a good chance of winning! The heart tells them the odds are even when the odds are stacked against them. The costs of the casino can only be recouped by having the odds in the house's favor.

While the odds are equal in trading, because of the cost structure involved, you have to perform better than 50/50 over time to be successful over the long term. You need to incorporate the costs of trading into figuring your leverage, your money management strategy, the types of trades you make, etc.

The Costs of Trading Through a Web-Based Service

Costs vary, of course, depending on the type of strategy you trade. Low costs on some aspects of your trading might not offset other higher costs.

For example, you can have low commission costs if you trade from home through an E-Trade account where you pay $12 to buy 10,000 shares of stock. In addition, E-Trade and other web services provide a variety of free research reports on stocks you can trade. As an E-Trade client, you need not be a broker-dealer or a member of an exchange. Some brokers have even rolled out commission-free trading in recent years.

On the other hand, E-Trade clients have to pay the interest rate that E-Trade charges to buy stock on margin. In addition, since E-Trade only shows delayed data, you may be putting your orders in at prices that are behind where the live market is trading. The lack of live data is a "soft cost" to you in terms of potentially poor execution of your trades. You will have to cross the bid/offer spread that E-Trade shows you on the screen. Even if you leave a limit order to buy shares instead of a market order, there is no guarantee that your order will be filled at your price. Some brokers will not fill your order until the market has moved low enough that your bid price is actually the same as the market offer price (or worse).

How can I get filled worse than the offer if I am buying shares? Many brokers offering low-cost or free commission trading need to recoup the costs of providing free trades somehow. They most often do this by sending your order to a market-making trading firm that pays them pennies per share to receive the order. In return, the market-making firm makes a bid/offer spread that is as wide as legally possible so the client gets a reasonable fill but not the best possible one.

Many non-professional customers will buy or sell stocks with a market order, which in theory means doing the trade at the best price. However, unlike futures exchanges, stock exchanges do not mandate what the best universal price is—only that the trade is executed at the best-posted price of the exchange where your broker sends the trade, costing you real money in poor execution.

Furthermore, in this type of arrangement with a web-based firm, if you don't pay for real-time data feeds or news services, you are at risk of having your orders filled when you don't want them to be. By the time you read the news that affects the stock you are trading, your order is already filled and it is too late to stop it. You either pay the fees and costs to be a top professional, or you should expect that the costs of "free" services will be built into your execution.

Trading Professionally Is a Job

Trading professionally (or like a professional) is a job in itself. A professional card counter or poker player knows that the number of hours he invests in being successful is time lost earning money another way (the opportunity cost), no matter how much fun it is to make money as a professional gambler.

Trading, too, is time-consuming, and whether you are doing it for fun a few hours a week or professionally for 80 hours a week, you need to incorporate the opportunity costs that you suffer by not drawing a salary doing something else.

Even if you choose to stay at home Monday through Friday instead of working at a job with minimum wage, you ought to at least earn the $20-an-hour minimum wage and incorporate that loss of salary into your overall cost to determine if you are profitable enough in trading.

If you work for a large Wall Street firm that pays you a salary, do not think for a second that this concept does not apply to you! You receive a paycheck, but it is essentially a draw against your future earnings. No Wall Street firm will keep you on the job if you are not ultimately profitable. And when I say "ultimately," I mean within a few months—maybe one year, tops!

Most Wall Street firms pay a percentage of what you trade back to you as a year-end bonus. The percentage is small enough so that the firm can recoup your salary and the benefits they pay you, the rental cost of the space you occupy, the cost of the computers they provide you, the data services you subscribe to, and the commissions you generate when you trade in the marketplace.

If You Do Not Trade for a Firm

Many readers of this book may not have the opportunity to trade for a firm. You may not have the background necessary to get an interview at a Wall Street firm or a large hedge fund. Many smart people are coming out of schools worldwide competing for those few new jobs each year handed out by the large banks, investment banks, and hedge funds. Most will not get hired.

But this fact does not preclude you in the least from being a trader. However, it does mean you have to study your costs intensely to determine the best trading strategy that will provide you with the highest net return after expenses.

Remember, if you are trying to trade as your means of earning a living, your profits must cover all your expenses. Start with your salary, any health insurance you want to buy for yourself, the implied rent for your home office (or actual rent for an outside office), the computer equipment and software you need in order to trade, your Internet access, etc. All these costs must be taken into account before we even consider the cost of the actual trade itself!

Finally, if you are a full-time trader, your trading income is taxable, as opposed to the long-term capital gains treatment you may be using when you hold your investments for several years. On the other hand, most of your trading costs can be subtracted from your trading profits to determine your taxable income.

The Cost of Data

Most exchanges long ago figured out the value of both historical and live data. Something as simple as getting the live bid-offer on a stock or futures contract costs money. As a trader, you will receive a menu of live feeds, along with the fees associated with each feed from the software vendor you use for information.

The largest market information data provider is the firm majority-owned by Michael Bloomberg, the well-known mayor of New York City from 2002-2013. In his earlier life, Mr. Bloomberg started a business called, simply, Bloomberg. He created a collection of pricing tools for most securities, commodities, stocks, bonds, and FX that traders around the world like to trade. He put it all in one place called the "Bloomberg Terminal." While the Bloomberg Terminal used to be a standalone machine that one would rent from his company, today, it's just another service you can download from the Internet.

Bloomberg charged a monthly fee for users to enjoy the convenience of one-stop shopping for news, pricing, and data that traders were interested in trading. The exchanges soon figured out they were providing data for free to Michael Bloomberg for him to resell on his terminal for a fee. Essentially, Bloomberg was getting rich by selling their data! However, the exchanges wised up and began to charge monthly fees for their information. In response, Bloomberg passed on the exchange fees to his customers lest those charges eat into his profits.

Data is the lifeblood for a trader. A body without blood circulating through it is just a corpse—nothing more. The market is the same way. Data is what makes everything work; it tells a story and provides information in real time that cannot be replaced by research alone. Live data is the window through which we see if something new or different is happening from what we expect. Therefore, you should expect to pay for live data and know that no successful trader can live without it.

A Young Trader Sees the Value of Data

Here is a story about the value of live data from my own past. When I graduated from business school, I got a job at Manufacturers Hanover Trust, a large New York bank that first merged with Chemical Bank and later merged with JPMorgan Chase.

I was hired as a trader and put on the Money Market trading team. Four traders traded short-term instruments like Certificate of Deposits, Bankers' Acceptances, and Eurodollar deposits. These instruments were hedged with Eurodollar futures, which was a small up-and-coming futures contract at the time (today, it is the most significant futures contract in the world).

Though the team had hired me right out of school, they had no particular product for me to trade. The other traders already had taken all the products available to trade, so they asked me to try to profitably trade just the Eurodollar futures and options. Since it was my first trading job after school, it took me some time to learn.

During the first few months at the job, I experienced losses. Next to me was an older, somewhat iconic figure named Bob Anczarki. Bob was one of the first traders interviewed by Marcia Stigum for her famous book *Money Markets,* which was, for many years, the bible on Wall Street concerning all the instruments that banks traded.

Bob had been a longtime trader at Salomon Brothers before he came to "Manny Hanny" (as we were affectionately known at the time). He took a liking to me, tried to teach me about the market, and gave me confidence I could handle trading at a bank.

Bob was a good trader. He was disciplined, knew his product well, and made money the year I arrived. The rest of my team consisted of three other traders, including the group's boss, all of whom were struggling to make money like me.

The boss, whom I will call Joe, decided to call a meeting to offer a forum where we could talk freely about what we thought was wrong with our trading approach. At least, *I* thought we could speak freely. It turns out that rarely do senior traders want to hear criticism from rookie traders, particularly those who do not make money themselves.

I was committed to making money and being successful. I had paid for half of my college costs and all my living expenses since college. I had paid the entire bill to earn an MBA from Columbia University. I was a rookie, yes, but I was studying the markets voraciously to be successful. It was clear to me that the reason I was losing was different from why the other traders were losing.

The other traders were trading large short-term bank instruments called Certificates of Deposits (CDs). When CDs started trading around 1980, the market was dominated by brokers who told the traders where the price of the instrument should be based on the most recent trade between one bank and another.

But the world was evolving, and data was becoming more and more available in real time. From my vantage point, I could see that every time Eurodollar futures moved, the prices of the CDs my colleagues were trading would also move, and in the same direction, regardless of what their brokers told them. My colleagues would often make the price lower when Eurodollars were going higher because their brokers told them that the last trade in the market was lower. When the customer would buy from them because they'd made the price too low, they would not even realize they had been picked off until a couple of days later. In short, there was a new sheriff in town—the Eurodollar Futures contract—and not watching it in real time was costing my fellow traders money because where the futures contract went was where the CDs were going to go. My fellow traders' brokers could no longer help them see where the market was going solely based on old information.

During the meeting called by Joe, each trader was asked what he or she thought the team could do differently to make money. One of the traders thought we should have better relations with the sales force to have more time when the customer called to make a better price. Another thought we should work more closely with traders at other desks to get their opinions on the market.

When it was my turn, I said we needed to get live data because we did not know what we were doing. That comment did not go over too well with the rest of the team, who immediately turned on me. They said, in essence, "You've been here just a few months, and you're telling us we don't know what we're doing?"

It was a multipronged attack, with all the traders yelling at me at once. How could I say such a thing, they demanded? I went back to my desk, vowing that if I survived this incident, I would never again tell a trader he or she did not know what he was doing, even if I believed it.

Well, a few days later, I was called into the boss's office. I could feel the tension in the room over the preceding few days, and I knew the storm had not blown over.

My boss sat me down and began to lecture me once again about how immature I was to think that experienced traders needed help in understanding the basics of their market. He felt I barely knew the basics of my market and asked me to come up with a price right there, on the spot, of where I thought the Eurodollar contract was.

I stood up to look at the screen to see where the futures contract was trading, but before I could see it, he sat me down again and said, "Don't look at the screen." I asked him why. He said, "You can't rely on screens. You have to 'feel' the market." Apparently, he meant like Yoda "feels" the Force.

In actuality, Joe wanted me to use my instincts to make a price instead of using live data and precise math. He explained that trading was about the "pulse" of the market, sensing what your customer wants to do and making your trades according to your gut. He said that compared to this "feel" of the market, pricing on a computer was of only marginal value. Until I learned that, he told me, I would not be a particularly good trader.

I walked out of the room feeling better. Though my boss did not like me much, I was less worried about my young career since I realized that my boss's lack of respect for using the best information available to make a trading decision was sure to be his demise. And I knew I would be okay not working and learning from a guy like that.

Sure enough, a few weeks later, I moved to another department. From my new location in the trading room, I watched all three of my fellow traders get fired one by one over the next few months. Bob, of course, did not get fired because he was making money.

The moral of the story: as a trader, you can turn a blind eye to live data, live news, and the best models, but you do it at your own peril, as you are sure to lose money over time.

Working for a Broker-Dealer and Being an Exchange Member: Pros and Cons

Sometimes, as part of your trading plan, it pays to work for a broker-dealer or be a member of an exchange.

Often, exchanges and broker-dealers are charged lower fees on their trades. This is a critical component of your cost structure if you pursue high-volume trading strategies such as market making or algorithmic trading.

Exchange members can receive additional advantages besides lower exchange clearing fees. They also get seniority rights on the trading systems that broadcast their products. For example, the Chicago Mercantile Exchange (CME) members get a slight advantage when they put in bids and offers on Eurodollar contracts, a contract owned by the CME. Members are also offered more leverage than non-members and thus need less capital per contract to trade.

These member benefits are no small advantage, but they come at a price. For instance, being a member of the CME is expensive. A trader has to either buy a seat on the exchange for several hundred thousand dollars or lease a seat from another member at a fee of several thousand dollars per month. In addition, members have to pass exams and pay yearly fees to maintain their license requirements. These costs have to be incorporated into your trading plan to determine if the benefits of exchange membership outweigh the costs that go with them.

Commissions on Trades

Nearly every trade has a commission associated with it. It can be a simple commission you pay to E-Trade or a commission you pay to your futures broker when you execute a futures contract. These examples reflect a "hard commission."

There are also hidden commissions known as "mark-up," which is usually an additional spread added onto the bid/offer price of a security that does not trade on an exchange. For example, retail traders pay a "mark-up" built into the price when they buy a bond or an FX contract.

At a bank, a trader usually pays his salesperson a commission for bringing a client to the bank. This is called a "soft commission" because the commission is not paid in hard dollars but in some form of credit system. The bank keeps records of that information and uses it to determine bonuses at the end of the trading year.

"Soft dollars" are often paid by giving preferential treatment to one firm over another. For example, traders at hedge funds usually pay soft commissions for good research by executing trades with that firm at a preferential price compared with what they could achieve by running a competitive bidding process.

Commissions are often reduced based on volume, but at some point, no amount of volume will reduce the price any lower. For example, it costs about 17 cents a share to execute futures trades, even for the most efficient firm. No trader can expect to avoid paying at least that charge even when trading in volume. Most traders should expect to pay significantly more than this per trade.

When traders work at home, the commission charge is right in their face on every trade. When traders work for banks or hedge funds, sometimes the only time they see the commissions is in the month-end commission report. At times, they are shocked by how much they have paid because they subconsciously ignored the charges when they conducted their trading during the month. After all—out of sight, out of mind.

Hard-dollar costs are subtracted one for one from your trading profits. Never let your guard down and become numb to your volume and your commission costs. High-volume trading styles demand particular attention. Often, algo-like trading or high-volume market making can be profitable pre-commission but unprofitable once commissions are calculated and factored in. Many traders who back-test their trading strategies do a poor job of figuring what their commissions would have been. When they go live with their trading, they are unpleasantly surprised to find how many strategies break down when commissions are included.

Moreover, most futures contracts and other products that clear on an exchange incur a "clearing fee" in addition to a commission. This fee goes to the exchange and is held by the exchange to build a secure pool of capital to guarantee all the counterparties' creditworthiness.

The bid/offer spread and the cost to borrow money on margin are significant enough topics that you remember they received their own chapters in this book. However, suffice it to say here that these are also significant costs to a trader that must be incorporated into any trading plan.

The Bottom Line on Costs

The more you trade, the harder it is to manage, on your own, all the things that you do. Trades need to be booked and settled, and reports need to be generated to show your trades, positions, remaining cash position, risk, profits, and losses. Technology can help track all your records, but that comes with its own price tag.

Technology can break down or become out of date, and support people are often needed to repair it. At a bank or financial firm, for example, support staff is supplied to traders. In return, the trader pays his pro-rata cost of the support team out of his trading revenues.

When a trader is on her own, she may need to hire an assistant or use an outsource firm to help manage her trading volume, risk reports, or other services. Often a trader needs to earn at least several hundred thousand dollars a year to have the luxury of support staff.

You will also need to allocate money to cover your accounting fees at year-end. Most traders will need a professional accountant to produce an appropriate profit-and-loss statement required to file for year-end tax returns. Finally, for those traders who either run money for other people or would like to run a fund, there is a significant amount of additional costs allocated to cover legal fees for the proper documentation needed to show to investors. There will also be fees for third-party vendors who provide independent reporting of your trades to verify, for investors, your performance track record. The expenses to start even a small fund can run into the $100,000 range annually and must be seriously considered before one decides to take other people's money to manage.

SECTION VI

THE BIG RISKS

CHAPTER 22

Mind the Gap: Jump Risk

T his section of the book is dedicated to the significant trading risks that go well beyond basic research or disciplined approaches to trade entry or trade design. Often the big risks play a major factor in outsized gains and losses. Understanding the jump risk in advance will help you navigate these all-too-common moments in your trading path.

A rising tide raises all ships, and big rallies with small retracements from time to time make trading seem easy. When a storm hits the markets, it is best to know in advance what your plans are: that is, your port in the storm!

Traders in training often want an explanation for how a market works and what the best rule sets are to use in managing their risks. When traders learn my first rule is that no rule is steadfast or applies to every situation, they often look for the second rule that applies when the first rule does not work!

Yet, rules do instill discipline as to how we manage risk, and I would argue that trading is a combination of the "art" and the "rules and disciplines" sides of our brain. The art side helps us: (1) envision new trends that bring new or accelerated market moves, and (2) design creative trades and approaches that lead to excess returns. After all, no rule will tell you how much money you should make!

On the other hand, the "rules and disciplines" side of our brain protects us from (1) sloppy execution, (2) missing opportunities to limit losses through the use of options when appropriate, and (3) avoiding losing precious capital by getting out of trades where the information set has changed. This side also provides us with the ultimate collection of disciplines to manage gaps and panics.

Gaps are a trading pattern in which price action moves suddenly or swiftly away from all recent levels at a speed many times greater than normal movement in the security. For example, let's look at Chart 29 for the price of Google around October 15th, 2013. The stock was hanging around its long-term resistance level of $875 a share, but on a surprise positive earnings announcement, the stock gapped from $880 to $1,010 in one day (almost 15% move!).

Chart 29
Price of Google Stock, February 2013 to February 2014

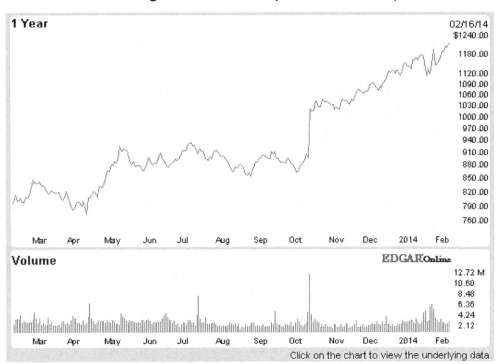

Gaps occur most frequently when the consensus view is heavily skewed one way. The market is surprised by information that completely contradicts this view. In addition to the new data, liquidity drops dramatically as the market tries to implement new trades to capture this gap movement. This illiquidity causes panic, as traders realize that the recent trading range was only an illusion of a well-balanced market.

We wish to distinguish between this random type of jump and the more traditional type of continuous price movement. When sufficient liquidity occurs at each price node along the way, all those who wish to clear their risk can do so. In the more random price movement, the market jumps from one price to another, at wide increments, preventing those who want to clear their risk from doing it easily.

The difference between these two types of price movement is so significant that we're dedicating this chapter to it. Ultimately, as a trader, you will dedicate your trading life to managing the problem posed by the gap or jump.

Dealing with Gaps Is Critical for Traders

I do not think I can overemphasize the critical nature of gaps in trading. A single gap is often manageable—sometimes expected.

For example, a trader holding a position through an 8:30 a.m. economic release about the latest jobs report can expect a gap one way or another. Based on his own research, the trader may be willing to bet that the gap will likely go in his favor. He may even be thinking far enough ahead to say that a short-term gap that goes against him will not ultimately cause the market enough consternation to change what is otherwise a trend in his favor.

Nonetheless, a gap—by definition—is a surprise event. Clearly, the larger the surprise, the larger the gap will be. This event has two consequences that must be understood to determine what to do.

First, there is the "surprise." As traders, we always need to make an honest assessment of what caused the surprise and determine whether it affects our belief in the trade.

The Importance of New Information

Although there is no absolute rule, greater weight should be placed on newer information over older information when a market gaps. Why is this?

First, as we have seen in previous chapters, our natural inclination is to stand by our old information because we bet on it. Our pride and intense desire not to be wrong prejudice us against new information that contradicts our belief system. We instinctively want to give new information less weight when we have already made a bet than when we have nothing at stake. However, now that the market is gapping away from us, we have less time to make critical assessments. Accepting that the new information has greater weight than previous research is prudent.

In some ways, surprises are not measured by the information quality but by the market's reaction function. The media will always report a gap from new information as "surprising" news. On the other hand, news that moves the market a little will either be reported as expected or will not be reported at all!

Here is where it gets critical for you as a trader. You should assess new information on how it relates to you and your system of beliefs, not on whether it gaps or not. If information comes out that contradicts your opinion in a trade, you should get out whether or not the market is gapping.

Many traders treat gaps as the information itself. They know the pain from a gap can overwhelm even the best thought-out trade. Therefore, you need to weigh the market's reaction function. Think about how the news is being treated by the press and fellow traders to determine the information's full effect.

Suppose there is little or no movement on information that is counter to a trader's trade. In that case, most traders will view this as a vote of confidence that they can remain in the trade because the damage was minimal. The trader's thinking goes like this: "I know that this new information hurts my trading idea, but the market hardly moved on it. I guess it wasn't that bad. Hopefully, the next set of information that comes along will be in my favor."

Avoid this type of thinking. For you, if information comes along that counters your belief in a trade, having the ability to get out without the market gapping is a wonderful opportunity to limit any further damage. While in theory, future information may come out that will be better, traders have to live in the here and now. Ask yourself, with this new information, would you put on this trade at the current price with the same price objective and the same stop-loss management levels? If the answer is no, hoping for better days is hardly a professional's path to success.

How Others React to the Surprise

Surprise information does not only relate to you—it relates to others as well. When a market gaps, it is often because others have collectively come to the same conclusion as you have. At the exact moment, you are all surprised.

The second key consequence you need to identify is that you are not just assessing the information on its own, but on how the surprise affects others. The gap reveals that traders have sprung into action. Traders who have not been involved now feel that the new information is compelling enough to trade in the direction of that information.

And those who were already involved in the security now have a choice. The market has gapped and some have lost money. Some have lost more money than they expected because they wanted to get out at a different price, but that price was skipped over in the gap. These traders who were already involved will be assessing the information just as you are, and you cannot be certain as to how they will react. Some will panic, some will try to get out in an orderly manner, and some will freeze and do nothing. Finally, some will fight and add to their position for one of two reasons:

(1) because their beliefs were not shaken and they see this as an opportunity, or (2) because their pride won't let them admit that they were wrong and they want to stop the movement against them by adding additional capital to the fight.

You must assess all these potential human reactions to the surprise news, not just the information itself. The other market participants' reactions can often be significant because the news set off a tipping-point reaction function. The tipping point is essentially a warehouse of pent-up power to move the market, looking for an event to trigger it. The human reaction from the tipping point event will invariably determine if you can stay in a trade or be forced out. Let us walk through an example to give these nuances some clarity.

How New Information Affects the Market: An Example

It is June 2013. The October 2013 oil futures contract has been trending downward slowly but surely for the past ten trading sessions. Based on your research, you have determined that oil should continue to drop and you have been short from a price of $96 a barrel. The current price is $93.

For several days, the market turns around and rallies on what appears to be little new news, and by June 15th, oil is trading back to $96 a barrel. But you are not deterred because you have done your homework. Production in the US was continuing to rise. Each month brought another record-high amount of production against a backdrop of stagnant US domestic demand for oil, natural gas, and gasoline. You understand that oil is a volatile commodity and rarely moves in one direction for long. You are prepared by owning put options struck at $92 a barrel instead of being outright short the futures contract.

On June 26th, after a series of massive protests against the Egyptian government, the military council of Egypt announces that the Islamic elected leader, Mohammed Morsi, has 48 hours to reconcile the differences between the government and the secular opposition, or the military will impose their own plan for governing the country.

The price of oil then gaps $1.25 a barrel on the move, breaking out of its two-month trading range and rallying further, making a new high for the year at $100.30 a barrel. Since you own the put versus being short oil, the price decline for you is much less—50 cents on your put versus the $1.25 loss on the oil itself.

Chart 30
Price of WTI Crude, May 22, 2013, to August 20, 2013

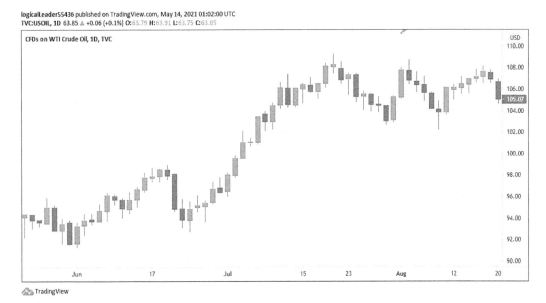

The news, at first, seems like a non sequitur to you. Egypt does not produce much oil, so why would this threatened military action have such a significant effect? As you learn within the next few minutes, though, much of the Arab world's oil bound for the US goes through the Suez Canal. Thus, any potential stoppage of the shipping lanes due to a conflict in Egypt could cause a shortage of oil in the global system.

This is news you have not counted on. Instead, you were patiently waiting for the weekly demand and supply numbers from the American Petroleum Institute to be released on June 23rd. Now the price has gapped and your trade is performing poorly before you even know what this data is.

You are projecting the data to show additional supplies with little demand. But you expected the price of oil to be around $95 when this information came out. Now it is at $100.30! Also, you look at the size of the gap; clearly, others were positioned the same way you were—i.e., they were short oil contracts. Remember, in futures contracts, it is a one-for-one game. That is, for every buyer, there's a seller, and as many people are benefiting from the gap as are being hurt by the move. In essence, those who are benefiting are long oil and they are getting a surprise gift from the fact that oil has gapped higher. Their mindset is one of calm. There is no panic for those who are making money.

When there is a gap in your favor, you have gains in your account that you did not expect to have in this timeframe. The longs can now secure these extra gains by putting stop-loss orders below the market. They can take an excessive risk knowing that their take-profit levels are at or above their original objectives. Thus, in the short run, those who are long the contract supply few sell orders at attractive prices.

Meanwhile, the shorts all have to make quick decisions. Some shorts intended to get out between $99 and $100.30, but were unable to do so because of the gap. These traders now become buyers at the higher price because they just have to get out. The higher price action results in buy orders at a higher price, which tends to drive the market even higher than the original gap price of $100.30.

The traders who are short and who now want to stop out have to bid higher and higher to entice: (1) those who are long to sell, or (2) those willing to enter the market with a new trade to take a chance and sell. In addition, the information, being new, is often given greater weight, so new traders are entering who want to buy on this news. They like the story, or they like the technical fact that the market is making new highs, and they know that this means there are probably traders who are short and feeling pain.

Some who are short have longer time horizons. They discount the news as something temporary in Egypt that the market will see as a non-event once it is clear that shipping lanes will not be affected. They don't add to the panic but hold on to their trade. Some may even sell more contracts to give themselves a better average price.

Still, other shorts are frozen. The data is not what they expected. The loss is already more significant than what they were planning to accept as a maximum loss. Instead of buying or selling, however, they do nothing. They wrestle with their instincts, knowing they should stop out, but hoping the situation somehow gets better. These traders are trouble for your position, as they act as a future source of panic-buy orders when the next piece of news comes along that supports oil prices going higher.

How Do You React to the Gap?

So what do you do? You have had a gap movement due to news you did not expect. You bought a put instead of going short to protect against unforeseen circumstances like this. You have lost as much money as you were willing to commit to on this trade.

You have not yet had the opportunity to get to the data you want to trade on. That data is still to come. As a trader, you can only assess in real time what you know in real time. You know there was news you did not expect, and clearly, it would have weighed on your confidence to go short now. You know that not only the news has gone against you, but also that positioning is now against you because of the gap price movement.

The gap has created a situation where some shorts are frozen and would have already gotten out had the price action been orderly. Therefore, you decide that the combination of the news affecting your belief in the trade and the fact that traders need to get out of their losses means it is not worth fighting. If you stop your loss, you can then continue to assess new information without affecting your capital. You can review the surprise information and weigh it against the data you expect to come in an unbiased way. You are no longer swayed by the positions you hold. Even if you choose to go short again, you can redesign the trade to have higher profit potential. For example, if you still want to go short oil, you may want to buy a December put. This will allow you more time to be profitable while the market takes all the information, bullish and bearish, into its thinking.

The epilogue to this story is that when the API reports came out on June 30th, and the report showed an unexpected rise in demand and a decline in supplies, oil prices gapped even higher. The pain from a second surprise gap can cause even more dramatic reaction functions. But applying the two-step process of managing gap risk allowed you to avoid further losses.

Gaps Often Indicate That Other New Information Has Caused the Move

This section brings out the third point about gaps. Gaps often hint at other information afoot that is causing the type of price action you are seeing. Almost no information is so secret that some people are not trading on it, even if they do so subconsciously. There are few news events and data releases that are not available to someone.

In the previous example, someone was watching the demand and supply of oil at the Hudson Oil refinery in Cushing, OK, the largest refinery in the United States. They didn't need a report from the API, like the rest of us do, to know what was happening on the ground.

Someone knows in advance of a scheduled news or data release whether oranges are growing above expectations, whether there is a disease among the cattle herds, or whether excess jobs are being created at Apple because of high demand for iPhones. Someone knows most information before it is broadly distributed.

Because someone knows, market prices get affected because people in the know can trade with confidence. They have a strong position. The market often drifts in the same direction, as revealed by a press release. This causes the gap because the market has already moved against one side or the other before the release of the data.

For example, in the oil contract case, the market moved substantially in favor of the longs prior to the news. The shorts quickly got into an unexpected loss before the story. The news itself broke the equilibrium of orderly trading and caused the gap movement.

Were you "fortunate" to get out of your oil trade when you did? No, you were "professional" about getting out. The concept of being "fortunate" using hindsight has no place in professional trading. Rather, you use professional judgment and discipline to assess the news and the reaction function of those who were hurt by the gap.

After your exit, you can assess the news and choose to get into the market again, long or short. The professional gets in based on her latest beliefs, taking in all the risks currently known, assessing the trading options available to her, and planning her objectives with an eye towards future expectations. These expectations include the notion that ultimately the longs could be in pain if the market has overpriced oil, even with all the positive data now outstanding. The trader never assesses her trade prospects based on emotions like revenge or desire to get even for past losses.

Planning for Gaps

Every trader's dream is to put on a trade—e.g., buy stock in Amazon and hope that some piece of news soon follows that causes the market to gap higher with little or no trading in between. Gaps in our favor allow us to avoid the pressure that occurs when the price only moves slowly, leaving us unsure of whether the trade will be profitable. We read about a record Christmas selling season and how Amazon is taking market share from other online vendors. Like magic, the stock opens up 10% higher than where we bought it the day before. No fuss, no muss. We reach our profit objective, and we put in a take-profit order and a stop-loss order; one cancels the other and we wait to get back our fill.

If we can imagine how we will act if the gap goes in our favor, we should then be able to analyze what to do if the gap goes against us. By imagining negative scenarios as part of our trading process, we will think much more rationally when they occur.

The first thing we need to look at is the size of potential gaps. Using historical analysis, we can calculate the percentage gap moves we have seen in the recent past. I like using percentage change over price change to allow us to equally compare historical movements. Further, the market thinks in terms of percentages change rather than absolute values. Stocks, commodities, and securities tend to gap in relation to their past history. This is due to a couple of significant reasons.

First, most market participants study past gap movements to determine when the move is large enough to begin market making/trading again. Therefore, we can take advantage of this tendency to anchor past movements and use them to quantify our risk.

Securities that gap tend to gap again, and those that are steady rarely gap. The latter situation may be because conservative traders like to "hang out" together in less volatile securities. It may also be that specific securities tend to be large, complicated instruments with many offsetting pros and cons, the news about them will rarely be so one-sided that they would gap. Whereas in the former case, stocks that gap tend to have an immediate unresolved conflict as to their value. Each piece of news changes the assessment heavily.

Deciding How to React to a Gap

Let us look at two years of Amazon's price action and identify gaps. We will define gaps as movements of 5% or more from their last traded price.

Chart 31
Price of Amazon Stock, March 2012 to March 2014

When you look at a chart, your eye can pick up the gaps because the line of prices will be broken instead of continuous. On Chart 31, we note that Amazon had roughly four gaps, (circled in grey for you on the chart), in the two years, one down and three up, greater than 5% per gap. We can use that as a guide to prepare ourselves for the worst. We think, "I own this stock, which could gap on average about 5%. Based on that information, let me ask myself a series of questions:

A.) Can I tolerate a 5% drop in the stock, or will I be forced by my clearing firm, boss, or me to liquidate?

B.) Would a 5% drop shake me out of my conviction, or am I positioned for a much larger movement that affords me this type of drawdown?

C.) Am I trading this as a pair trade against another security or a hedge against something else, and how has that other security performed in the past when Amazon gaps by this much?"

These are just starter questions. As you delve more deeply into your style of trading, you may get more intricate. For example, an algo trader may want to calculate whether gaps happen after the market closes when no trading can occur; or during the day, when a fast computer might be able to get you out during the few moments the gap is taking place.

Depending on your answers, you may need to consider how you have designed the trade. If the answer to question "a" is no—i.e., you cannot tolerate a 5% drop—maybe you have to express your trade in option form, so a large move will not force you out.

If the answer to "b" is yes—i.e., that your conviction would be shaken—you need to look at your entry point or trade size. You can also study the timing of gaps—perhaps they are most common around earnings announcements. You can choose to close out your trades before earnings reports.

If the answer to "c" is yes—i.e., that you are trading this as part of a pair trade—then you need to look at gaps in parallel time with the other securities you're hedging Amazon with to see how the two stocks perform as a pair. Perhaps the ratio of how much you hold of each security needs to be modified, depending on which security tends to gap more or tends to gap in a bigger size.

Even without historical data, you can look at the options market to solve the gap risk. For example, out of the money options that expire within a few weeks can be examined. The higher the value of the out of the money option, combined with the short time remaining before expiration, will calculate for you the probability of potential gap risk.

Using historical data and current option pricing, you can quantify the size of a gap move and study your ability to stay in your trade as designed. If you do not believe you can stay in the trade, you need to have a better entry point or redesign it.

Most traders avoid this type of analysis. Gaps are the non sequiturs of trading. Except for crisis trading, they are the hardest emotional losses to deal with and can make a trader feel stupid for such poor trade management. Sometimes gaps occur right before your eyes because you chose to take your position knowingly before a planned announcement. Some gaps arise out of nowhere and would have been difficult to foresee.

It is a challenging emotional exercise to go through your current trades and imagine them being blown up quickly. But that damage control is the crux of what we do as professionals. It is easy to manage winners; losers take our full attention.

CHAPTER 23

Crisis Trading

I t was 1995. I was a senior trader at Deutsche Bank, trading Forward Foreign Exchange. It was a busy time. European countries were fighting to get into the European Union and its single currency, the euro.

This was a time of high inflation around the world. Interest rates were rising. The market was attacking various countries' currencies in Europe to see how much conviction they had about keeping their currency strong. A strong currency meant the risk of losing exports to their peers, but weakening their currency meant the risk of not joining the euro. The French had a reputation for defending their currency, the franc, in times of trouble. They called this defensive position "Franc Fort." Their motto was strong currency over anything else, including growth or jobs, for what the French feared most was inflation.

I had a great boss in those days, Tony, who taught me a lot about trading. He taught me an excellent trading technique, a more practical way to apply George Soros's theory called "reflexivity." Tony's idea was that the market would anticipate a specific risky outcome that might arise from an upcoming economic event. Since the market consensus usually had a bias one way or the other as to what the data release might be (either bullish or bearish), Tony realized you could make a lot of money trading up to the time of the data release because the market would keep leaning towards its bias. This trading style would also allow you plenty of liquidity since you would get out before the official number was released. In essence, you could make money without having to take the risk that the actual data release would go against you.

Tony also taught me a lesson about crisis management that has so clearly stayed with me that I can still hear him saying those words as the day he told them to me.

In 1995, the French Crisis was blowing up. Short-term interest rates were rising higher and higher, even though economic growth was slowing and inflation was steady. The currency was under attack, and the market was getting weary of what the

French central bank, the Bank of France, might do. Defend the currency with really high interest rates and hurt the economy or save the economy, keep rates low, and let the currency weaken, even at the risk of being kicked out of the European Union?

The UK had let its currency weaken during the famous attack by George Soros rather than risk that the UK economy would slow further in 1992. By 1995, the British pound had weakened by 15%. In France, Franc Fort (strong currency) was near and dear to the French. As rates went higher and higher, I began to worry about my trades because I was reliant on using a model to determine the prices at which I would trade.

"Why Can't It Get Stupider?"

Based on the math of my model, I assumed the French would keep short-term rates unchanged. It was clear that I should sell French francs and repurchase them in the forward market to take advantage of the high rates. But each time I tried to do this, the rates would be even higher than before and it became painful to suffer losses to stay in the trade.

I turned to Tony, who had much more experience in FX than I, for help. I had spent my career to date at that point only in the US markets. I said to him, "Tony, this is really getting stupid how high these rates in France are going." Tony looked at me and said, "Dave, I know it's stupid, but let me ask you this: why can't it get stupider?"

In a second, I realized he was right. In a crisis, it was not about math—it was about who is in pain and what they will do about it. In that situation, arbitrage and math theory goes right out the door, while panic and job preservation march right in.

Tony explained that the smart players were positioning their trades for the Bank of France to dramatically raise short-term rates to screw over the speculators who were shorting the currency. The French even had a phrase for it: "closing the window." It meant that the Bank of France would limit the amount of money banks could borrow in the open market. Once that limit was reached, the Bank of France window would close for all other borrowers. If they were still short... oh well, it was their risk what interest rate they would have to pay to borrow the currency.

Tony also explained to me that traders come and go, and the new ones do not remember how tough the central bank can be. As a result, they get caught in these crises, not knowing what to do.

I began to study how the other banks were acting. I saw that several banks were calling me desperately every day, looking for francs to borrow. I soon realized I could actually charge much more than I was charging and still get paid because there wasn't enough money to go around.

I studied the Bank of France's comments and what they had done in the past and made some new calculations. I realized that I should go long French francs even if the current price was already "stupidly" high. Why? Because I realized that if the Bank of France did nothing, I would lose a little bit of money, but nothing I could not handle. But if the Bank of France did close the window, I would lose so much money that I would lose my whole year's pay—maybe even my job.

Chart 32
US Dollar vs. the French Franc, June 1995 to February 1996

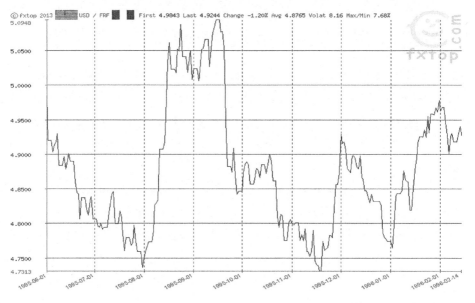

I made my decision to go long French francs on a Tuesday. Sure enough, it only took three days for something big to happen. On Friday, knowing that the speculators would have to borrow money not only for Friday but also for the weekend, the Bank of France closed the window around noon, Paris time. That was three hours before the market customarily closed, and it left the entire US market desperately looking for francs to borrow.

Interest rates, which had been trading at 7% the month before and at 20% in the past week, were now trading at 1,000%. That's right: 1,000%! And even though speculators rushed to close out their shorts against the franc, they still needed to borrow francs up to the number of days it took for their trade to settle. In this case, their trades settled on Tuesday, so they needed to borrow francs at 1,000% for four days. It turned out that interest on a $10,000,000 trading position for just four days was almost 1 million dollars! That was a massive loss on a trade where traders were trying to make $250,000 at best.

It was a painful lesson for those who got it wrong. And it was an experience with advice I have never forgotten. Crisis trading is its own animal. I have seen many crises: the 1987 stock market crash to the Asian Currency Crisis, to the Russian Bond Crisis, to the LTCM (Long Term Capital Management) blowup, to the financial crisis of 2008, COVID-19 of 2020, and many, many more that many non-professionals didn't realize were happening.

Chart 33
Russian Ruble Crisis of 1998 (500% in One Year)

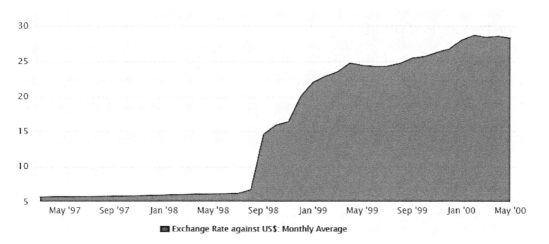

Exchange Rate against US$: Monthly Average

Chart 34
Stock Market Crash of 1987
(The Dow-Jones Industrial Average dropped 42% in just two months!)

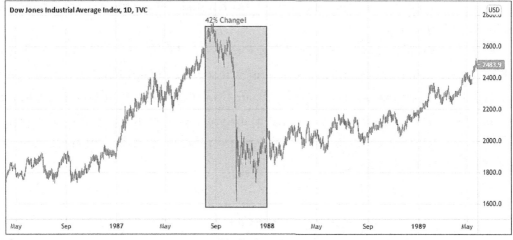

logicalLeader55436 published on TradingView.com, May 14, 2021 11:45:56 UTC
TVC:DJI, 1D 34021.5 ▼ −52.3 (−0.15%) O: 33624.7 H: 34181.8 L: 33623.5 C: 34021.5

TradingView

Three Lessons in Crisis Trading

Crisis trading is defined by abnormal market conditions that extend beyond a few days. Markets gap for a few days when you have an unexpected data point or a surprise move by a central bank. Markets go into crisis when traders question when, if ever, normal conditions will return for a specific market. Consider these three lessons I had to learn on the job.

Lesson 1: The First Bid Is Your Best Bid

When we begin to question a company's creditworthiness, a bond, or a country, the markets start to enter crisis mode. After all, what is the value to someone else to let us out of a trade we are holding if the new buyer will own an asset that is failing?

The answer is: not a lot. The first rule of thumb is: "your first bid is your best bid." This expression means that when you are trying to get out of a bad trade during a crisis, usually the first bid you get is the best bid because minutes count.

Every minute you waste trying to get out gives your counterparties time to rethink what price, if any, they should make to let you out of your problem. After all, they can see very well that a crisis is here. They may be making a price to you solely out of an obligation to keep the markets trading. They may have positioned themselves for the crisis and are now taking a profit by making the trade with you.

On the other hand, in a crisis, many traders need to get out of bad positions, not just you. Every extra moment you take means that someone else can call this market maker and get out before you do. If that happens, your price will be worse.

Lesson 2: Panic Trumps Models

Another vital lesson is panic trumps models. This is because the model is not considering the new information that is causing the panic. Eventually, everyone will recalibrate their model to a new fair value. However, for the moment, the security you own is caught in a crisis and the value will be measured by the degree of panic in the marketplace.

For example, if an accounting scandal is unveiled in the stock that you own, do not model the price using a cash-flow model. Instead, look at the history of accounting scandals and how far traders will panic to get out. If that is too much risk for you, try to get out as soon as possible.

Just as recently as June of 2020, a fintech wonderchild called Wirecard, a member of the prestigious Dax 30 Index in Germany, suffered an accounting crisis. The accounting scandal had been flagged several months earlier. Still, the market assumed the reality was not as bad as the news articles claimed. After all, this was one of the greatest new financial startups in a generation.

But when news broke on June 17th, 2020, that Wirecard was missing two billion dollars from its payment accounts, panic set in. Traders who refused to hit the first bid or turned to their model instead of just getting out paid a heavy price.

Chart 35
Wirecard Sells off in June of 2020

Lesson 3: Diversify

The third lesson is diversification. In a crisis, never trade a large amount of capital on one trade. Survival is your goal, not choosing sides when your assets are involved. Study the correlation of the trades you put on. You can have a basket of trades, but if they are all based on one theme or asset class, then a crisis can bring them all down.

Try to mix in long option strategies whenever possible so you can benefit from a crisis, or at least have your options limit the loss of your capital. For example, when I find myself very bullish on stocks, I will try to buy at least some put options, even if they are way out of the money. Not specifically to protect me against a bad trade idea, but to give me a floor I can count on if I awake from sleep and find the stock market in a general crisis mode.

Often, markets in crisis go far beyond your expectations of what you could lose. You may lose a week's worth of trading profits, a month's worth, or even your entire year's worth of gains. What you care about more than losses is your overall ability to keep trading, whether it is your personal account or your job at a trading firm. To do that, you have to be out of the crisis trades that are hurting your account to focus your energies on what has changed for the worse and what will go back to normal. Remember, crises come and go often enough that sooner or later, one will bite you.

Like gaps, crisis conditions are the markets that can destroy your business. It does not mean you should not be in the business, but it does mean you need to think about the possibilities. Think about what could go wrong and play out those scenarios. How would your portfolio do under your scenarios? Are there any hedges, no matter how far away from your current position, that will at least get you out at some price if you need to do so? Of course, any hedge is a hidden cost of your business.

Incorporate all these possibilities into your thinking and make them a natural part of analyzing your overall trading plan.

If you can manage through gaps and crises, you are now ahead of 99% of all traders. That's a huge competitive advantage to your trading style over others. Use that positive thought to motivate yourself to do the difficult things, thinking about blow-ups and thinking about spending money on hedges that will be worthless most of the time. If your biggest problem is that you never had to go through a crisis and wasted a lot of money on hedges that never paid off, you will be one successful trader!

CHAPTER 24

The Uses and Costs of Leverage

Understanding leverage is essential because all professionals use leverage in one form or another. Leverage is prevalent in all of economic society. For example, most of us use some form of leverage when we buy a home. We put down a deposit and then borrow the rest from a bank. Often, the bank will lend a willing and qualified buyer up to twice their annual gross income. Given that the average homeowner pays about 30% in state and local taxes, that means we can borrow about three times our net income.

Now, most homeowners have expenses other than their house payment—e.g., property taxes, utility bills, food, and entertainment. The bank considers those expenses as well when it makes a loan. Assuming one-half of our net income goes to other costs besides our mortgage payment, we borrow up to six times our net income when we buy a house. That is a lot of leverage! But we do it because we have a high degree of confidence (as does the bank) in our ability to earn that income over the next several years.

The bank also has something else that gives it confidence: the mortgage on the house is collateralized by the home itself. If you do not make your mortgage payment, the bank can seize the house. If the bank did its homework correctly, it knows it can sell the house for at least the mortgage cost based on the previous sale price.

Leverage Example: Purchasing a House

For example, say you have a job that pays $100,000 a year gross salary. You decide to buy a house for $250,000. The bank may ask for a $50,000 deposit and offer you a $200,000 loan, or two times your gross salary.

The bank has two things to fall back on when it makes the loan. The borrower has a job that pays $100,000, so you have a good chance of paying the monthly mortgage payments on time. However, if you lose your job or fail to make your payments, the bank has the right, through the mortgage, to seize your house.

The bank figures that since the previous sale took place at $250,000 and only owed $200,000, it has a good chance of selling the house for at least $200,000 if it seizes it from you. Since $200,000 would represent a 20% drop from the previous sale price, it would take an abysmal housing market for the price to drop that much. Thus, the bank offers significant leverage when it feels it has a strong chance to be repaid.

Beyond houses, consumers and businesses make decisions about leverage all the time. Companies borrow on lines of credit to help fund short-term cash crunches, often leveraging their assets to meet their cash needs.

On the other hand, some businesses will bet it all on a capital project they deem worth the risk. For example, oil speculators may borrow ten times their capital in the hope of finding oil. Manufacturers may borrow five times their capital to retool their assembly line in the hope of achieving a considerable productivity gain in the form of lower variable costs. This investment could pay dividends for years to come if it is executed properly.

As a professional trader (or even a stay-at-home, part-time trader), you will often employ leverage in your trading. In Chapter 20, we touched on leverage and how to use it with options. This chapter will explore a more technical but equally critical topic—the cost of financing your trades.

The Cost of Financing Trades

Every trader faces a different and unique cost to finance the leverage she chooses to take. Using an account at Interactive Brokers or Fidelity Investments, a stay-at-home trader borrows cash at treasury bills plus 300 basis points when she buys FX using leverage. A trader at a bank putting on the same trade may borrow at treasury bills plus 25 basis points. A trader at a hedge fund may finance bonds he buys at the prevailing repo rate plus ten basis points. In contrast, his counterpart in the repo department of the securities firm he trades with may finance the same bonds at the prevailing repo rate minus a few basis points.

The cost to buy or sell stock on margin is not fixed for everyone. In fact, it is just the opposite—every trader pays a different rate to borrow stocks or buy bonds on margin depending on whom they use as their clearer or prime broker.

The interest rate at which you borrow money then becomes a variable cost, which must be considered in estimating the potential profit of the trades you consider. I emphasize the word "estimating" because most borrowing costs are variable. The lender has the right to raise (or lower) the interest rate based on current market conditions. When calculating the risk of the trade and incorporating the cost to borrow money to leverage the transaction, you must also add in a factor for the risk that borrowing rates will rise over the life of the trade.

Consider some examples of the financing of various assets to help you understand the nuances of managing funding leveraged trades.

When you buy stock shares, you must decide whether to pay: (1) cash for the stock or (2) borrow money and buy stocks using leverage. The expression commonly used for the second alternative is "buying stocks on margin." But "margin" has various meanings in the professional trading world depending on the context. To avoid confusion among these meanings, for now, let us simply decide whether to pay cash or borrow money to purchase stock.

Most long-term investors (as opposed to traders) who buy stocks or bonds will choose to pay cash. They do this because, over time (e.g., a multi-year period), a bond or stock will deliver a return only slightly better than the cost of borrowing money. Over the long run, stocks or bonds will usually perform the same as borrowed money. Otherwise, we would all borrow money to make investments. Then when those investments return more than the cost of the money borrowed, we would make even more investments, borrowing even more money than before. We would basically all have a money machine and quit working! Therefore, borrowing money for investment typically has a short-term benefit when returns appear to exceed borrowing costs.

For traders, the rate charged matters. If you can borrow at zero or near zero, most investments with any thought behind them will return more than zero. When you borrow at excessively high rates, like 19% on your credit cards, the interest is so incredibly high that your investment is sure to lose money. And if you think zero is low or 19% is high, then wait until you get to the world of professional investing, where there are instances in which interest rates are negative—yes, negative! For certain assets, someone will pay you to borrow money from them! And there are instances where rates have gone to 1,000% to borrow money for a day or two. Even if it is only for a day, 1,000% percent can be very painful.

But despite the potentially wide range of interest rates charged, most professional traders borrow money when they trade. Why is that? The answer is they want to generate the maximum return on the capital used, particularly relative to the holding period of a typical trade. While holding a bond for many years will generate a return that closely monitors the cost of borrowing, professional traders often have trading ideas whose time horizon is much shorter. Ideas that profit in a few weeks or months will likely outperform the cost of the leverage used to put on the trade. The more successful the idea, the less the capital will cost to generate a large return. The less the capital costs, the more leverage can be taken.

Trading With and Without Leverage: An Example

Here, in Table 10, is an example of how trading with and without leverage works.

Table 10
Three Strategies for Buying Home Depot Stock
(Margin Rate of 7%)

Price	Date Bought	# of Shares	Interest	Price Sold	Date Sold	Total Profit	Annual Return
$35	Jan–1–11	1,428	0	$61.85	1–Jan–13	$38,341	24%
$35	Jan–1–11	2,856	–7,000	$61.85	1–Jan–13	$69,683	46%
$47	May–1–12	2,127	–2,014	$61.85	1–Jan–13	$29,571	101%

In this table, we see three trading strategies for Home Depot executed over a two-year period. The first was to buy the stock on January 1st, 2011, paying cash for 1,428 shares and selling the stock two years later on January 1st, 2013. Over that period, the trader invested $50,000 in capital and got back $88,341 at the end for a total return on his capital of 24% per year.

In the second case, the trader bought 2,856 shares with $50,000 in cash; plus, he borrowed $50,000 at an annual interest rate of 7%. Since the stock price rose 24% per year on average over the two years, borrowing money was a good choice. After interest costs, the investor was left with $69,683, or a 46% return.

Chart 36
Price of Home Depot Stock, 2010 to January 1, 2013

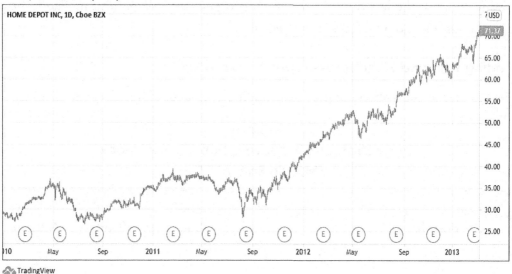

logicalLeader55436 published on TradingView.com, May 14, 2021 11:50:02 UTC
BATS:HD, 1D 325.42 ▲ +8.42 (+2.66%) O:319.00 H:327.42 L:318.69 C:325.42

TradingView

Finally, in the third case, we see an investor who had a short-term trading idea and bought Home Depot after it had declined to $47on May 1st, 2012, and sold it at $61.85 on January 1, 2013. In addition, she felt confident it was a good trade and borrowed money at 7%.

Her return was the best dollar amount of all three trades. She made $29,571 in trading gains and she also borrowed money to leverage the trade. Her holding period was only eight months and her interest charge was only $2,014. Her annualized return is a whopping 101%. Remember, annualized return assumes you would make the same amount of money you made in the eight months of the trade for the other four months of the year.

The deciding factors in taking on leverage should be: (1) the confidence level of the trader, (2) the interest rate charged, and (3) the length of time the money is borrowed. The third trader could have borrowed at a much higher rate, given she planned to have a short holding period—just long enough for the stock to bounce back after a selloff.

The same cannot be said for Investor 2. For example, if he had borrowed money at 40% (instead of 7%) to buy and hold Home Depot for two years, he would have paid $40,000 in interest and only earned $36,685 in total. Therefore, his return would be worse by borrowing money to buy more shares than if he had simply paid cash for the shares and not borrowed at all.

Most professional traders assume they will borrow money. Buying on leverage is often needed to generate the kind of returns required to earn a full-time living when trading. Most traders with less than $1 million in capital will need to borrow money and leverage up their trades to make enough money annually to trade full-time.

Borrowing money is not without its risks and is not cost-free. The higher the confidence in your idea and the shorter the holding period, the more likely that borrowing money to leverage your position will pay off. Be sure to calculate your cost of leverage in advance and monitor the borrowing costs over the life of the trade, particularly if your interest charge is a variable rate

The Cost Incurred by Margin Requirements

Another cost that must be considered is the margin requirements. As we stated earlier, buying on margin is a common phrase in the stock market. Still, for most of the professional trading world, margin means the amount of capital that must be posted by the trader to a bank, broker-dealer, or Futures Commission Merchant to protect the trading counterparty against any losses the trade may incur.

Margin works as follows: depending on the law, regulatory requirements, or the margin department of the broker-dealer involved, you will be asked to put up a certain percentage of the overall capital needed to buy or sell a security. For example, if you are buying shares of stock, the law says you will need to post 50% of the stock's value as margin. If you buy a US government bond, you may only be asked to post 5% of the bond's value as margin. The bond, which can be used as collateral with which to borrow money, is considered very safe, with low volatility. In other words, there is little risk of default.

As another example, if you buy a contract on orange juice futures, you may be asked to post just 10% of the contract's value. That is because the exchange trusts the Futures Commission Merchant (FCM), with whom you have an account, to collect any losses from you. Otherwise, the FCM will pay the exchange themselves.

If a position goes against you, the initial margin may not be enough to cover the loss or the potential for future losses. In this case, you will have to post more margin, which is often referred to as "variation margin." This variation margin can be a significant risk for traders, and it is usually where traders will experience pressure to exit a trade.

Traders who are either undercapitalized or unprepared for losses will often discover that margin calls (i.e., requests for additional margin) are a very time-sensitive issue. In most instances, you will have only one day to meet a variation margin call. If you do not meet the call, your position will be closed out for you and you will not be allowed to trade further. Having someone else decide whether you close out your trade or not is a surefire way to lose lots of money.

Remember, even if your trade becomes more profitable as the market moves in your favor, you will still have to post a variation margin once the notice is sent out.

There is an old adage in the market to "never meet a margin call." In other words, the saying goes, do not pay the margin. In the old days, stock speculators would get a margin call, not meet the call, and would simply let their firm close out the trade for them. The logic was that the trade was going bad and to meet the margin call meant staying in the trade—only to lose more money and thus have another margin call to meet.

This strategy worked fine 50 years ago when the rules or punishment for not meeting a margin call were less stringent. The broker would close your position and ask you to settle your account before trading again. However, in the last 50 years or so, the rules have tightened considerably, and it is now your obligation to meet a margin call or face sanctions from your broker-dealer, fines, or even regulatory punishment.

Due to the speed in which money can move, banks and brokers offer more leverage today than they did in the past because they know clients can wire money almost instantly to meet a variation margin call. Meeting a margin due to a small change in the price of an asset you are holding is no longer in itself a reason to close out a trade. However, it does mean that your overall excess cash is reduced and it may be difficult for you to continue to meet future margin calls.

Determining a minimum cash balance, which you will need to support a portfolio of your trades, is a critical part of the preparation of sizing your trade and determining your stop-loss parameters. At the extreme, your stop-loss level needs to be above the level where a margin call would draw your cash below your threshold limits. Overall, the minimum level of cash you want to hold at any time has to be your highest priority. Stop losses need to account for the level of cash you will have remaining over and above the price action you are willing to tolerate.

Margin Requirements and Your Return on the Trade

As a cost of trading, the margin you put up affects your return on the trade in the same way that interest rate changes affect your return. The more margin you put up, the larger the denominator when determining your return on capital.

For example, if I put up $10,000 to buy an orange juice futures contract and make $1,000 on the trade, my return on capital is 10%. If, however, the trade initially goes against me and the exchange sends me a variation margin notice to send in another $5,000, and soon after that the trade comes back and I make the same $1,000, my return on capital is no longer 10%, but instead $1,000/$15,000—or 6.7%.

The risk of having to pay variation margin will force you to keep a cash reserve when trading on margin. For example, imagine that you have $100,000 in your trading account and you invest in 10 futures contracts, putting up $10,000 each, which leaves zero in your account. Seven of those trades go well, but three do not and you are asked to send in $5,000 in variation margin for each of the three trades going against you. To meet the margin call, you will have to close out some of your winning trades. Remember, if you close out a losing trade, you still need to meet the margin call.

Based on margin considerations, you will have to choose how much capital you will need to meet your initial margin and the potential for variation margin calls from time to time. You will have to study your strategies very carefully and look at trends and short-term volatility to determine the risk of variation margin. To be prudent, you must calculate that risk not just over some long-term average, but you must stress-test your trades under extremely volatile market conditions.

The failure to meet a variation margin call can be devastating to your trading performance and your reputation. You should, therefore, assume the worst-case scenario. This concept even applies when working at a bank, hedge fund, or other capital management organization, as a variation margin call may send a red flag to a risk or compliance officer. Even if another department handles your margin calls for you, it's good to know what controls are in place when variation margins are needed. Your expectations of how you will manage the risk of margin call match the rules and risk metrics the firm has put in place.

Traders are often ignorant of this subtlety, to their own detriment. Even to the traders themselves, it is not well-known that they may be measured on how frequently their trades are asked to meet margin calls. Risk managers will often use this metric as a critical measure of a trader's performance in determining whether to keep them around or not. In extreme cases, traders are the last to know they are being fired for overuse of capital.

Always explore and understand what rules you are working under when you trade someone else's capital.

CHAPTER 25

The Best Practices to Protect Your Capital

I n a vacuum, when trading for your account, you can set your risk tolerance levels for whatever amount of risk with which you are comfortable. The management of your capital over any time period that is meaningful to you depends solely on your disciplined approach.

Most often, trades "blow up" when conditions in the market become "stressed" and losses seem to be coming without respite. Often, this is the moment when traders have a choice: (1) stay in the set of trades that as a group are not working and violate their risk parameters, or (2) get out of the trades and live to fight another day. Surprisingly, many traders choose the former and fight on, holding their positions, supported by the notion that the current situation is illogical and temporary. Hence, they feel justified in doing so. In other words, the exceptional environment allows for exceptions to risk management rules. These traders suspend their standard rules of risk management because getting out would mean admitting that unexplained price movement tops fundamental thinking.

Managing Your Capital

When facing a run of trading losses, you must not be deceived by the idea that a portfolio of trades is less likely to blow up and therefore garners special exceptions when losses begin to pile up. Your portfolio's value based on your research or its diversification is not the only rule set you are operating under. Instead, you are also managing capital—i.e., you are determining the risks of losing significant amounts of your money.

You must always identify when further substantial losses may affect your capital in a way that prevents you from business as usual going forward. You must consider not only the capital you could stand to lose by holding on to losing positions but whether you are putting business as usual at risk by not closing out trades.

Your job is to deal with your portfolio, not your personal view or your reputation. You are merely dealing with trades you no longer think are prudent, and you are in full capital-protection mode. This is no time to let pride about being wrong have a place in managing your capital.

When thinking about your capital management, you must consider two levels of capital preservation. First, ask yourself what level of capital will continue to let you operate business as usual. In other words, regardless of your losses, what amount of money will allow you to initiate the next set of trades with the same size and risk tolerance as before? This first level of capital must be protected to the best of your ability since it allows you to focus on trading and not the preservation of your business. Generally, this level will equate the average amount you would need to trade for a block of time that is meaningful. For example, your answer to this question may be: "With at least $100,000 in my account, I can trade my normal way for six months without having to draw that money away from trading to manage my personal life."

The second level of capital preservation comes when losses are large enough that you cannot afford business as usual. In that instance, you have to triage your trade designs and ask yourself: How many trades can I switch from trading the stock to purchasing the option instead so I can reduce the potential for surprising large losses? Can I choose trades where the asset I am buying or selling has lower volatility and I can assess incoming information with less stress?

Notice I am suggesting trade design improvements over trade idea improvements. Striving to analyze fundamental information and coalescing that information into a trade idea is an independent process that never ends. However, risk tolerance goes up and down—it is the nature of the market. Volatility is not in your control; trade design and risk management are in your control.

I will give kudos here to one of the best sayings ever written about markets and money management. This saying was coined by Dennis Gartman, the publisher of a well-regarded commodities investment newsletter, so all credit goes to him: "The markets can remain illogical longer than you can remain solvent."

You must always have a separate control for capital preservation that supersedes your desire to keep trades in place. Losing trades may seem illogical, but they lose capital nonetheless. Capital is the heart of your trading business.

Remaining solvent and preserving your ability to keep trading is the one rule I have in this entire book that has no exception!

Capital Management Rules When You Manage Other People's Money

When managing someone else's capital, capital management has a different set of constraints beyond those of managing your own capital. The rules are unique to the owner of that capital.

For example, if you work at a hedge fund, the head of the fund will have completely different capital management rules for himself than you as his portfolio manager, even though the capital pool belongs to the same set of investors. If a trader works for a bank or an asset manager, he may be subject to risk constraints to which he might not otherwise subject himself. One of the most common constraints bank traders suffer from is the inability to hedge trades using instruments that are not designated as part of the trader's "approved product list." For example, the head bond trader at the bank who is trading US government treasuries may not be authorized to trade the S&P 500, even though a selloff in the S&P is positively correlated with a rally in US Treasuries.

Even if you are the owner of a fund that manages money for other people, you have rules that apply outside of your own views because in your descriptions of your trading style, you may have explicitly or implicitly claimed to have limits in your trading strategies. Investors who give you money to manage may ask you to assign loss limits to preserve capital. These limits will obligate you to close out trades perhaps sooner than your own risk rules would suggest.

Other Ways Capital May Be Restricted

The risks involved in regulation, compliance, or accounting may also restrict capital usage. For example, the costs of doing trades in a new area for a bank that involves setting up controls for regulators far outweigh the benefit of giving the trader the ability to make a few extra bucks! Your broker may restrict trading from home because of rules stemming from compliance departments. Also, traders are frequently prevented from trading options without meeting a suitability assessment.

Capital that comes from a retirement account often has different restrictions on what assets can be invested in versus money that is free and clear from the retirement account designation.

Other rules can be temporary but just as restrictive. For example, in times of stress, stock market exchanges will put in a rule preventing short selling. If you run a long-short equity strategy, you can be out of business for months until the ban is lifted.

Moreover, in times of stress, the Nymex may put a position limit on oil traders to reduce speculation. The Federal Reserve has likewise placed restrictions on how many bond contracts a single account can take for delivery.

Algo traders often have different restrictions on the number of orders they can send to an exchange. Exchanges often set these restrictions to prevent a flood of computer orders that would overload a system meant for access by all traders.

There are often bans that prevent traders from trading "on-shore" in local markets. Countries as large as Brazil and as small as Latvia have rules to prevent foreigners from flooding the market with capital one day and leaving the next. Breaking the rules can get you fined, even arrested, and, yes, extradited! As recently as ten years ago, traders from Deutsche Bank in Singapore and Hong Kong were extradited to South Korea for breaking South Korea's stock exchange rules.[40]

All in all, it is a free country but not a free market. Capital that is not your own has many restrictions, depending on its source. You need to match your trading acumen with the organization or structure that will best allow you to execute your trading strategies. When you choose that organization, you must be prepared to abide by their rules for capital preservation in a timely manner and without exception. Even for your own portfolio, maintaining minimum capital levels to keep your business going needs to supersede staying in trades they have not played out as you expected.

---

[40] "Deutsche Bank Employees Indicted over Stock Manipulation," *The Korea Times*, August 21st, 2011

SECTION VII

THE END GAME

CHAPTER 26

Post-Trade Reports: After the Trade Is Done, Your Work Is Just Beginning

O nce you have completed your trade, the world of trade processing begins. This world has a multi-faceted effect on you, the trader, and failing to understand these facets can whittle away the difference between success and failure.

As always, the purpose of this chapter is simply to make you aware of the risks involved to you if your post-trade analysis is not done correctly. It would be impossible to cover every contingency, but you must learn to be obsessive about the details of your reports. Whenever possible, get more—not less—detail about what you did, what you own, and how your positions are accounted for in your profit-and-loss statements. This way, when you do find problems, you will have the relevant information at your disposal instead of having to recreate it after the fact, which can be quite tricky even for the most sophisticated trading firms.

In this chapter, we will review four main aspects of post-trade analysis:

- Trade Reporting

- Risk Reporting

- Mark-to-Market Reporting

- Accounting

Once your trade has been completed—whether it's a trade on the stock exchange, the futures exchange, the options exchanges, the FX market, or a derivative trade between you and another financial institution—a confirmation is created to explain the exact details of the trade. This confirmation is a legal document. In most cases, it overrides the voice orders, email discussions, or chats you may have had when you placed the order. It may even override your electronic order entry systems.

Needless to say, your confirmation is an extremely important document and your goal within 24 hours after it has been generated is to make sure it is right.

While sophisticated venues such as E-Trade or a bank platform rarely make a mistake in creating the correct confirmation, errors do occur. My experience is that the best that organizations can hope to achieve is a 99% success ratio in generating accurate confirmations. A 1% error ratio is not a lot when you are manufacturing building supplies or taking the SATs, but it can be devastating to traders.

Confirmations Should Always Be Checked

Confirmations should always be checked. You should review the trade details and the trade date, the commission (if any), and the correct names and accounts of each counterparty.

Your most significant (first-order) risk is that the confirmation does not match what you thought you traded. The error can run both ways. The broker-dealer can make a mistake by sending you an incorrect confirmation, or you could make a mistake by not realizing that your expectation of what you traded does not match the confirmation.

Here are some common examples to get your mind thinking about these issues and the risks associated with them.

Let's say you go to buy options on oil futures. You buy 100 call options at a limit price of $1.50. You get a partial fill of 80 contracts. The broker says he can get you filled on the balance but is unable to do so at the current time. He sends you a confirmation for just 80 contracts he has executed so far. You assume you got the other 20 based on your broker's confidence and his assurance that he could fill you, but in fact, he is not obligated to fill you on the last 20 options—he was simply rendering his opinion. Without reviewing the confirmation, you may not realize your expectation does not match the real world.

A standard error is when you modify your order's size but fail to check if the new amount was accepted. Exchange rules require the broker to leave the old amount on your order, unless all the steps to modify are done correctly. Often, traders find errors in the confirmation only to realize then that they failed to modify the amount correctly.

Finally, you are using an electronic platform to trade stocks where the buy and sell buttons are remarkably close together on the screen. The price on the bid is very close to the price on the offer. Many times, a trader will execute a buy when they meant to sell. Immediately the trader sees the fill price and assumes the correct side was done. Without reviewing the confirmation, this will go unnoticed until the position report is reviewed.

Risk Reporting

Risk reporting is the requirement that at the end of each trading day, all the positions that you hold overnight, until at least the next trading day, need to be fed into a computer that maintains the records on your portfolio. This recording can be as simple as your brokerage e-account statement at Schwab or as sophisticated as a top-of-the-line proprietary relational database that holds the records of thousands of open trades you have put on.

Regardless of your positions' size, they must be reported to everyone relevant in your organization. For example, if it is just you trading for your own account, you need to see the positions in an orderly fashion, with closing marks and the daily change in value clearly marked. More importantly, you need to be able to produce a risk report. Almost all online trading firms now provide some form of risk reports, and you should read them and understand them.

A risk report shows your portfolio's risk profile using various standard metrics to help quantify the risk you have. For example, if you are trading in options on Facebook stock, you might have a report that looks like the one below:

Table 11

Option Risk Report: Facebook Calls, Stock Price= $28, 44 days to Maturity

Strike	# of Options	Closing Price	Dollar Value	Delta	Vega	Gamma per 10%	Theta
25	700	5.10	$357,000	0.67	27%	0.25	$(2,700)
30	500	2.30	$115,000	0.39	28.20%	0.13	$(2,500)
35	−1,000	1.00	$(100,000)	0.15	29.10%	0.07	$2,000

This report shows that the trader is long two different call option strikes (25 and 30 strikes) and is short one call strike (35) on Facebook stock. This report helps the trader learn various risks concerning his positions to quantify his risks as the market moves away from the closing price.

For example, if the market is unchanged but a day passes, he will lose $3,200 in time decay. If Facebook stock rallies 10%, his deltas will change to 92%, 52%, and 22%, respectively (add the delta and the gamma to get the new delta after the 10% move).

Some of these metrics may be intuitive and even obvious to an experienced trader. Still, the computer program provided by your clearing firm can compute the metrics better than you can on a spreadsheet. The risk report acts as your trading partner, providing you with a sanity check by displaying your risk in a consistent format every time and helping quantify what your risk is. Seeing your risk in black and white is often better than letting your gut tell you how much risk you have.

Reviewing your risk report at the end of the day or first thing in the morning also provides you with an excellent opportunity to reconcile the portfolio with the risks you thought you had or were trying to attain. "To err is human," and errors are most often found by reviewing the risk report. Sometimes, a keystroke error causes the trade to be input incorrectly. Other times, you took on more or less risk than you intended, and the risk report reveals what the current metrics are so you can compare them to your intent.

The Risks in Risk Reporting

When a trader is part of a bank or hedge fund, the reporting process has to be organized so all team members can access the data to get the information they need without affecting others.

In a typical trading room, a trader, a trading assistant, an accounting clerk, a risk manager, and a credit officer, among others, might all access the same raw data to construct risk reports that suit their needs in support of the trading organization as a whole. The trading assistant may need to access the trades to correct booking errors or generate risk reports. The accounting clerk needs the data to settle cash payments and produce P&L reports. The risk manager needs to blend the data with other traders in the firm to produce Value-at-Risk (VaR) reporting. VaR is one measure of the amount of risk or potential loss in an investment portfolio. It is discussed more fully in the next chapter on performance benchmarking. The credit officer needs the data to see how much credit is being used with certain counterparties to determine if there is excess exposure to a single firm.

Clearly, a lot can go wrong in this process. If the data is not protected, data can be overwritten or modified, creating errors where none previously existed. Each report has to be reviewed on its own and compared with other reports that used the same raw data to see if the reports reconcile with each other.

Often, reports help reveal risks that were not easily understood when the trade was put on. For example, VaR reports show where trades that seem to be independent of each other are quite correlated in specific economic environments. For example, a position short on oil contracts and long on S&P 500 futures may both perform poorly if there is a threat to oil supplies in the Middle East.

The most critical aspect of risk reporting is accepting the facts as a trader and incorporating them into your risk management. This statement may seem like a tautology, but it is often the Achilles heel of most traders.

Most traders tend to subconsciously deny they have correlated risks concerning specific market movements or potential news shocks. For them to acknowledge these risks would usually mean that they should consider changing their position or risk less—but risking less means making less money!

Optimism often trumps prudent risk management. If your reporting is insufficient, you cannot have strong risk management. On the other hand, being open to accepting the information the risk report produces, particularly if it is quality reporting, can significantly improve your trading. That is because this information can help you make an informed decision about managing your risk and ultimately prepare you for how market movements, which will invariably come, will affect your trading performance.

Mark-to-Market Reporting

At the close of each business day, a closing price or "mark" is used to measure your profit-and-loss change from the previous day's close. For securities that are traded on an exchange, the "mark" price will be set by the exchange and, when compared to the previous day's close, will produce for you a mark-to-market profit or loss for each position held.

For trades that are done over the counter (OTC) with other financial institutions, the mark will either be derived by your counterparty, who will send you his marks, or you will mark your positions to your model. A third way may be to use a third-party source that everyone agrees is a knowledgeable source for the closing mark.

But regardless of how the price is obtained, the trader must understand that the closing price is not necessarily tradable. Instead, the mark is just a moment in time consistent each day—such as 4 p.m. Eastern Time—to fix the end of day price. By having a single closing mark for everyone, regulators and accountants can compare profit and loss on a level playing field.

Accounting Reports

Even after the risk has been taken and the trade is long closed out, the trade requires a series of accounting notations to officially recognize it as a loss or a gain. The accounting process is vital because there are different tax consequences depending on how, where, and when the trade is booked.

For example, some solo traders trade out of their retirement accounts to create tax-free income. Traders who trade out of a taxable account need to consider the accounting implications of trading stocks versus options. Depending on the holding period, there is risk of having short-term trading income, which is fully taxable, as compared to having it treated as a long-term capital gain, which is taxed at the lower capital gains rate. Accounting also needs to take records of all your trade-related expenses so they can be used to offset trading gains when available.

In summary, reporting is an integral part of successful trading. It takes organization and discipline to review your reporting daily in order to manage your risk appropriately. The market has no idea what you think your risk is. And, like the ocean, it just keeps moving whether you have the correct risk report or not. It is up to you to systematize your reporting.

You should establish a routine for creating your reports and be consistent with reviewing them. After all, it is your risk, and you will invariably find risks you did not intend to take. It is better to correct those mistakes in a controlled environment than under the stress of moving markets when incorrect positions tend to reveal themselves through unexpected trading losses.

CHAPTER 27
Benchmarking Performance

L ong-term success in trading is measured using indexes as benchmarks. Bench-marking helps traders understand how their capital has performed over a given time period. Performance comes in many flavors, with profit and loss being just the tip of the iceberg.

For purposes of efficiency, we will focus this chapter on the assumption that the trader has a profitable collection of trades over a specific time period, net of brokerage and expenses.

First, it is important to take a second and address the concept of "profitable trad-ing" because it is easily lost on many new traders. Particularly among those traders who are back-testing a theory and feel confident they will perform profitably when put into a live trading environment.

Profitability in trading means net of the brokerage costs and the costs of running your operation (your expenses). When you are trying to sell yourself to others to manage their money, it involves the costs of managing their money as well. These costs include legal, compliance, marketing, accounting, reporting, banking, and other expenses.

Many traders run back-tests on a historical database and assume that they will have the ability to enter a trade, pay minimal bid/offer spreads, and not suffer any slippage. Even if all this were true, they still need to assign brokerage costs to the trades and es-timate a cost structure to running the business once they begin live trading.

For example, how much more will data cost you when you need live feeds and have to pay monthly exchange fees? Maybe you will need a much faster Internet con-nection, and possibly, your strategy will have to be adjusted when eliminating small trades that go from profitable to losing when brokerage costs are included.

How to Measure Performance

Taking the just-completed discussion as a given, we now have to level the playing field. We all know we have to measure our total costs and subtract them from our gross trading profit to produce a true net profit. The question then becomes, how do I measure this performance? And more importantly, how will others measure this performance?

Finally, we will address the question, "How do I measure my performance when I am trading someone else's capital, say, at a bank or a hedge fund?" Suffice it to say, we can only touch on the subject of measuring returns. My job here is to arm you with a basic understanding so you can pursue the subject in greater detail as it suits your trading style.

Even if you never plan to work for a trading firm or manage other people's money, benchmarking can be helpful in understanding the risks you are taking and improving them. It can also be useful because having this data will give you the ability to gain more leverage with capital providers (your brokerage firm, your FCM, or your bank), who will see that you have a semblance of control over your trading and your costs.

For example, suppose you are trading from home. In that case, you may decide after a while that you want to move from a fairly basic trading platform like E-Trade to a more professional platform like IB (Interactive Brokers). Brokers offer different amounts of leverage for the same amount of capital, based on the experience and knowledge that the trader represents to the broker's account representative. Having a benchmark of your performance and historical risk reports can go a long way toward getting more leverage and professional services from these firms.

Measuring Your Return

To measure your return, you must determine the amount of capital you have to risk. You may have a fixed amount of cash and securities in a trading account, which makes the calculation simple. Often, as an individual trader, you may be drawing on that same pool of money to pay personal expenses that have nothing to do with trading costs.

A simple way to adjust your capital is to determine an annualized amount of money you need to live on for a year and add that amount back into the total amount in your account at the end of the year. You can then compare this number with the beginning-of-year balance to determine your net profit and your simple annual return.

For example, imagine that you start the trading year with $250,000 in your account. This amount is all you have. You also know you need to draw on about $50,000 for living expenses over and above any expenses related to your trading. Now, add that amount back into your trading account at the end of the year to determine what your total would be had it not been for living expenses. Suppose your account has $250,000 at the end of the year after all trading costs were paid. In that case, you add the $50,000 of living expenses you drew out to this number and then divide by your starting balance of $250,000 to determine that you made 20% for the year (i.e., $300,000/$250,000 gives you a 20% gain). A fine performance!

Figuring Returns When Trading for a Firm

Determining how much capital you are managing when you work for a bank, where you are given trading limits instead of capital, is a bit more challenging. It is common for these types of firms to assign the trader a set of limits. Limits may include things like a total dollar value per basis point change, a position limit measured in units of stocks or bonds, or a limit based on a Value-at-Risk calculation (VaR).

Traders may also be assigned a simple dollar amount stop-loss limit that is set with daily, monthly, or yearly limits. Even with just these simple metrics, a trader can solve for the equivalent amount of capital under management.

For example, imagine that a hedge fund manager assigns a draw-down limit of five million dollars. Armed with this limit, a trader can simply invert a year-to-date stop-loss limit and multiply by her percentage of loss limits per traded capital to solve for the total capital she is managing. Let's say this trader is determined to close out her portfolio after a 2% loss, and that equals five million dollars, which means she is comfortable managing 250 million. If, on the other hand, she loses 5% before losing five million, then she is managing 100 million.

On the other hand, if she has only a limit based on total dollars at risk per a one-basis-point change in her portfolio return, or she has a limit in VaR terms, she can also make like comparisons to a total notional of capital under management. For example, many hedge funds limit VaR to 2% of capital managed, so whatever VaR limits the trader is assigned, she can multiply by 50 to estimate the amount of capital she controls.

Table 12
Calculating Hedge Fund Parameters

Method 1	
Stop-Loss Limit	$5,000,000
% Loss on the portfolio before hitting 5,000,000	5%
Then take $5,000,000/.05 = Equivalent Capital of	$100,000,000
Method 2	
VaR Limit of:	$2,000,000
Industry Standard VaR per Capital of 1/100	100 multiplier
Then take $2,000,000 X 100 = Equivalent Capital of	$200,000,000

Now that we know our capital, we can calibrate our returns to industry standards to benchmark our performance. Often, we want to know how we did versus a standard benchmark such as the S&P 500 Index, which represents a potential return using an index of stocks with no active form of management. Vanguard and other investment firms offer ETFs based on the S&P 500 and replicate the index return within a few basis points while charging a mere 25 basis points of yearly fees.

Thus, if the S&P 500 is up 10% and this was your only holding, you would most likely have a return in your account of about 9.7%. As I said above, we assume five basis points of slippage trying to match the index and 25 basis points of costs, both costs reducing the return. Technically, if you want to compare your returns to the S&P 500 in this example, you should use the achievable rate of 9.7%. But most people in the industry use the actual index rate of 10%, making the comparable hurdle rate a little harder for you to achieve.

Many use the S&P 500 as their benchmark, even when trading other assets such as FX, bonds, or commodities. Benchmarking using the S&P is clearly wrong, as you should benchmark your return using comparable trading styles. You are better served to find an ETF that better matches your asset class. Today, there are many specialized ETFs covering specific sectors within asset classes so you can create an even more targeted benchmark if necessary. For example, suppose you are only trading technology stocks. In this case, you can compare your holdings to the Vanguard technology ETF (symbol VGT) to prevent your comparisons being mismatched to the more broadly defined S&P.

Alpha and Beta Returns

Why compare your returns to these indexes? The answer is, by doing so, you can determine how much "alpha" was created versus "beta."

Alpha refers to first-order returns—i.e., returns you generated through your trading that are unique and would not have been made through passive investing. Beta refers to returns that were a consequence of your being in a particular market. Beta returns would have been generated if you were a passive investor in the index that represents your investment style.

Your total returns are the sum of your alpha plus beta returns. Let's look at Table 13 below to track how two traders traded utility stocks in 2012. The index went from 467 to 446 over the year.

Table 13
Annual Return for Traders Who Try to Beat the Dow-Jones Utility Index

Trader	Index Start	Index Finish	Percent Change	Alpha	Beta
Index	467	446	-4.49%	0	-4.49%
Trader A	10,000	13,400	34%	38.49%	-4.49%
Trader B	10,000	8,700	-13%	-8.51%	-4.49%

The difference between a trader and an investor is that an investor is a passive participant in the market. An investor is willing to accept whatever the market returns for the types of investments he makes. Thus, the investor only earns the beta of the market.

A trader tries to outperform passive investments. To do this, she must generate alpha. From the table above, we can see that alpha can be a net positive or a net negative contributor to total return. By definition, negative alpha means you underperformed your benchmark and, therefore, you underperformed a passive investor. Positive alpha means you contributed returns greater than merely the market return. Thus, your alpha is your gross return minus the market's beta for your trading style and minus brokerage costs. The costs of running your business are usually calculated separately.

In all of these comparisons, it is essential to note that we cannot say similar gross returns are equal when comparing which trader outperformed. For example, let us compare a trader focusing on utility stocks with another trader focusing on information technology stocks.

From 2004 through 2013, the Utility sector's annualized return was 9.47% during the ten years, while the annualized return for the information technology sector was just 7.37%. Both beat the S&P 500, which had a ten-year average annualized return of 7.16% (these data provided by S&P and Dow Jones). As one might expect, the annualized volatility of the Utilities was only 13% compared to the higher annualized volatility of Info-Tech of 18.63%.

We cannot say that Utility traders are better than Info-Tech traders just because the Info-Tech Index had lower returns and more volatility over the period. We can only compare how a trader focusing on Utility stocks performed compared to her benchmark of annualized returns and the volatility of her returns compared to the volatility of the same index. Technology stocks have been all over the place during this timeframe, with three years of near-zero gains, one year of a massive loss of 43%, and several positive years. Thus, a trader who is adding lots of positive alpha to a portfolio of technology stocks could still return a negative total result for the year if her beta, the index she is trying to beat, is significantly negative.

While generating positive alpha is generally considered a good thing, we cannot thoroughly compare one trader versus another based on alpha alone; we also have to look at how much capital was applied. At the extreme, if one trader kept his capital in the bank when technology stocks were declining, then he created alpha only by not trading. If that was a prudent decision, then kudos to him!

But we must also see if the same trader will take his cash out of the bank when the beta of the market is positive! Suppose this same trader produced positive alpha in an up market as well. In that case, he can be considered a great trader who is worthy of managing capital. If, on the other hand, he only generates alpha in down markets, then he is simply being paid to keep the money in a bank. His benchmark should be the return one gets on a bank account rather than the return one gets from an active index such as technology stocks!

Comparing Degrees of Risk

Another essential metric in comparing our performance with that of other traders is to compare the way we took our risk versus how others starting with the same amount of capital took theirs. In other words, who earned the same rate of return with the least amount of risk?

For example, if Trader A and Trader B each earned 14% returns in 2012, and each created the same amount of alpha, it does not mean that the traders' performances were equal. Trader A could have deployed very little capital and taken little risk. Yet, because he was such a good alpha producer, he returned the same amount of profits as Trader B, who deployed nearly all her capital, traded often, and took considerable risks. Clearly, we would want to go with Trader A's style because any trader who allocates all her capital is more at risk of losing it one day versus a trader who uses much less capital to trade.

How Significant is "Value-at-Risk?"

"Value-at-Risk," or VaR, is one measure of the maximum potential losses a portfolio can incur when capital is put into the financial markets. It uses statistical probabilities based on historical movements to quantify the level of the financial risk involved. It is universally used by institutional traders to manage and limit the degree of risk they are taking.

VaR measures the potential loss in value of a risky portfolio over a defined period with a given level of confidence in its most general form. For example, suppose the VaR on a portfolio shows the largest expected loss over a five-day period is $1 million, with a 95% confidence level. In that case, the probability is that there is a 5% chance that the value of the portfolio will drop by no more than one million dollars on any given day. Since VaR measures the risk of a portfolio rather than summing up the risks of each individual trade, traders may reduce their potential losses by either adding or subtracting trades to the portfolio.

The invention of VaR analysis was considered a significant advancement because it allows traders to think about a portfolio of trades rather than simply adding the risk of each individual trade with no regard to its effect on the portfolio risk.[41] However, while VaR helps to standardize risk, it is also a backward-looking methodology. It

---

[41] "The History and Ideas Behind VaR," Peter Adamko, ScienceDirect, *Procedia Economics and Finance*, 24 (2015)

produces risk metrics using past data. Because many traders anchor their views on the relationships that held in the past, capital usage may be too dependent on correlation and the attempt to reduce risk, irrespective of current market conditions.

A trader with a large, diversified set of trades can be deemed to have much less risk than a trader with just a few large trades. Due to the efficient frontier theory, a large portfolio, having a variety of asset classes, should move more independently and ultimately create a portfolio effect on returns. Even if the amount of capital deployed for a portfolio of trades is greater than the portfolio with a few trades, it can still have less risk. Theoretically, of course!

Here is a real-time example. Below is a chart of the Nasdaq index, with actual daily returns since 1999 and a normal curve distribution using the daily returns to calculate the standard deviation and the probability distribution.

Chart 37
VaR of the Nasdaq 100

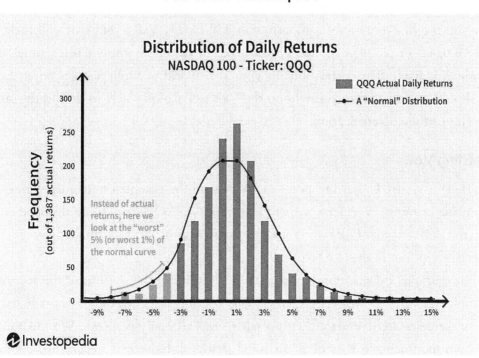

Assuming your trade portfolio consists of the Nasdaq 100, you have a diversified portfolio of 100 stocks, which have some correlation since all the assets are stocks. If we use either the bars (actual data) or the normal distribution (the black curved line), we can see that with 95% confidence, one is likely to lose around 4% in the worst-case scenario on any one day. [42] Even though there are worse days, the probability of it happening in any one day is less than 5%.

Given the historical negative correlation between stocks and bonds, the trader can reduce his VaR by adding a negatively correlated asset such as bonds. Though adding bonds takes more capital, the VaR model would calculate that a 5% loss would now only be approximately 3% or less since bonds historically make money when stocks go down.

In reality, VaR at any moment is just a prediction using past data as a guide. Your real VaR for the trades you put on will reveal itself as the trades produce positive or negative returns each day. The actual returns will be used to determine how well the VaR predicted your risk. If you ultimately lose much more in a day or a month than the VaR analysis would have expected, you cannot get your money back. If you use VaR as an analysis for your trading risk, have your antennae up for deviations between actual performance and the VaR model.

For example, if you have a VaR of $100,000 with a five-day, 95% confidence, then you might expect once a month, you will have a VaR event that will make or lose $100,000 on your portfolio. If you make or lose that amount three times in a month, it is likely that correlations in your real-world portfolio are breaking down and should be studied, less you rely on the VaR calculation solely to defend the safety of your portfolio diversification.

Adjusting VaR

As a trader, we need a starting point to understand the potential outcomes with some reasonable certainty. We need ways to adjust the VaR. One way to do this is to compare the VaR standard deviation assumptions with what was implied by current observable options in the marketplace.

For example, by examining the implied volatility of the options of the securities we trade, we can solve for the expected daily or monthly movements as predicted by the marketplace and compare them to what the VaR analysis shows. We must make our own judgments as to which is correct. If the difference is significant, consider taking an average of the two instead of leaning one way or the other. Implied volatility may not always be accurate—it can be skewed upward by increased demand

---

[42] "An Introduction to Value at Risk (VAR)," David R. Harper, Investopedia, January 30th, 2020

for hedging, or it may be skewed downward by increased demand by traders to take in option premium.

A second method in adjusting VaR is to consider giving more weight to recent correlations and less weight to past correlations. Correlations break down over time and even switch signs on occasion. The breakdown of correlations is often what causes trading opportunities in the first place! Without broken correlations, every trade would hedge every other trade. There would be no need for active trading, just passive investing.

A great example is the Brazilian currency, the real, versus the price of oil. Over a ten-year period, the real has been as much as 50% positively correlated with the price of oil and been as much as 50% negatively correlated! It just depends on which data set and timeframe you look at.

Leverage as a Measure of Risk

A third way to adjust VaR is by measuring the amount of leverage used. Leverage is a handy risk metric because, generally, more leverage equals more risk.

In trading, leverage is the ratio of the amount of notional assets (the total value of a leveraged position's assets) used in a trade divided by the amount of initial capital involved. Investors have long known that they can trade stock on margin and receive "two times" leverage on their stock portfolio. In other words, they can buy twice as much stock as is in their initial capital account as long as they sign a margin agreement and pay interest on the borrowed portion of the money.

However, leverage can grow significantly when one is trading instruments other than stocks. In commodity futures, for example, exchanges offer traders 20-to-1 leverage. In that case, one need only put up $5,000 to control $100,000 worth of gold. In foreign exchange, certain brokers offer their clients 50-to-1 leverage!

One can derive their average leverage ratio in their risk reporting. Imagine that Trader A and Trader B each have $100,000 to trade. Trader A and Trader B each trade FX, but Trader A always trades in $1 million amounts. In comparison, Trader B always trades in $2 million amounts. Trader A, in theory, can still make more money than Trader B if his trade ideas are better while still using less leverage—i.e., 10-to-1 for Trader A versus 20-to-1 for Trader B. By measures of comparison, Trader A has better trading performance in terms of both risk and leverage.

Summary

Benchmarking can be a daily, weekly, or monthly calculation. The frequency of it should depend on your resources, requirements from organizations you work for, and your own desire to measure risk and performance as accurately as possible.

Leverage can be measured pre-trade or post-trade. VaR is most often calculated daily and almost always measured post-trade with a one-day lag. This is because it takes a lot of computer power to run the correlations on a portfolio of trades and create tables showing the results. Benchmarking returns is always done post-trade and is typically done month over month to better measure long-term performance over a one-day statistical blip.

There are two goals for benchmarking. The first is to help us better understand the risks we are taking, particularly when a portfolio of trades is involved. Great traders try to identify areas of risk that they may wish to modify to improve their potential performance. We do this by thinking about limits to risk via a nominal VaR limit or a leverage limit.

The second goal is to help us compare <u>our</u> performance with that of others, regardless of the amount of capital we have to deploy. You can be a great trader with any amount of money. Using a series of metrics, you can compare small and large traders, and find out whose returns are truly market-beating and whose are optically good but have underperformed in reality.

For small and novice traders, benchmarking your performance is not only a valuable tool in managing your risk, but it is the key method that you can use to promote your performance to others who might provide you with greater capital to manage.

CHAPTER 28

The Conclusion—But What's Next?

A t the outset of this book, I set out to accomplish one goal: to provide a complete starting guide to fundamental trading. Hopefully, I have provided you with enough philosophical and fundamental building blocks, which I call best practices, to become a profitable trader.

Expanding on this goal was my attempt to equip you with core processes on where to look for trading ideas and design an appropriate trading strategy around those ideas. You should now understand the challenges that come with dealing with your heart, your body, and your mind, which in many cases interfere with your ability to employ your best practices.

I want you to be a trader who knows how the game works, why bid/offer spreads cannot be taken for granted, and the real cost of doing this job for a living. I want you to understand what it takes to make enough profit to overcome those costs.

I want you to be: (1) a trader who quantifies the risk and builds a system that tells you what information you need to manage your positions; (2) a trader who understands who the participants are in the market and refuses to empower them with any more knowledge or foresight than they deserve; (3) a trader who understands that your unique perspective on how to develop ideas gives you an edge if that perspective is deployed with discipline; and (4) a trader who understands that trading is a business where winning and losing are a natural part of the process, as opposed to the notion that winning gives you a reason to feel superior and losing gives you a reason to feel ineffective or hopeless.

You may feel empowered by this book, but understandably cautious that things may not go as smoothly as you hope in actual practice. And for the most part, you would be right. There is nothing smooth about trading. To understand trading is to know that it is not a smooth skillset that one learns and applies in all cases. Instead, trading is like surfing, as we discussed in Chapter 1. In surfing, one never feels in total control throughout the day, but as you prepare more and more, you become more professional in your approach. We can execute flawlessly from time to time, but just as easily, we can hit a wave that we cannot manage or control.

Trading is the same way. Being trained does not alleviate the bad trade—it is just the opposite. You are armed with the knowledge that losing trades are part and parcel of what defines someone who is trading like a professional. Managing bad trades just becomes more natural in the same way that a surfer manages to recuperate when a wave knocks him over.

Feeling empowered and having trepidation can be natural coexisting feelings for you to have. Accept them as a normal pair versus something that should always make you question your skillset.

Delve Deeper and Challenge Yourself to Learn More

I have a second goal in mind for you. That goal is to ask you to take inventory at this point and figure out which areas I have covered in this book that still require a more in-depth understanding for you.

Suppose you are an accountant who wants to be a trader. You may feel empowered and confident because of the sections about creating reports or understanding the costs involved, as those sections are familiar to you. However, you may feel overwhelmed at the thought of trading options without more training.

In contrast, an experienced options trader who reads this book may feel quite confident in trading options and may already be an expert on Value-at-Risk reports. Yet, this options expert can still think that this was her first exposure to the concept that the mind and heart can be working to undermine her best practices. She may feel that this is an area she needs to explore further lest she trade irrationally when the market gets stressful.

I implore you to delve further into the footnoted material or seek out books with direct application to areas in which you feel you need improvement. This book is intended to be a prequel to your lifetime of learning about trading. If you have read my book and are preparing yourself to trade, know that I gave you many ideas in these pages you can use to succeed. If you decide that there may be even better resources out there than the books I referenced, then I will have accomplished my third and final goal: for you to challenge yourself to learn what you do not know, wherever that search leads you.

That is the ultimate motivation for a successful trader: to question what she does not know when a trade is ongoing and challenge herself to learn new ways to think about the market. She is always increasing the quality of her trade-idea generation and execution.

One of the many ways traders judge other traders is to listen to the stories others tell about their trading prowess. Interestingly, one thing seems to stand out over and over again with the best traders—their stories are mostly about losing trades instead of big winners.

Good traders expect to win over time. They do not remember their winning trades because it is what they expect of themselves. Instead, they recall their losing trades. They focus on what they did wrong or how they realized the market was capable of reacting in ways they did not expect. They learned how to manage their losing trades, so those trades are incapable of knocking them out of the game.

A Glorious Feeling

Imagine doing something where the older you get, the better you become?

I relish playing team sports. I played football until I was thirty-two in a local flag football league. One of my best teammates went down with a knee injury on the last Saturday of a cold December. He was lying on a muddy field waiting for the ambulance to arrive. I remember thinking, *Wow, that could have been me.* Maybe I am running out of time to play the sport I love. I played volleyball until my arm gave out from too many spikes, and I played baseball until I could no longer run the ball down with any speed.

But boy, oh boy, that computer is always waiting for me, seeing all the possibilities flash across the screen when the market is open. No video game in the world can replace that feeling! Trading will give me that high into my very old days. I hope it will for you as well.

As we say in every trading room around the world at the beginning of each day:

GOOD LUCK and HAPPY TRADING!

Index

Made in the USA
Las Vegas, NV
30 September 2021